IMAGES
of America

HENDERSON HARBOR AND HENDERSON

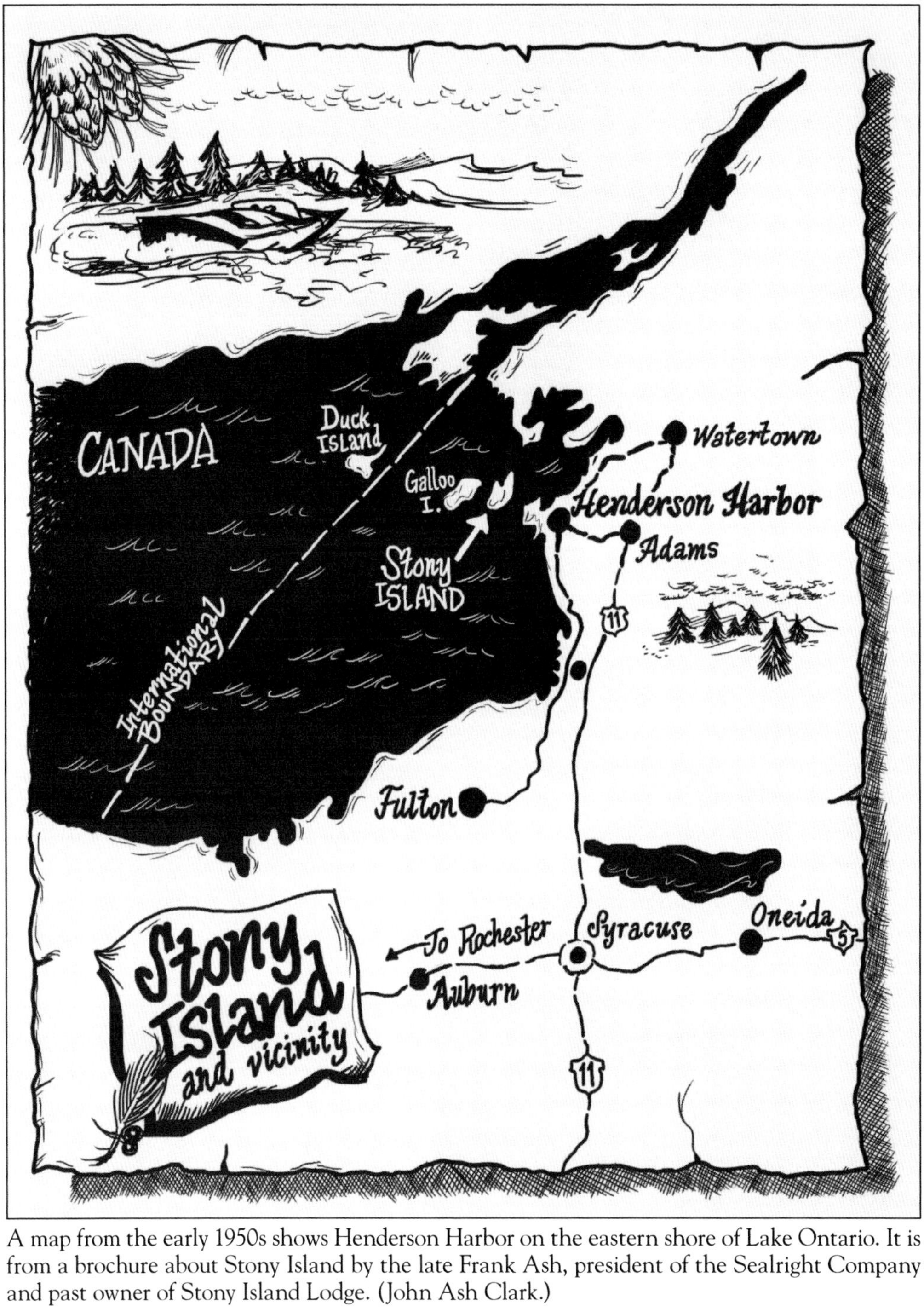

A map from the early 1950s shows Henderson Harbor on the eastern shore of Lake Ontario. It is from a brochure about Stony Island by the late Frank Ash, president of the Sealright Company and past owner of Stony Island Lodge. (John Ash Clark.)

On the Cover: Pictured prior to 1920 diving off the original Highland Park dock in Henderson Harbor are, from left to right, Kenny Hart, Allen Dodge, John and David Fairchild, Anna Barnes, Morton Pickslay, and Edgar "Bill" Averill in the water. (Jeff and Harriet Averill.)

IMAGES
of America

HENDERSON HARBOR AND HENDERSON

Timothy W. Lake

ARCADIA
PUBLISHING

ISBN 978-0-7385-7685-5

Published by Arcadia Publishing
Charleston, South Carolina

Printed in the United States of America

Library of Congress Control Number: 2011936169

For all general information, please contact Arcadia Publishing:
Telephone 843-853-2070
Fax 843-853-0044
E-mail sales@arcadiapublishing.com
For customer service and orders:
Toll-Free 1-888-313-2665

Visit us on the Internet at www.arcadiapublishing.com

This book is dedicated to the memory of Jayne Warren McGowan, who spent nearly every summer of her life at Henderson Harbor.

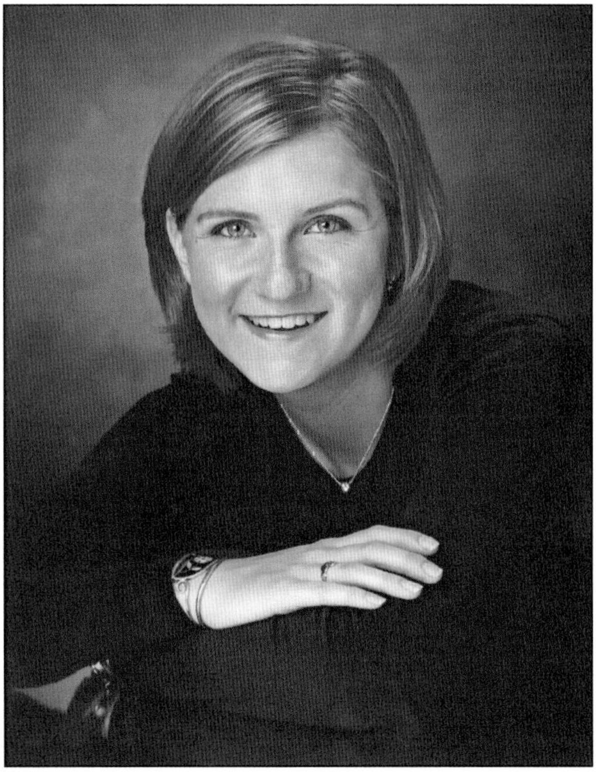

Contents

ACKNOWLEDGMENTS

Upon deciding to write this book, the first person I reached out to was John B. Johnson Jr., copublisher of the *Watertown Daily Times* and lifelong summer resident of Henderson Harbor. In 1937, Johnson's grandparents purchased Underbluff, the large Victorian waterfront cottage of former US Secretary of State John W. Foster. Through the newspaper, the Johnsons have recorded every significant, newsworthy, and social event in Henderson Harbor history. Allowing my use of the *Times*'s archives and Johnson family photographs has been invaluable.

Photographs and research materials were compiled from the following: the GE collection at the Schenectady Museum (GE); the Dwight P. Church collection at the Owen D. Young Library, St. Lawrence University (Church); the LaGuardia and Wagner Archives at LaGuardia Community College (LCC); the Grinnell 100, Jefferson County Historical Society (JCHS); North Coast New York Coast Guard Association (NCNYCGA); US Coast Guard Historian (CGH); Oneida County Historical Society (OCHS); Crawford and Stearns 1987 survey of Henderson Bay Cottages; Jefferson County Journal; and, unless otherwise noted, the author's collection.

Thank you to the people who provided photographs and stories and helped with research. They include James and Signe McGowan, Maryanne Giangobbe, James and Mary Parke Manning, David and Jeri Joor, the late Ann Dulles Joor, Stan Hovey, Harriet and Jeff Averill, John and Jill Stevens, Ed Davis, Jennifer Davis Rogers, Jack Machold, John D. Marsellus, William "Sandy" Conde, Alma and Frances Eastman, David and Paulyn Eastman, Torre Parker-Lane, Gordon Koscher, Dan Lake, Jill Lang, Greg Smith, Lamar Bliss, Lyn Matteson Jr., Lyn Matteson, III, Virginia Matteson Taber, Mary Louise King Morrow, Lydia Miller, Ann Montague Maurer, Janet Williams, Diane Henchen Gamble, Brian and Mary Lee Bettinger, John Dunk, Gatra Wehle, Barbara Tifft, Jack Major, Sue McKenna, Sarah Haun, Candace Clifford, James Bettinger, Joel Bettinger, Chris Hunter, Lenka Walldroff, Emily Anthony, Marge Beaver, Janine Smith, Art Bronstein, Paul Haggett, Mark McMurray, Ann McConnell Williams, Rachael McConnell, Sue Washburn, Grover Moore, Arlene Dana, Claude W. Hunt, John Ash Clark, Jeanne Fitzpatrick, and Mike Franklin.

Introduction

In 1756, gunfire erupted near Galloo Island, Lake Ontario, between the French and the British at the first naval battle on the Great Lakes. During the height of Prohibition, the US Coast Guard opened fire on a family out fishing in their Chris Craft boat near Galloo Island. In a modern battle over fishing rights, shotguns blasted away near Galloo Island, killing hundreds of cormorants. Each of these historic events put the tiny hamlet of Henderson Harbor, New York, on the international map; however, the remarkable history of this entire cottage community has not been compiled in a book of photographs until now.

Henderson Harbor was originally called Nioure Bay by the French, who had settled on Lake Ontario. In the 1750s, French troops built a log stockade on what is now Association Island. Camp de L'Observation was used to watch for English warships and Indians in the channel leading to Henderson Harbor. Later, Henderson Harbor was briefly called Naples after the Italian port city, but it was eventually named for early settler and landowner William Henderson.

The beauty of this small fishing community is enhanced by the view from the rocky bluffs and ledges along the shoreline. Deep and easily navigable water with few obstructions make it a boater's paradise. Many visitors, some famous, have raved about the fishing while enjoying its shoreline inns, guesthouses, and cottages. Bass and perch are eaten during a shore dinner or prepared in one of Henderson Harbor's cottages and restaurants.

Boaters, who travel around Six Town Point into Lake Ontario, are treated to the harbor's secret—the vast acres of wooded forest and the steep, rocky cliffs of Stony Point. This mostly public landscape, so generously donated by late beer company heir Robert G. Wehle, was long off-limits during its many years under government and private ownership. Further west and visited by even fewer people are Stony and Galloo Islands, surrounded by some of the best fishing grounds in the east. The offshore islands have long been the playground of corporate executives, statesmen, politicians, and their fishing and hunting guides. The islands have a rich history of farm families who combined sheep herding with fishing, boating, sailing, and guiding, which still continues today, to some extent. These islands were also the summer purlieu of American diplomats from the Foster, Lansing, and Dulles families.

The jewel of the many islands around Henderson Harbor is Association Island, now open to the public as a camping resort and marina. Best known as the corporate retreat for the General Electric Company from 1912 to 1957, Association Island is part of Sixtown Point, a string of islands connected by rocky shoals and gravel bars. *Henderson Harbor and Henderson* reveals the little known details of how the Association Island Corporation was formed.

Around Stony Point and along the sandy beach of Lake Ontario is the mouth of Big Sandy Creek, believed by some historians to be the 1684 location (others believe Salmon River) of La Famine, a council between the French and Iroquois Indians where many French soldiers nearly died of starvation and disease. For 50 years, the mouth of the creek was home to the Big Sandy Life Saving and Coast Guard Station, consisting of many local men who risked their lives to save shipwrecked schooners on Lake Ontario. During Prohibition, the Big Sandy Coast Guard helped apprehend some of the most notorious rumrunners on the lake, including Anthony "Tony" Kane, who was captured at Henderson Harbor. Guardsmen made regular patrols around Henderson Harbor, which included an incident in 1928 where guardsmen opened fire on a boat loaded with the family of a Henderson Harbor resident with friends in Washington. The publicity of this incident played a minor role in America's increasing disdain for the interdiction tactics of Prohibition.

In the 1990s, Henderson Harbor fishing guides claimed that newly imported double-crested cormorants, a type of seabird, were destroying their fishing-based income. In response, several of them took a moonlit cruise to a cormorant nesting island in Lake Ontario and performed a shotgun massacre. After trial, conviction, and sentences of home confinement, the result was a long-term scientific cormorant management run by the State of New York. It was a clear example that professional wildlife management strategies must consider fishing-based economies of small communities like Henderson Harbor.

Today, Henderson Harbor remains virtually unchanged. Through fluctuating conditions, the economy is still based in fishing and boating, tourism and cottagers. On a hot summer day, the water remains cool, sometimes cold. Visitors can stand on the shoreline, still hear the chug of a small wooden motorboat, and imagine the early days of Henderson Harbor.

One

Early Days and Cottages

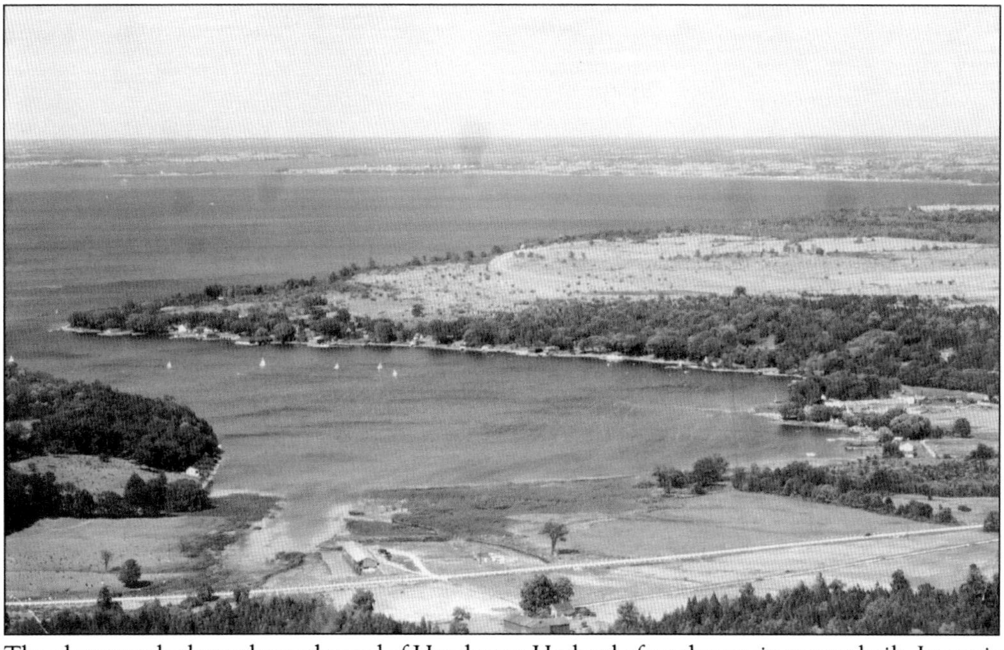

The photograph above shows the end of Henderson Harbor before the marinas were built. Iroquois Indians used Henderson Harbor as a canoe route to bypass the rocky shoals of Stony Point. After crossing Henderson Bay, they would carry on from the end of Henderson Harbor to Stony Creek and Lake Ontario. A newspaper article published in 1898 describes the remains of an old log wharf at this location used by the Indians to start their carry. (Church.)

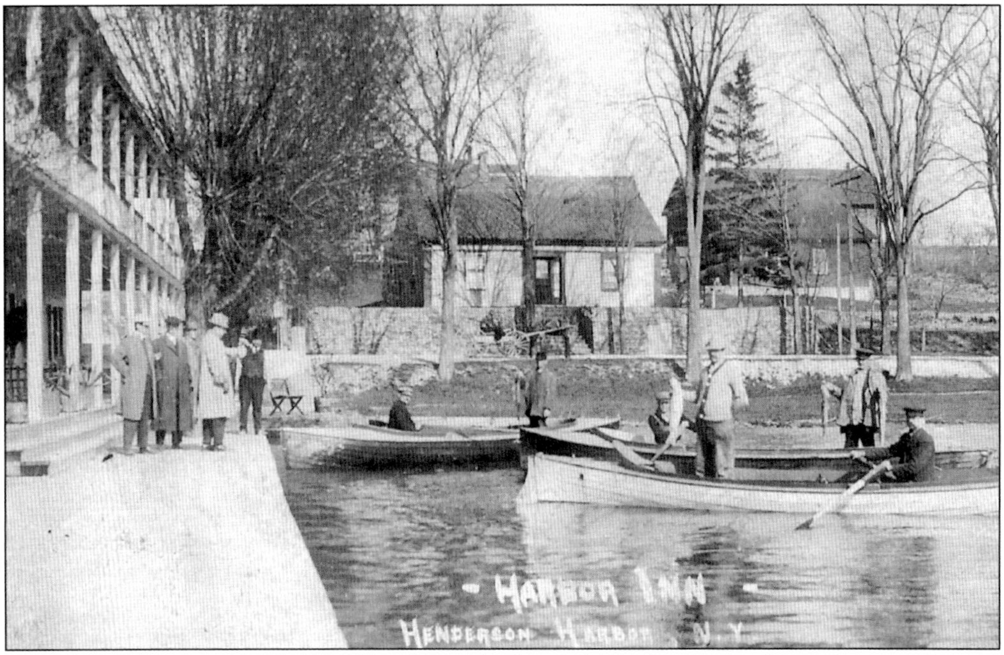

Trout, salmon, cisco, perch, and bass have challenged Henderson Harbor fishermen for two centuries. Prior to motorboats, guides rowed fishermen from hotels, such as the original Harbor Inn (left), for overnight trips to the fishing grounds. The double-ended rowing skiffs pictured here were dragged over the gravel bar of Sixtown Point on wooden skids to reach the open waters of the lake.

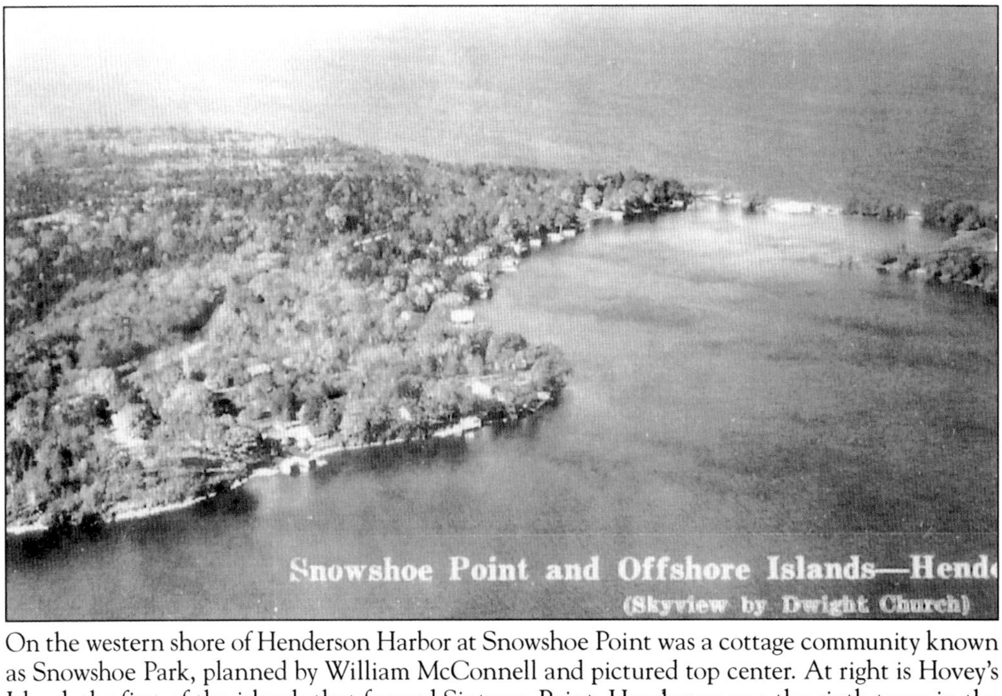

On the western shore of Henderson Harbor at Snowshoe Point was a cottage community known as Snowshoe Park, planned by William McConnell and pictured top center. At right is Hovey's Island, the first of the islands that formed Sixtown Point. Henderson was the sixth town in the Macomb land purchase. (Church.)

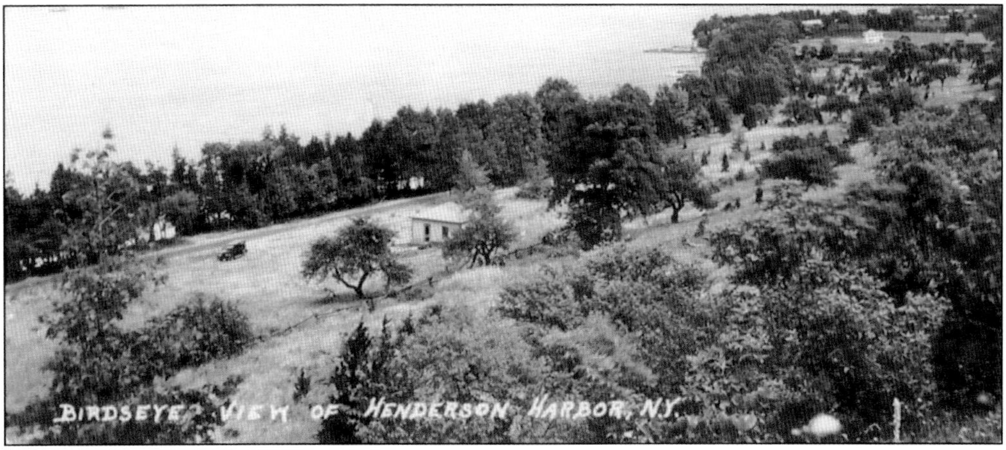

From Chestnut Ridge looking north, this area along Harbor Road was proposed in 1912 to be a large cottage community known as Henderson Harbor Park. Many Watertown and Syracuse residents built their cottages here after first staying at Warner's Inn, top right. (Church.)

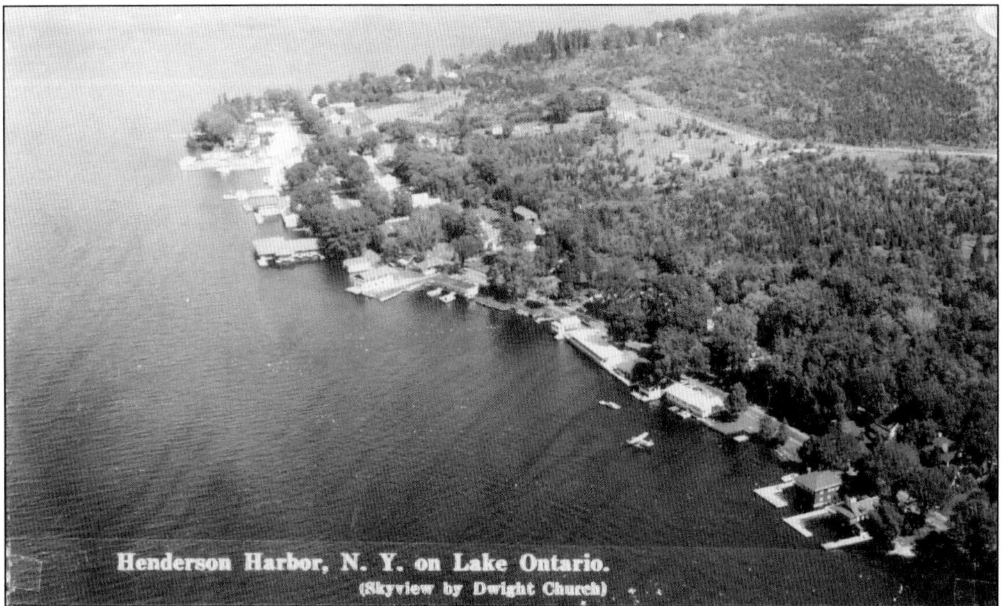

This c. 1960 photograph shows the eastern shore of Henderson Harbor at its heart, from the Gill House, top, to the former Tyler's Inn, bottom right. Notice the float plane, right center. (Church.)

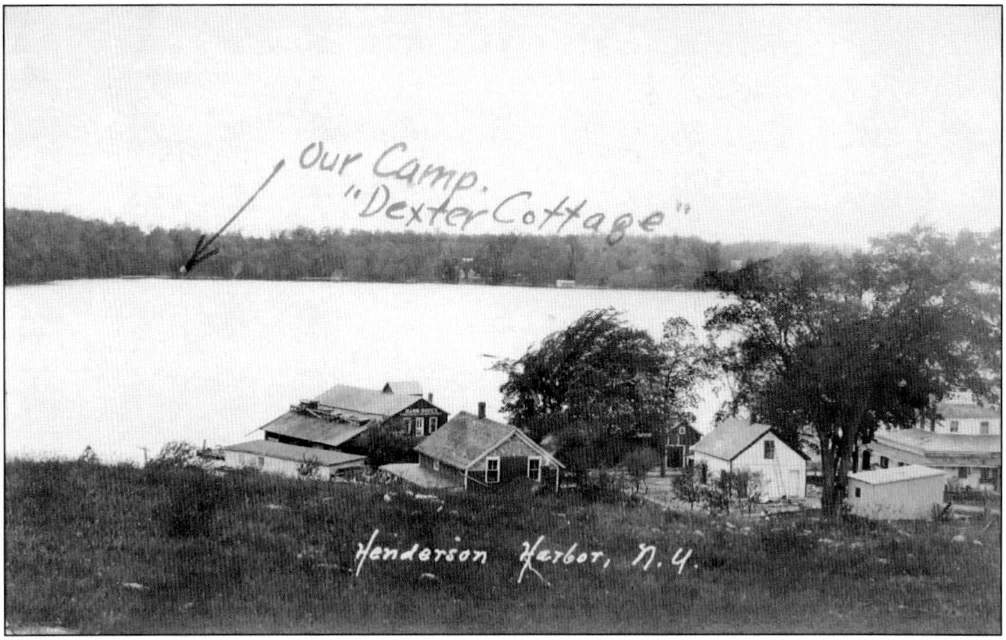

The Hamm and Hovey coal and feed dock was owned by Fred Hamm and Harold Hovey. At the far right is one of the most historically significant houses in Henderson Harbor. It is the c. 1835 Federal and Greek Revival R.J.W. Morgan house, also known as the cup and saucer house. It was owned for many years by John Austin, manager of GE's resort on Association Island, and by his daughter Alice "Allie" Austin until the 1990s.

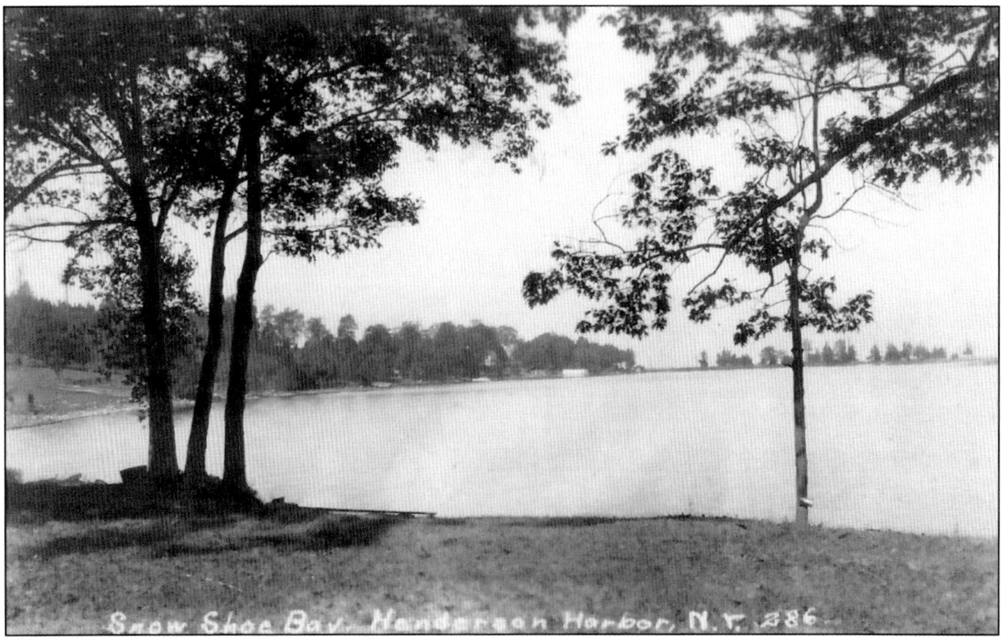

Snowshoe Bay offers the most protection from the often violent northwest winds of Lake Ontario. It is mostly farmland in this photograph but is now the most densely populated section of the Henderson Harbor shoreline. This view looks across Snowshoe Bay toward the gravel bar that once joined Snowshoe Point and Hovey's Island.

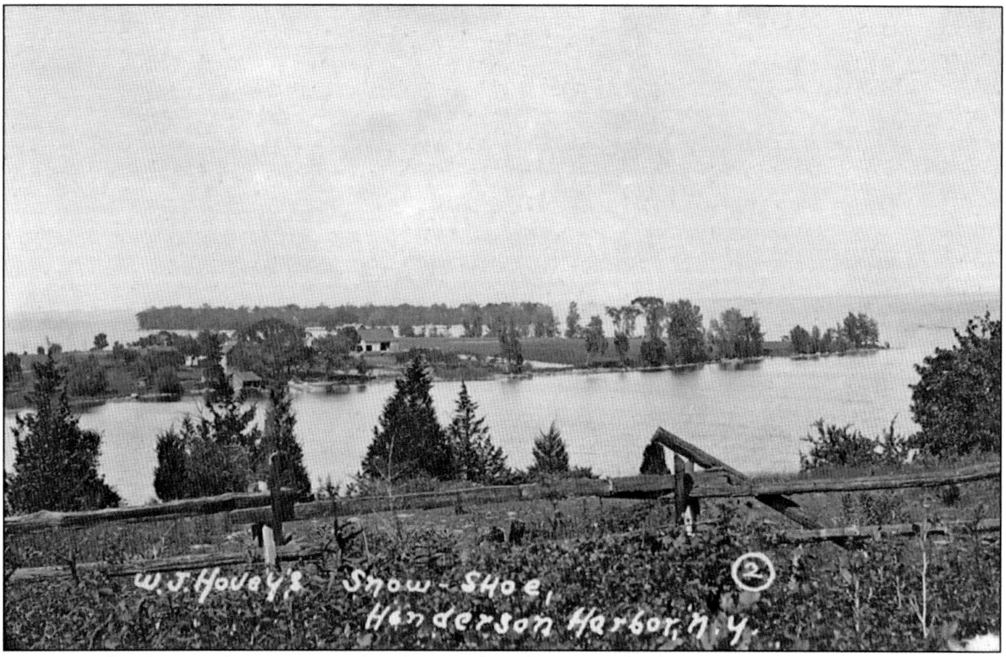

Hovey's Island is on the eastern side of Snowshoe Bay. Winford J. "Winnie" Hovey and his wife, Martha, ran a farm and guesthouse on the island. The island was owned by Hovey's brother George S. Hovey, a Kansas City, Missouri, banker. Association Island is seen in the background.

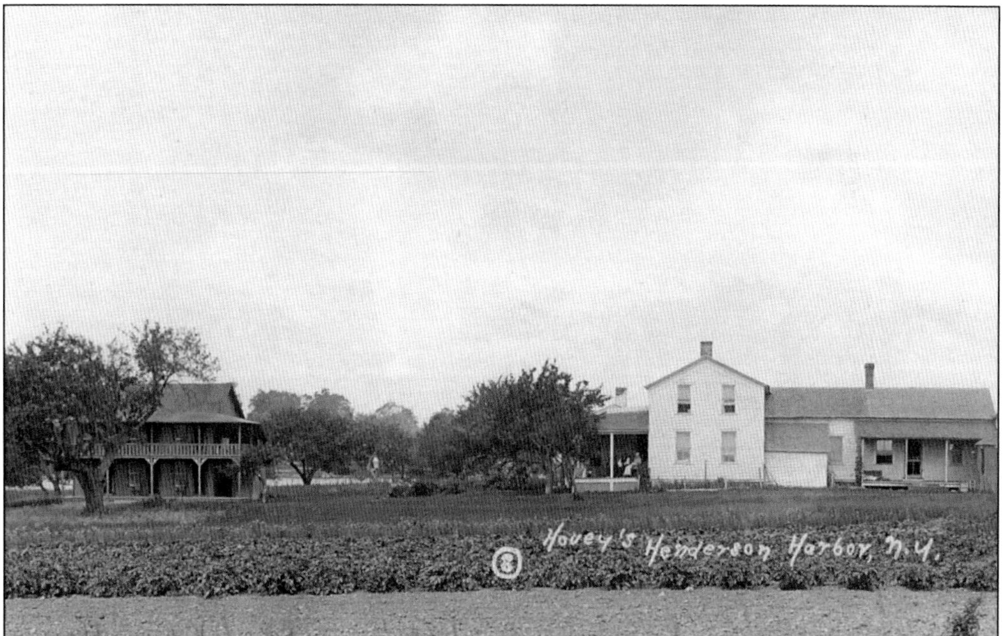

Although Martha Hovey died of a heart attack on July 25, 1916, the family continued operating the Snowshoe Inn for another decade. When Winnie Hovey retired, his brother George sold the island and other land on Snowshoe Point to GE's Association Island Corporation in July 1926 for $22,500.

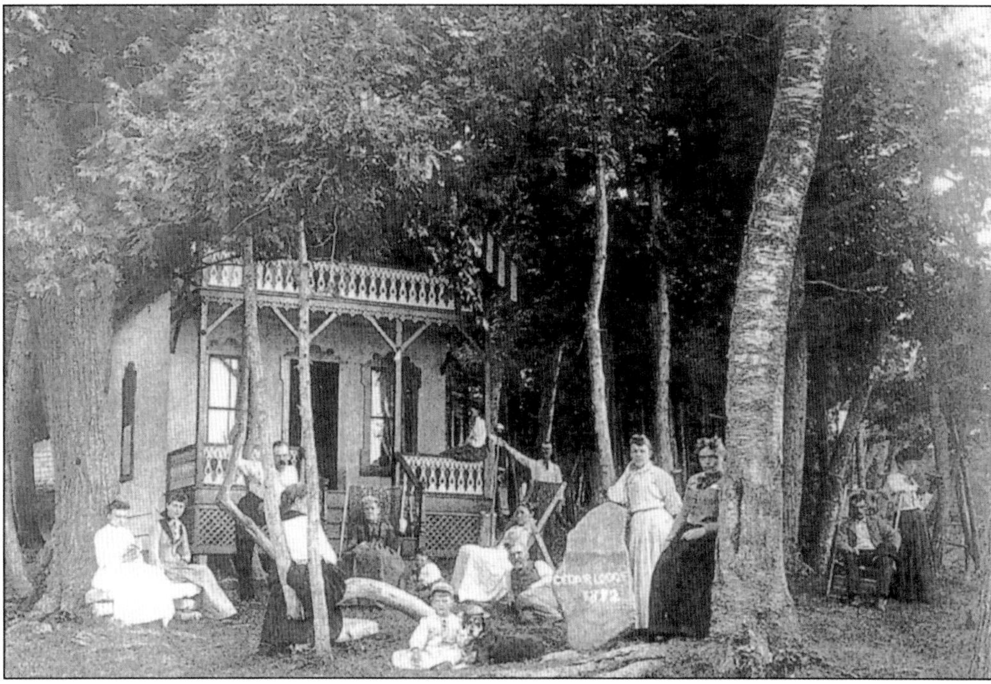

William McConnell of Sandy Creek and Pierrepont Manor, New York, built Cedar Lodge in 1882. It was the first Victorian cottage erected on Snowshoe Point. It is a classic example of Stick architecture that was popular among Henderson Bay cottages prior to 1890. McConnell is in the right center with his arm extended to the corner column of the porch. (The McConnell family and Sarah Haun.)

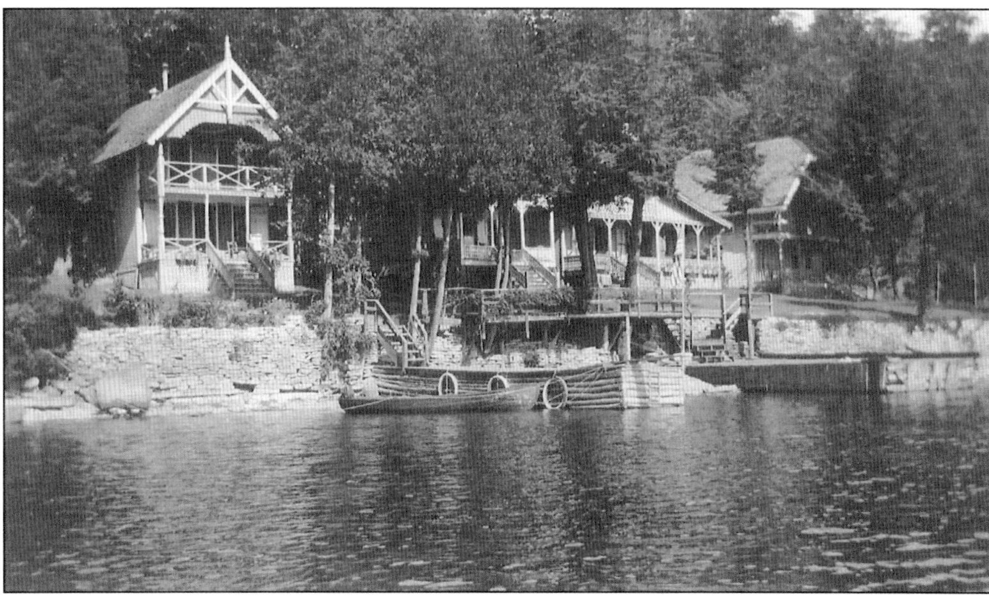

Another example of Stick architecture often seen in Henderson Bay cottages is at Highland Park on the west side of Henderson Harbor. Established in the 1880s by the Arms, Jones, and Manville families of Adams, New York, this small colony soon flourished with members of the Averill and Waite families, also of Adams.

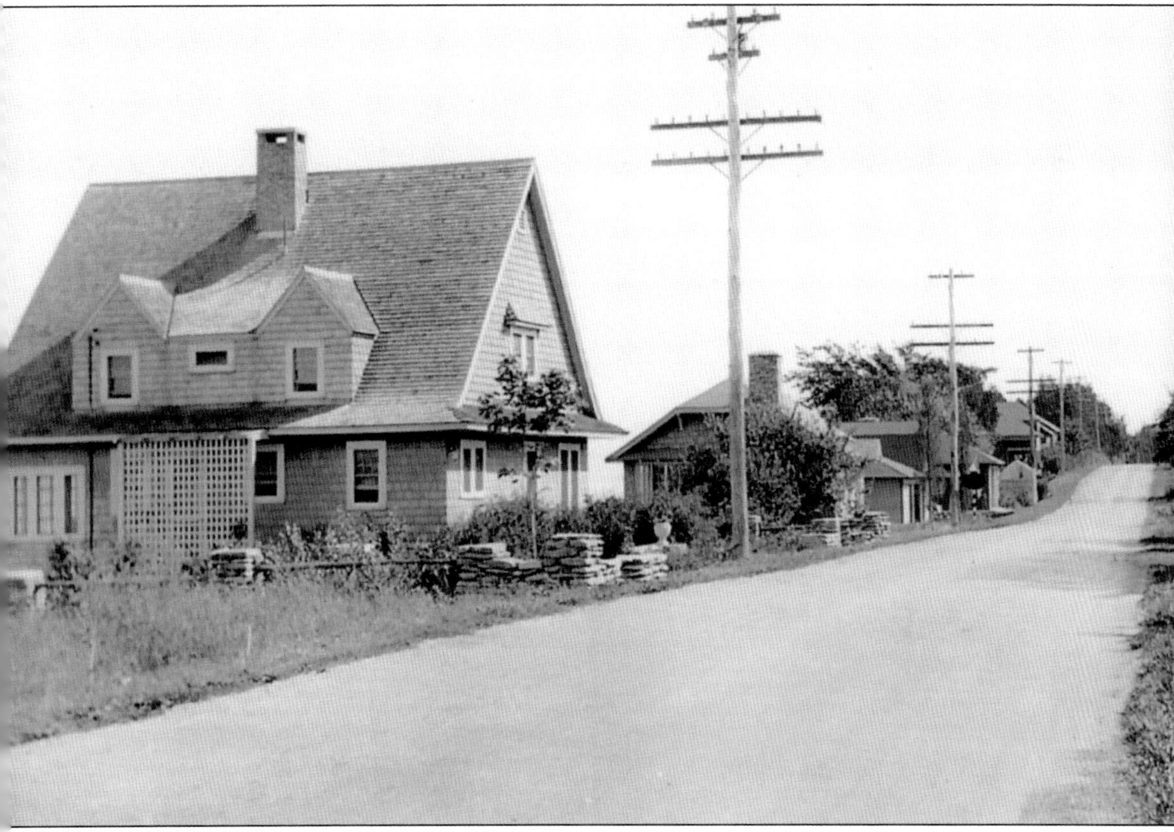

By the 1920s, Harbor Road was dotted with bay-side cottages. The shingled Craftsman cottage in the foreground looks much the same 100 years later. Many of the cottages were actually built with their foundations in the bay, a method that would not be permitted today. This location was slightly north of the curve in Harbor Road and near the beginning of what was planned, in 1912, to be a cottage community called Henderson Harbor Park.

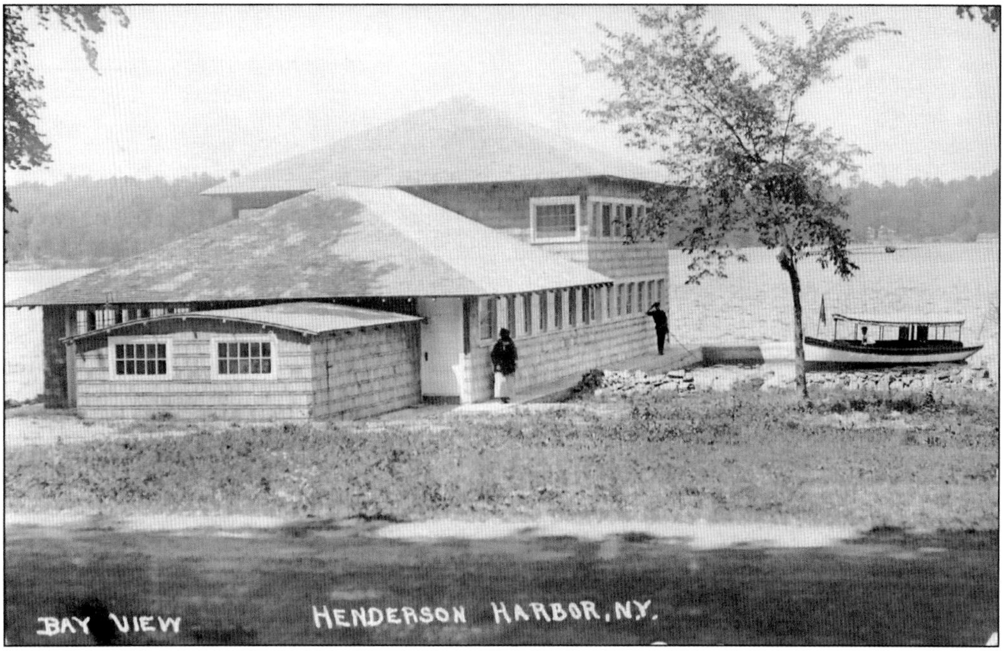

Oliver J. McConnell's boathouse was located on a prominent point in Henderson Harbor. One large slip could accommodate small steam- and naphtha-powered launches, such as the one pictured here. The boathouse later became Henchen Marina, the most popular marina in Henderson Harbor.

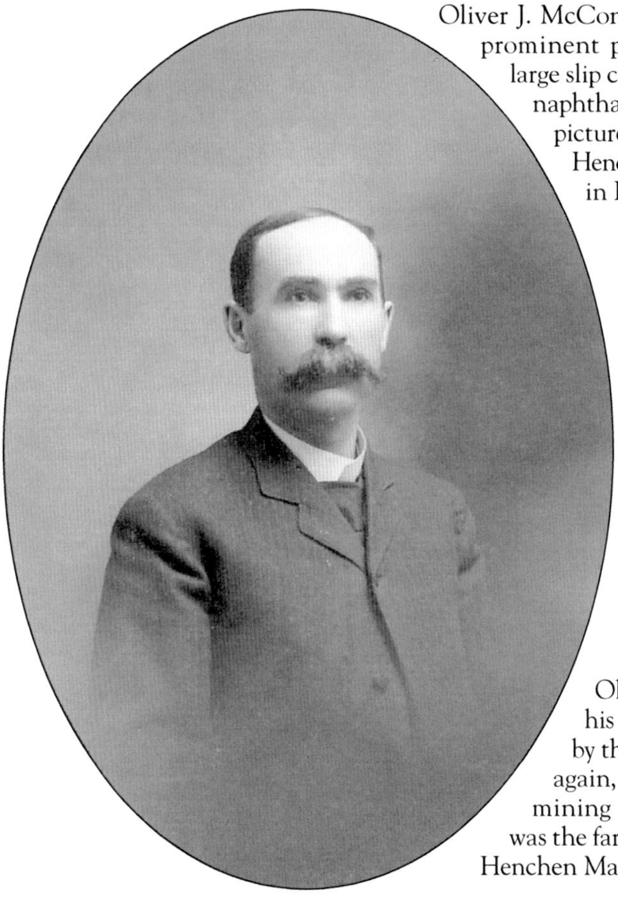

Oliver J. McConnell went west to seek his fortune but was forced to return home by the great Chicago fire of 1871. Leaving again, he found success in lumbering and mining in Montana. His retirement home was the farmhouse and boathouse that became Henchen Marina. (The McConnell family.)

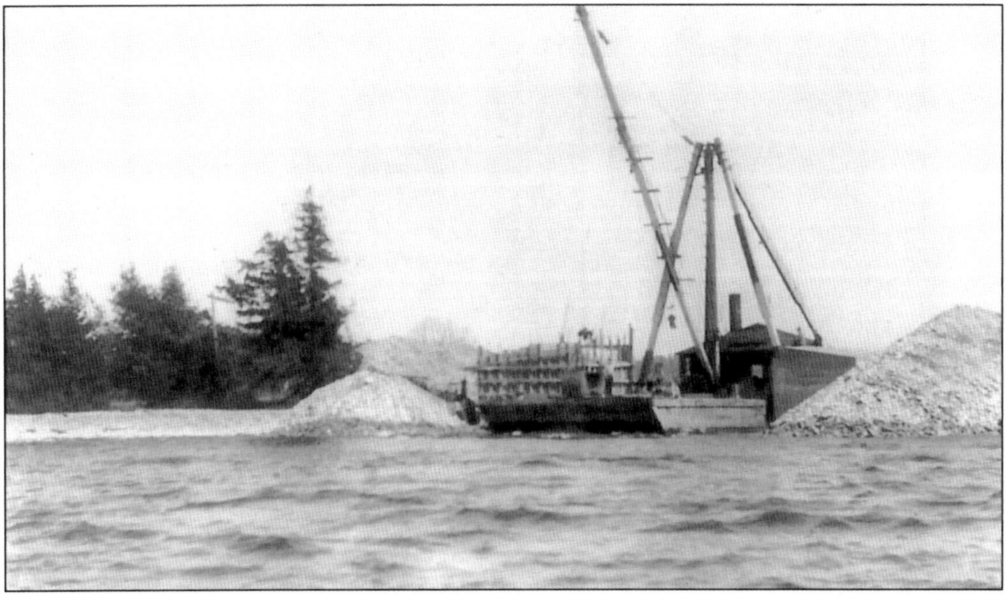

On August 20, 1927, many Henderson Harbor residents met at McConnell's boathouse and organized the Henderson Harbor Improvement Association. After raising $7,000, they hired the Hinckley firm of Cape Vincent, New York, to build the cut, or a navigation channel, through the gravel bar between Snowshoe Point and Hovey's Island. (John Dunk.)

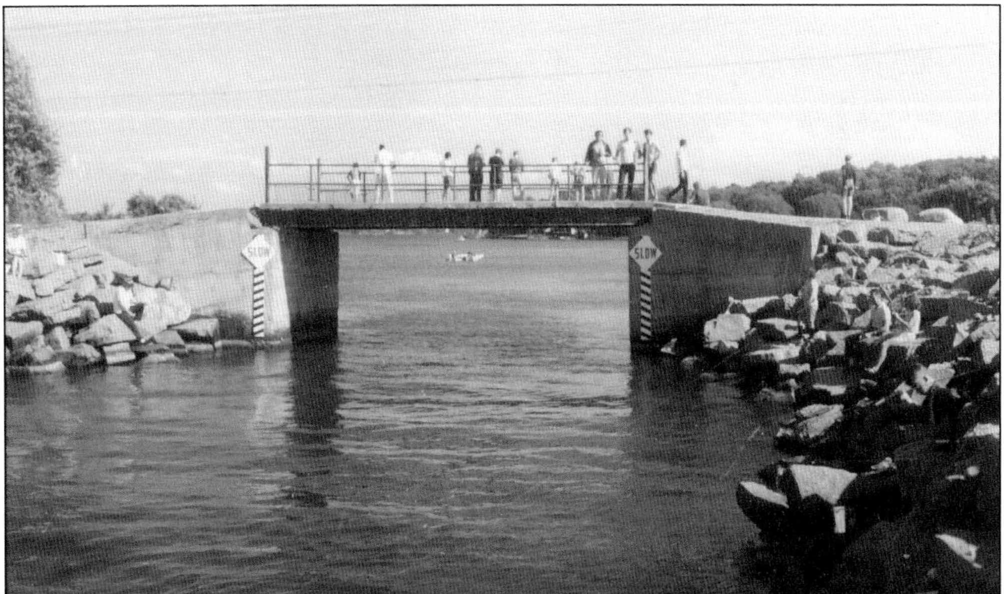

When the cut was completed, it provided a faster and safer boat trip to the fishing spots of the lake. This view from the lake end of the cut is the same as the previous photograph but many years later. Snowshoe Bay is through the channel. (Church.)

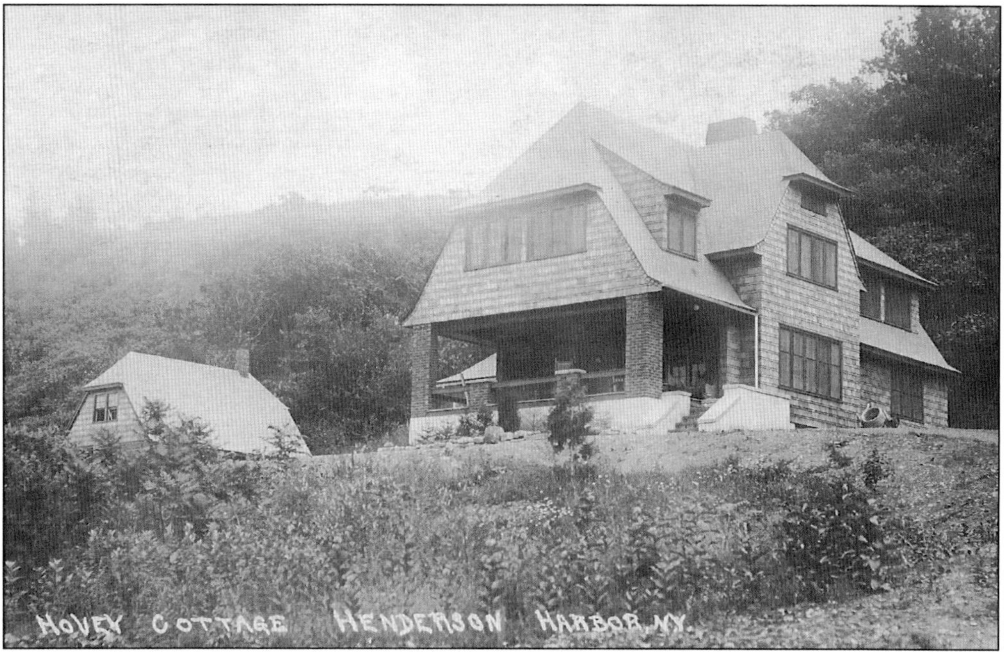

The George I. and Clara Hovey Bay View cottage, built on the ridge along Harbor Road in 1921, is the finest example of shingled Craftsman architecture in Henderson Harbor. It is the largest of the original properties subdivided for Henderson Harbor Park.

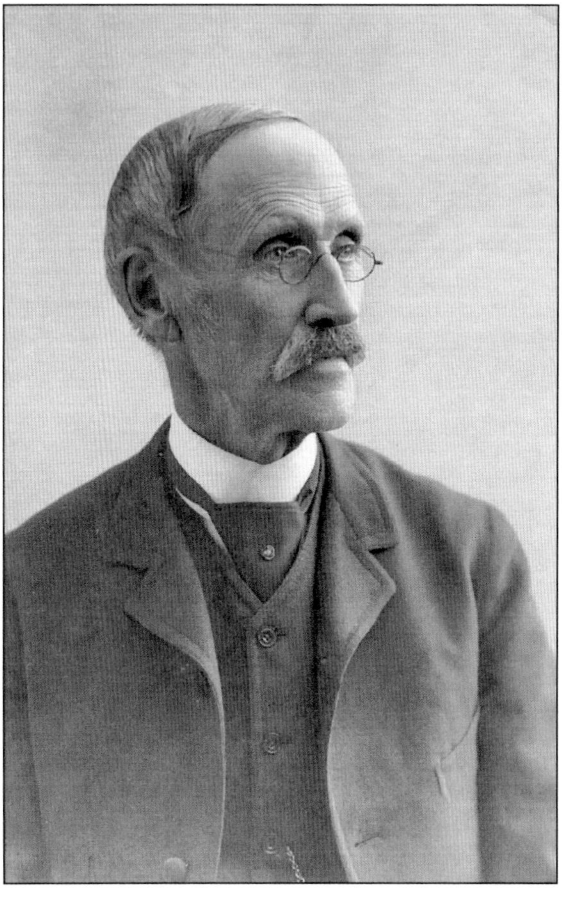

George I. Hovey was a banker and textiles manufacturer from Deansboro, New York. He became embroiled in a securities fraud lawsuit by Francis A. Cody, a descendant of "Buffalo Bill" Cody. Bay View cottage was auctioned off during a sheriff's sale in 1940 to settle a judgment won by Cody. The cottage was purchased by the John Riordan family of Drexel Hill, Pennsylvania, and is still in the family. (OCHS.)

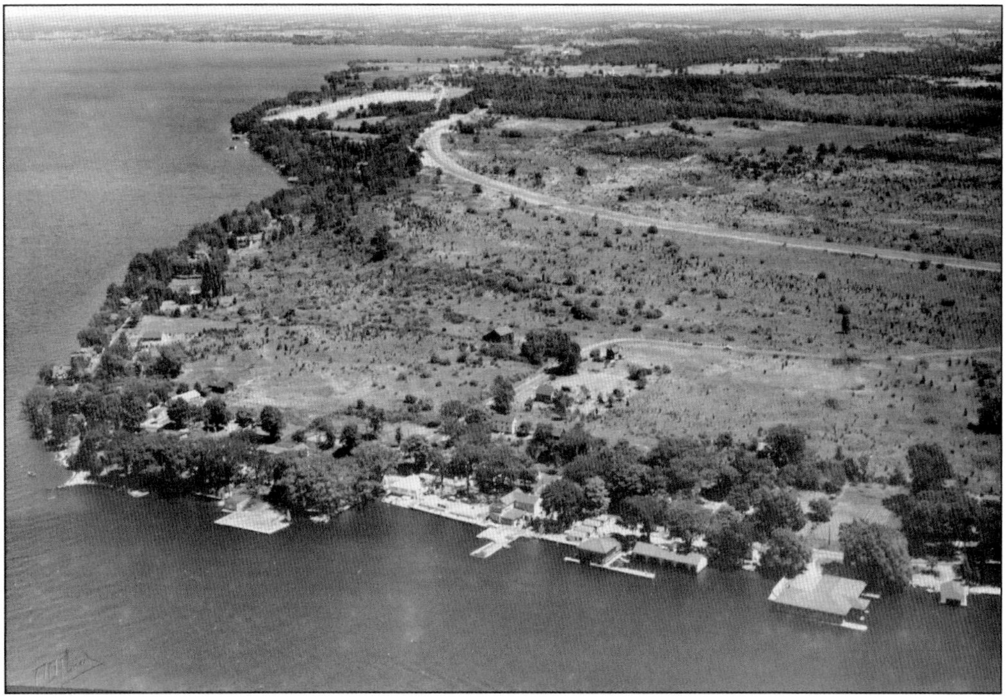

In the early 1930s, Henderson Harbor residents lobbied New York State to locate NYS Route 3, top right, on Chestnut Ridge and not through the hamlet. They even led state officials on a hike up the ridge to see the spectacular view; it worked. This section of the highway was completed between 1933 and 1934. (Church.)

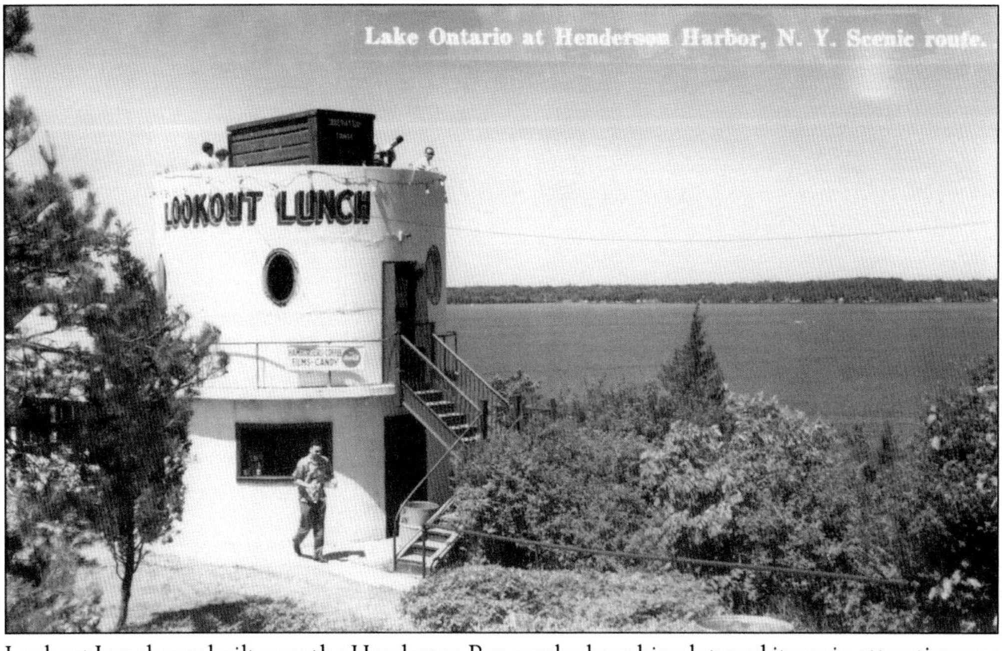

Lookout Lunch was built near the Henderson Bay overlook parking lot, and its main attraction was the lookout tower. On a clear day, tourists could see Stony and Galloo Islands and the Canadian shoreline. Lookout Lunch closed in the 1980s and is now a private residence. (Church.)

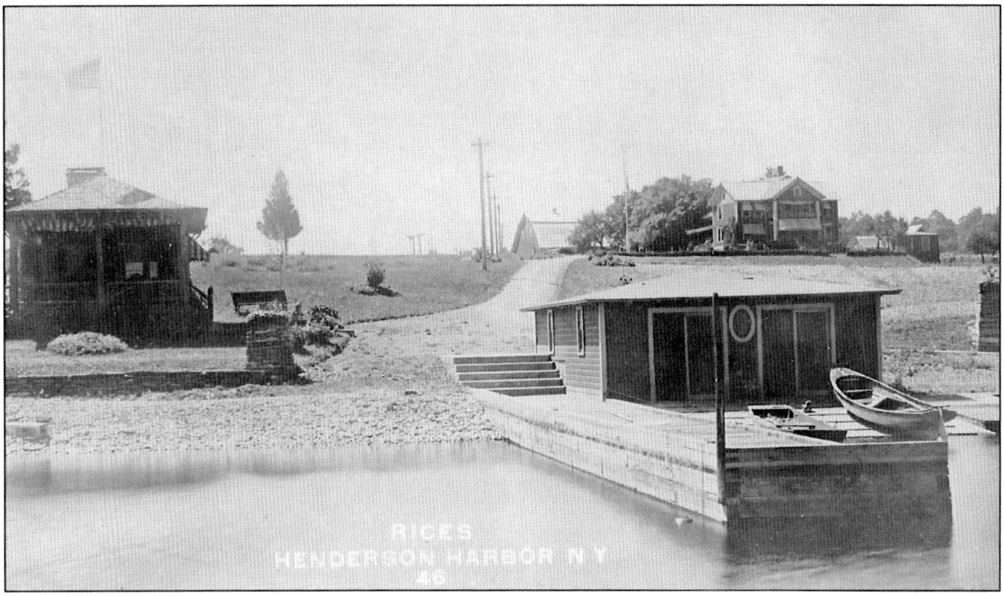

Dr. William S. Rice, a corset manufacturer from Adams, New York, owned Rockledge Farm, a large waterfront property along Henderson Bay on the northern edge of Harbor Road. In August 1904, Dr. Rice returned to his dock from Oswego, New York, with one of the first naphtha boats in Henderson Harbor. In 1918, Dr. Rice leased out Rockledge Farm for an inn. In 1924, Rice's 90-acre waterfront apple orchard was sold for cottages, and in 1928, the entire farm was listed for sale.

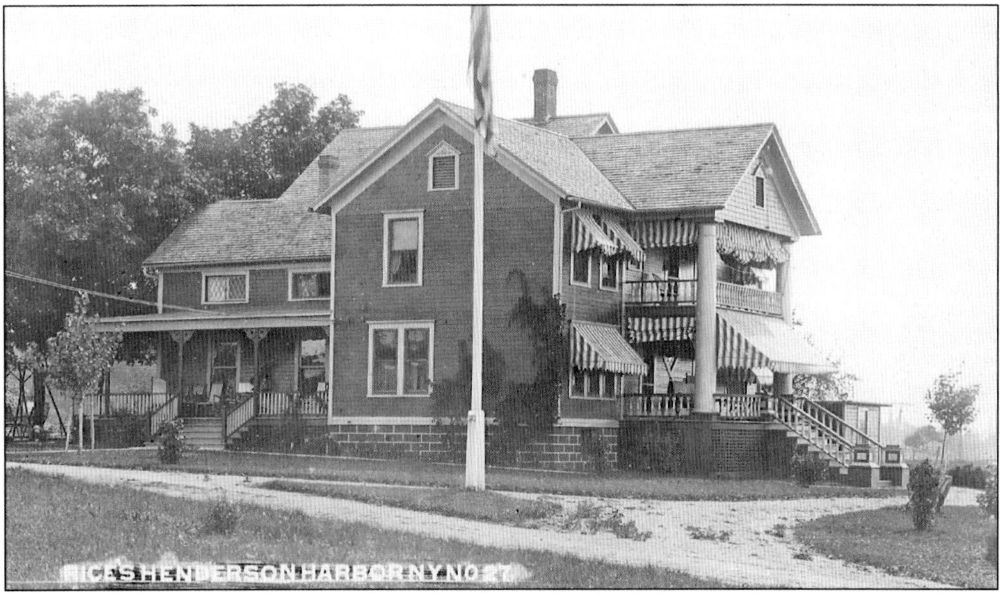

The Rice cottage at Rockledge farm offered panoramic sunset views across Henderson Bay. It was first purchased by Cleveland, Ohio, steel magnate James W. Brainard and later by New York City surgeon Dr. Robert S. Bickley and his wife, Georgia A. Bell Bickley. They expanded the farm to nearly 1,800 acres. Following the Bickleys' deaths in 1957 and 1963, Rockledge Farm was taken over by Dr. Paul M. Read and his wife, Georgiabell Bickley Read. In the late 1990s, their son Paul B. Read sold the remaining waterfront land, including the Rice cottage, for private homes.

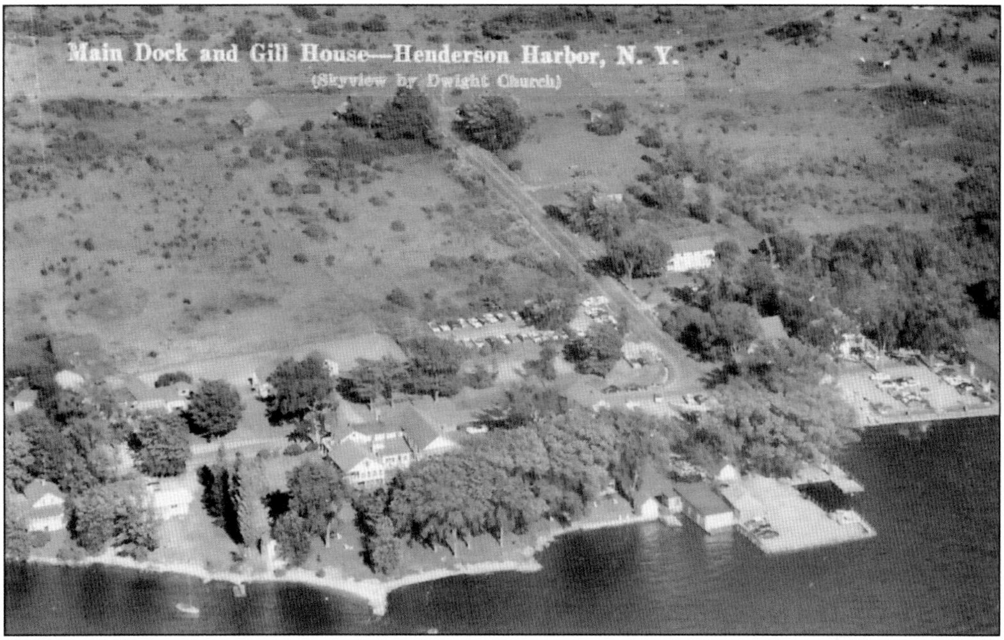

By the 1950s, Henderson Harbor was a busy summer resort. Visitors would arrive by car or bus to the GE dock (pictured bottom right), which was the site of the former Harbor Inn, for a boat ride to Association Island. The Gill House (center) was a thriving hotel with daily fish dinners of locally caught bass and perch. (Church.)

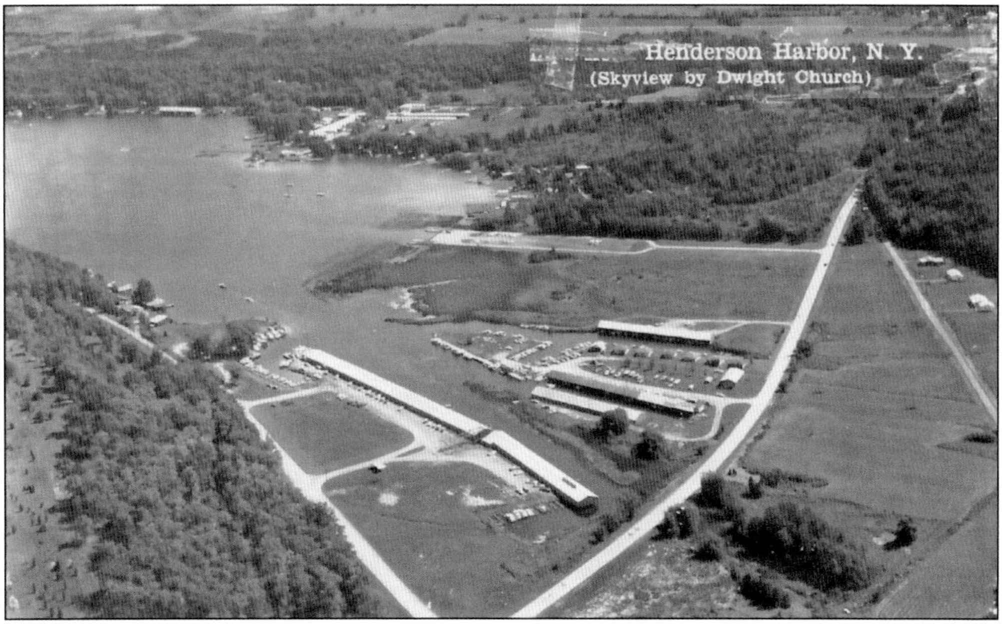

At the southern end of Henderson Harbor, commercial boathouses had taken over the location of the Indian wharf by the mid-1900s. Eastman Marina is the longest. Harbor's End Marina is on the right across the channel, and the Town of Henderson's boat launch is at the wishbone feature above them. At the top left is the Larry Smith boathouse, later owned by Phillips Petroleum and ConocoPhillips for Stony Island Lodge. (Church.)

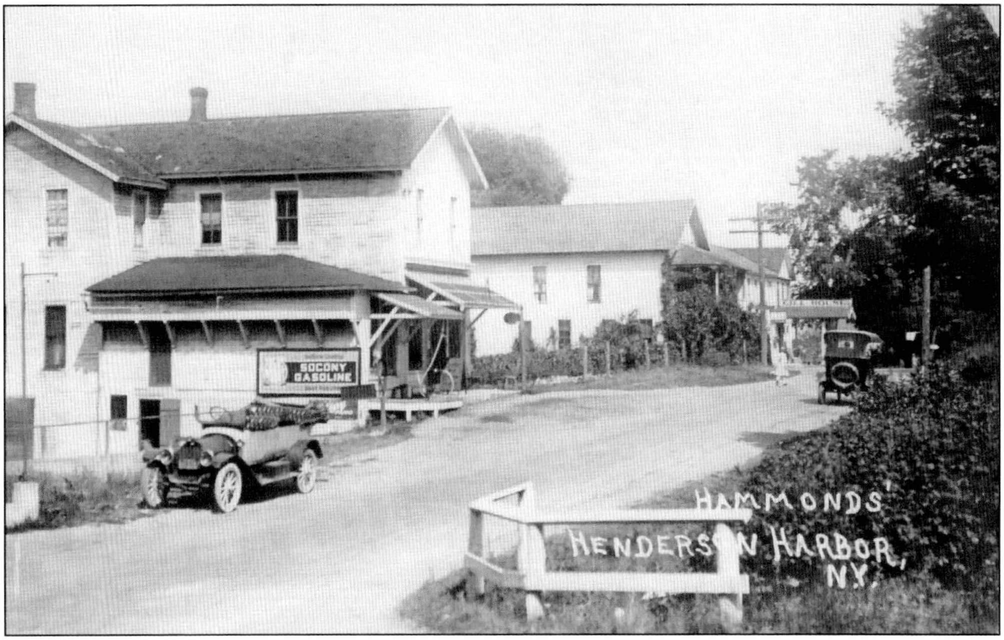

Hammond's Store was a fixture along Harbor Road between the Gill House and the Harbor Inn as early as 1910. Originally operated by Wilbur W. and MaryAnn Hammond, their daughters, Pearl and Hazel Hammond, later operated the general store with a popular ice cream parlor. (Church.)

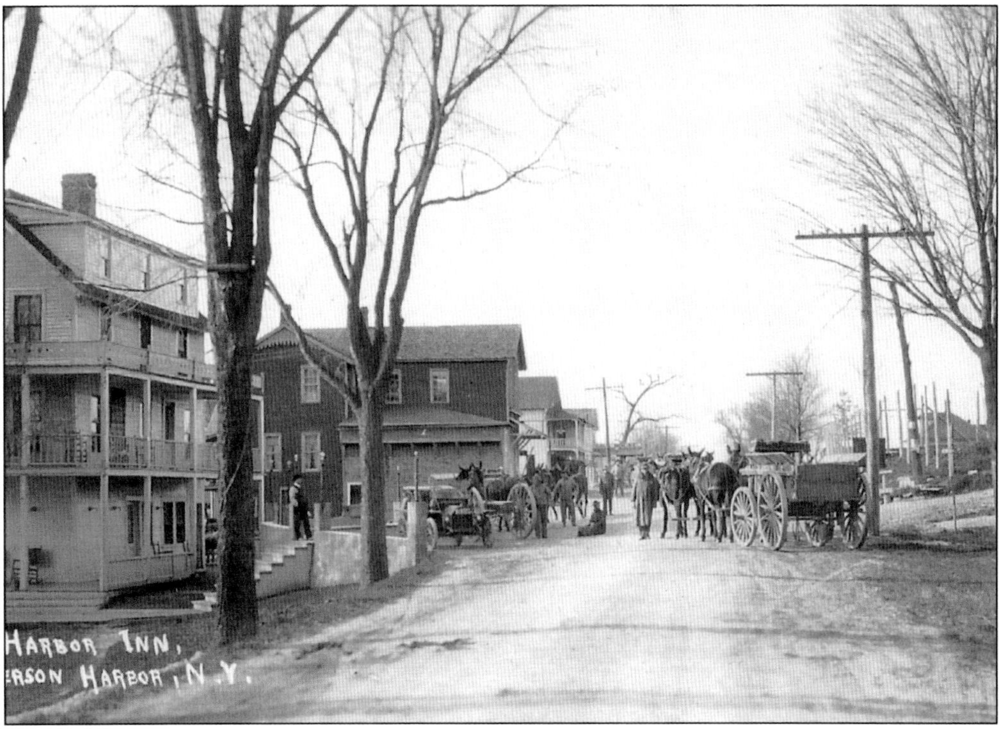

In this view from around 1905 or 1910, Hammond's store is in the center. The Harbor Inn is at left, and the Gill House is in the distance with the upper porch. Looking north, the camera would have been located in front of today's Westview Lodge.

Two

INNS AND GUESTHOUSES

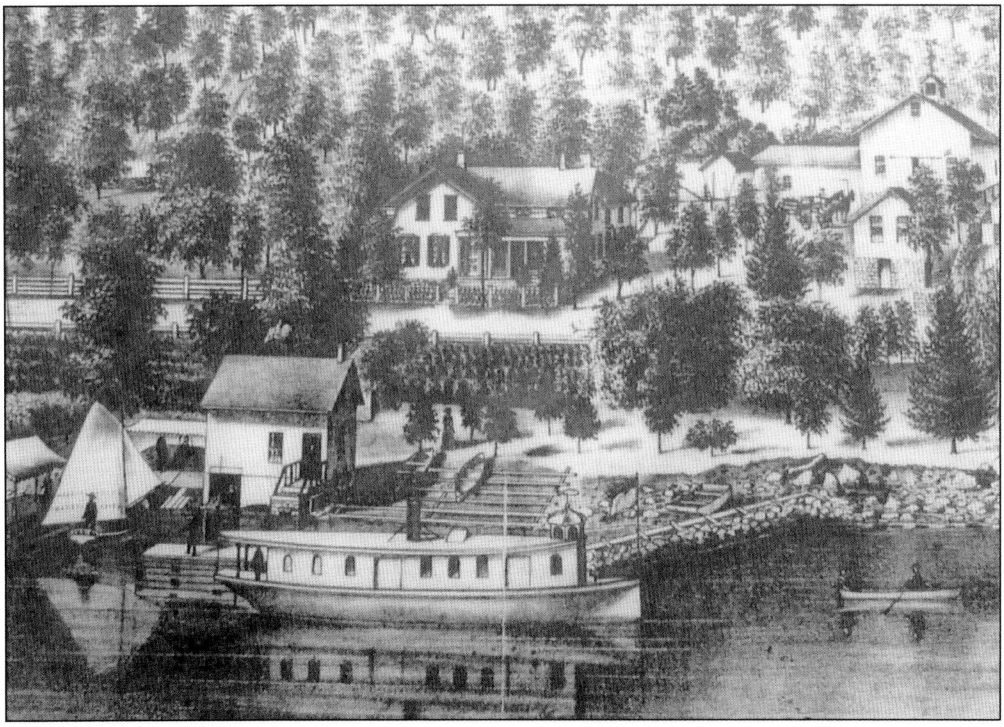

Warner's Inn was located on the north side of Henderson Harbor. Great Lakes ship captain Henry R. Warner purchased his farm in 1843 and was hosting guests by the 1860s. The steamer ran between Kingston, Ontario, Sackets Harbor, and Henderson Harbor. The farm on the east side of Harbor Road included more than 40 acres. (Sandy Conde.)

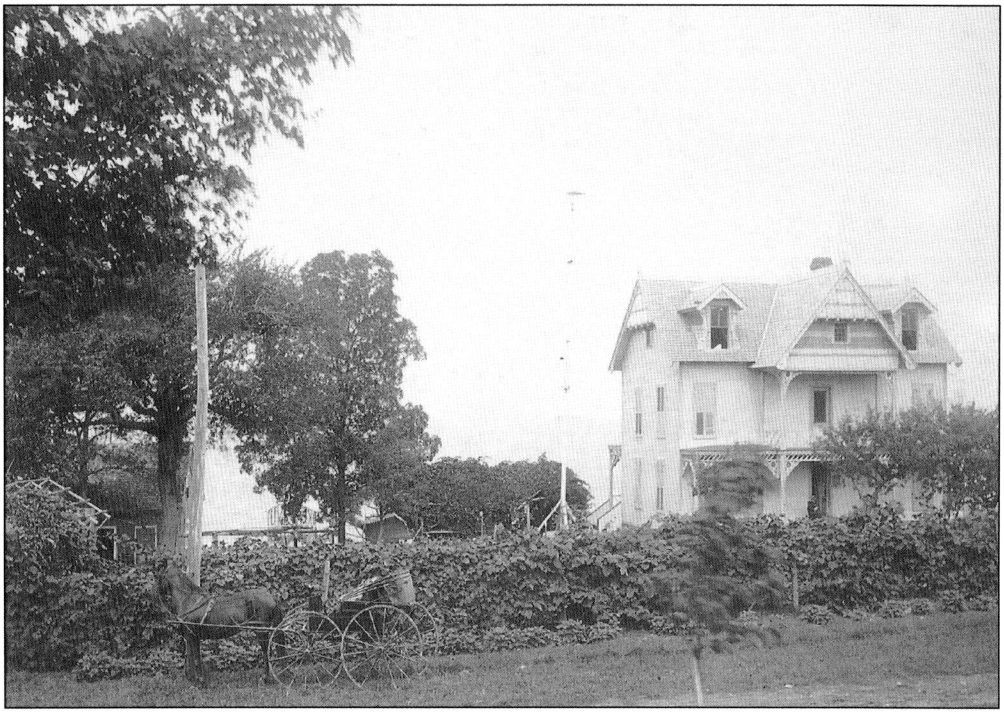

Henry Warner's son George H. Warner expanded beyond the farmhouse inn to accommodate regular guests, such as Secretary of State John W. Foster, piano company heir Henry W.T. Steinway, and Syracuse casket company owner John Marsellus. Warner built Edgewater, a three-story Victorian cottage on the edge of the bay. (JCHS.)

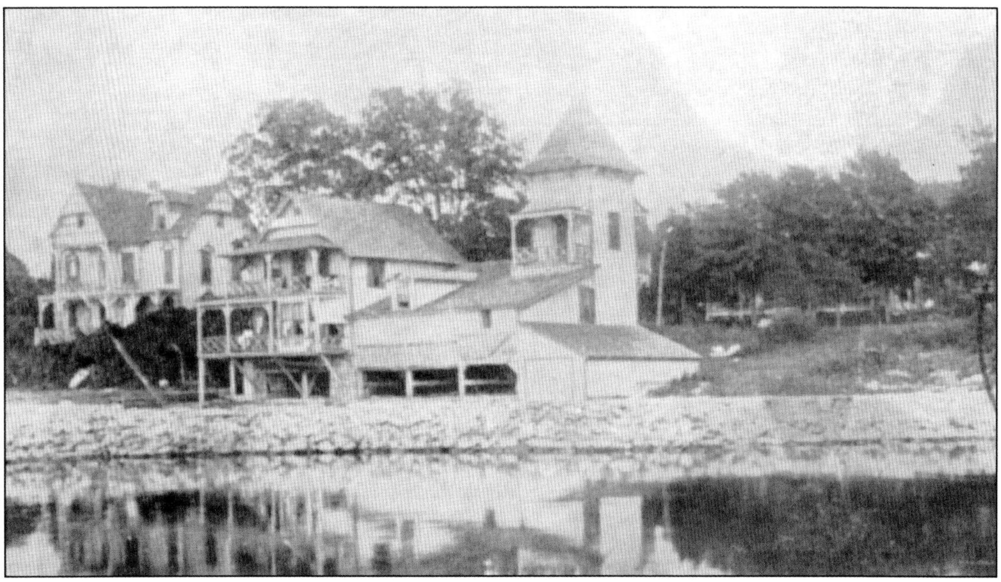

George H. Warner also built a large boathouse, with a cottage and tower above it, next to Edgewater, left. It was destroyed by fire in August 1902. Warner's Inn farmhouse is in the right background. This is an extremely rare photograph of the Warner's Inn boathouse complex, which stood for just a few years. (Maryanne Giangobbe.)

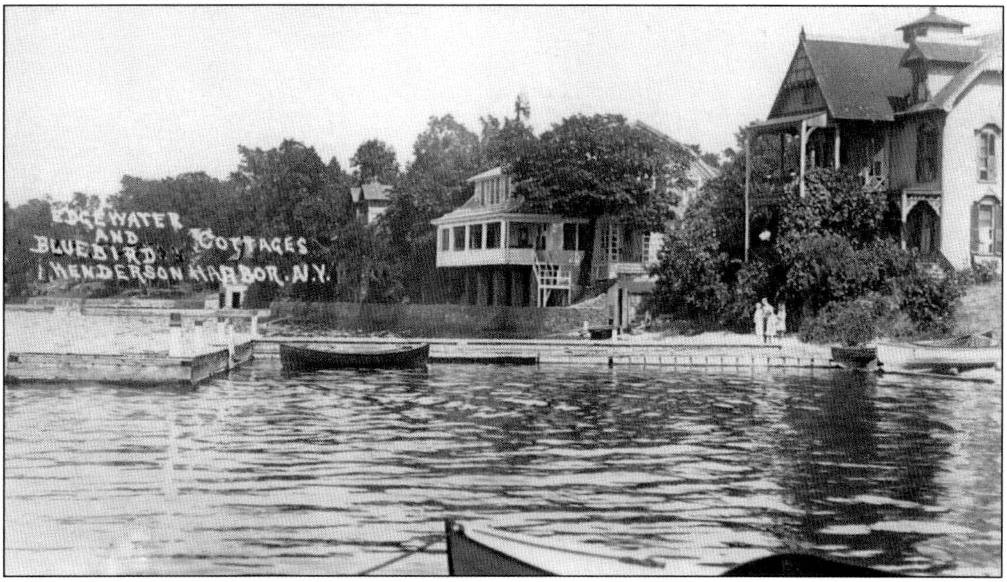

Edgewater included a large dock complex for double-ended rowing skiffs that were popular around 1900. To the left of Edgewater is the Bluebird cottage, which still stands today.

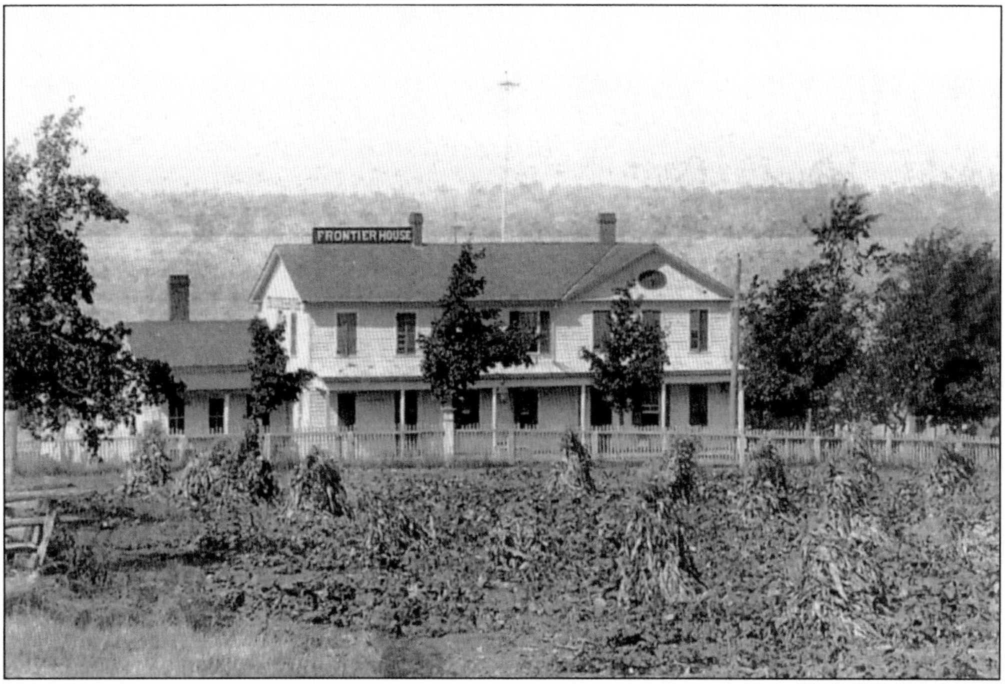

Around 1850, the Frontier House was owned and operated by Great Lakes ship captain John S. Warner, brother of Henry R. Warner. The house was located on a prominent point where Henderson Harbor becomes Henderson Bay. This hotel eventually became the most popular hotel in Henderson Harbor after it was purchased by Hugh H. and Minnie C. Gill and renamed the Gill House. (JCHS.)

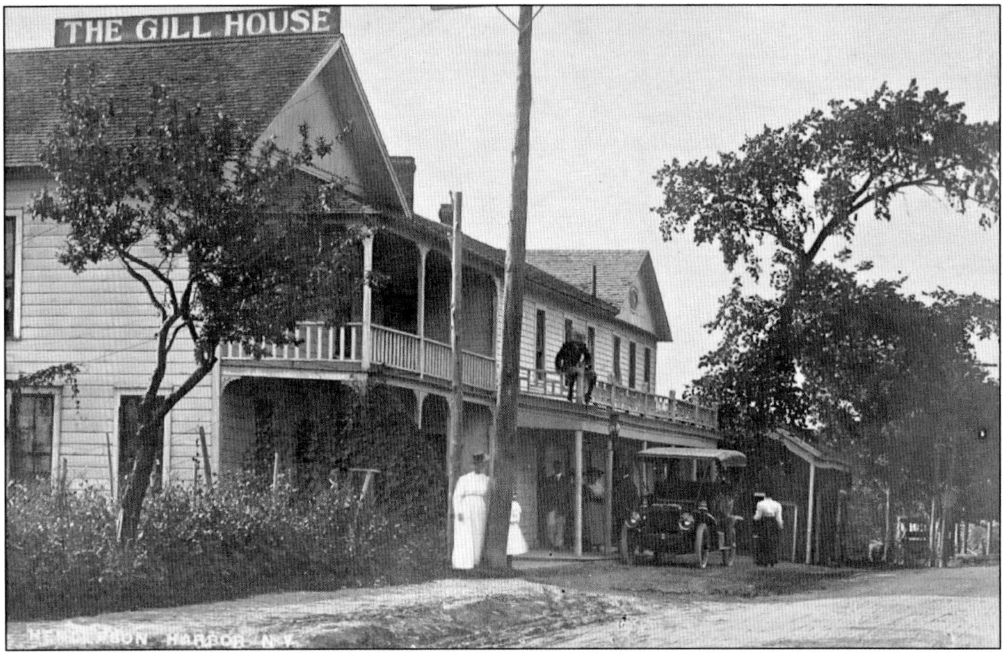

The appearance of the Gill House changed dramatically when a boathouse was moved to the south side of the inn, below the sign. This post-1900 photograph was taken before the addition of the large stone fireplace and chimney. The Gill House would soon become renowned for its fish and chicken dinners and many celebrity guests.

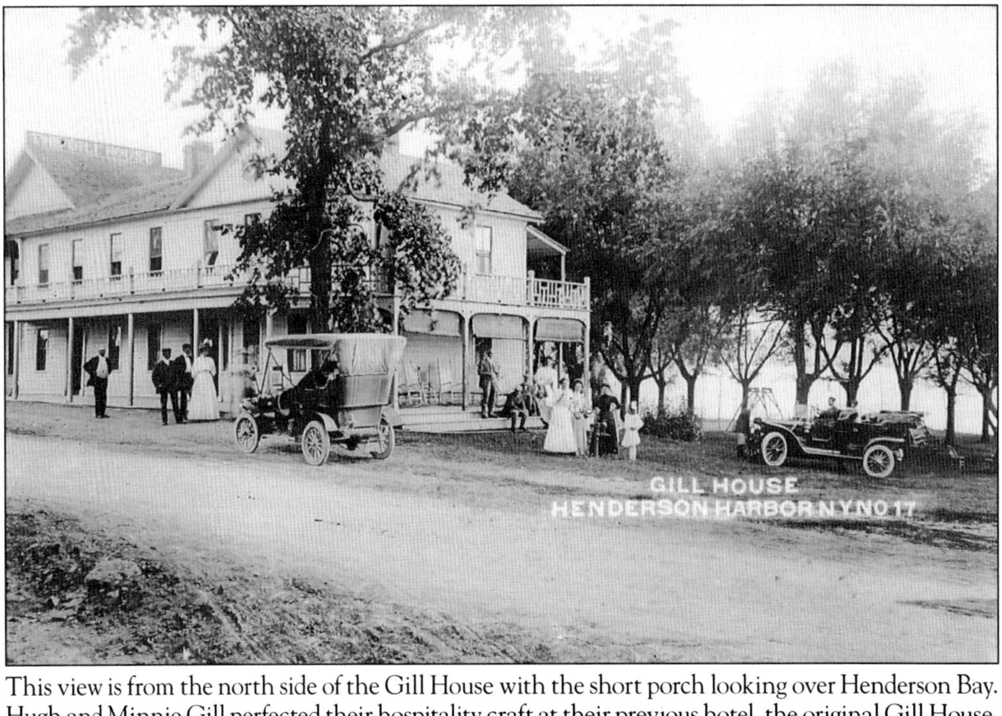

This view is from the north side of the Gill House with the short porch looking over Henderson Bay. Hugh and Minnie Gill perfected their hospitality craft at their previous hotel, the original Gill House, located at the head of Aspinwall Shores, which much later became the O'Donnell's Hotel.

New York City actor Joseph Jefferson was a regular visitor to the Gill House in the early 1900s. Jefferson was well-known for his stage performances as Rip Van Winkle. He made regular trips to upstate New York theaters and spent many fishing vacations in Henderson Harbor.

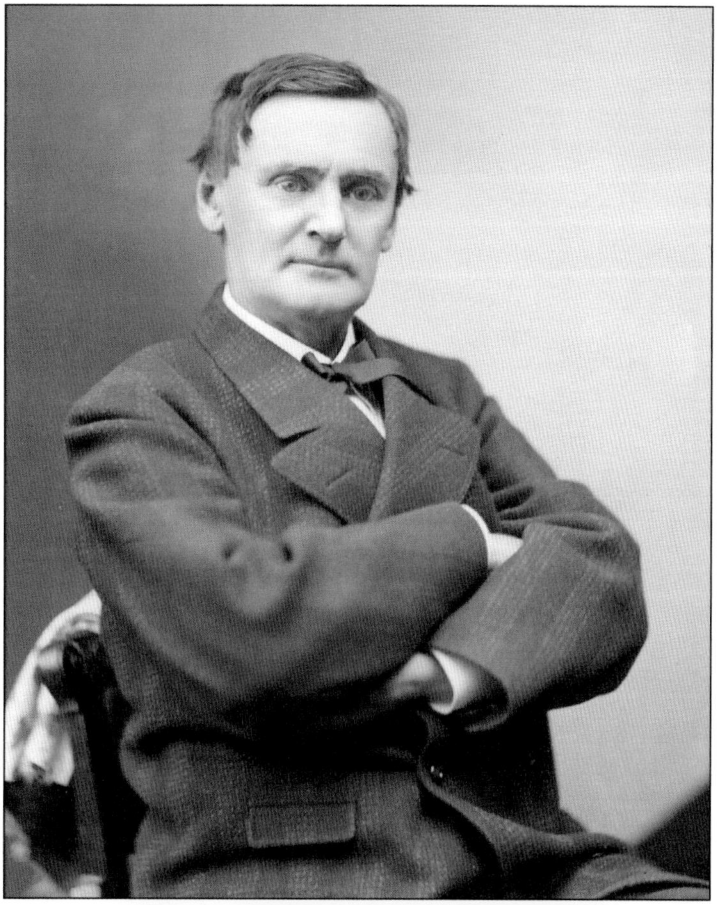

By 1917, Hugh Gill was suffering from poor health and took his own life in the barn next to the Gill House. His daughter Bessie, who was a trained nurse, found him. Bessie Gill assumed operations of the Gill House and continued its highly respected reputation for the next 44 years.

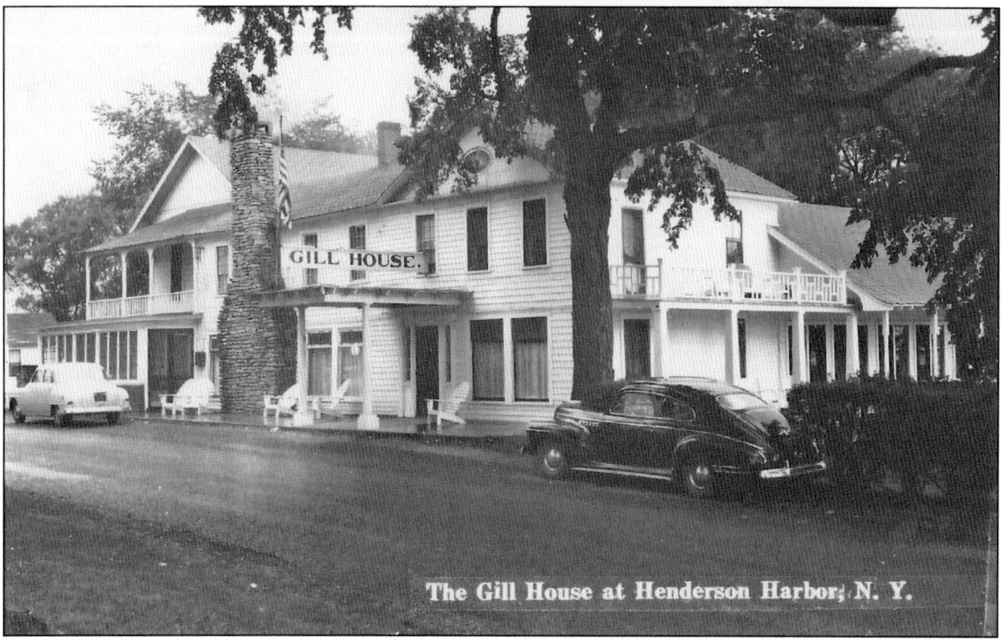

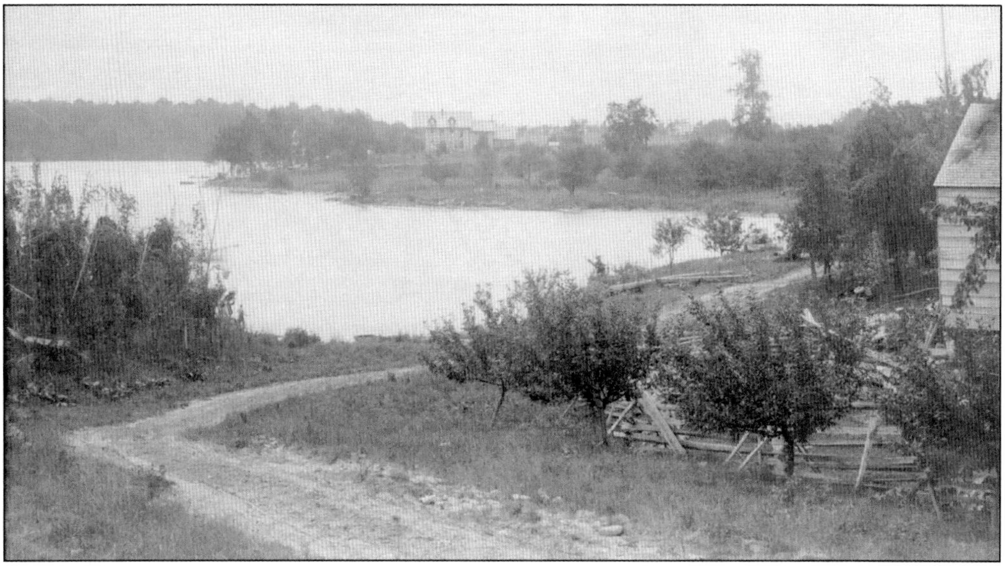

On the west side of Henderson Harbor, between Ding's Cove (foreground) and White's Bay (left), was the Brooklyn House, built by Albert Wilkinson in 1884. On the bluff to the left of the Brooklyn House was the three-story Van Dyne House hotel. It was built by O.W. Van Dyne in the spring of 1875. Eight months later, it was destroyed by a kitchen fire. (JCHS.)

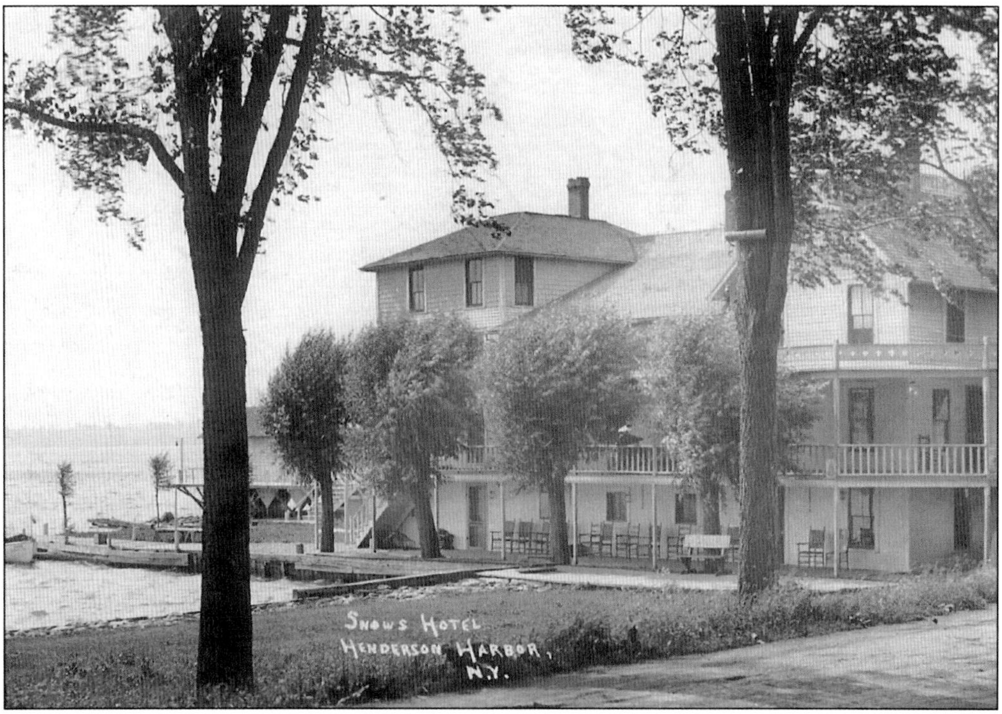

The Hotel de Snow was located in the heart of Henderson Harbor south of the Gill house. Built by Goodwin M. Snow around 1895, it was very popular because of its central location. In 1902, Stony Island Club boatman Michael Lynip was staying at the Hotel de Snow when he was wounded while hunting ducks on Calf Island. Fishing guide Myron Barney carried Lynip back to the hotel in his naphtha launch, where innkeeper Snow cared for him until the doctor arrived.

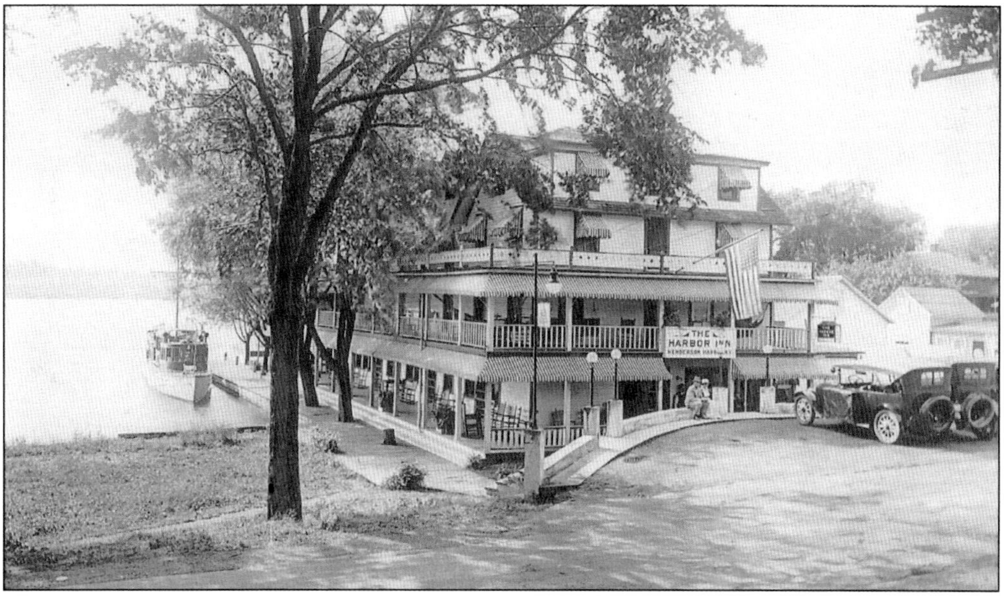

The Hotel de Snow suffered a major loss when four feet of water flooded into the ground floor and the bar on June 12, 1908. In 1912, Snow sold the hotel to Charles J. Purdy of New York City for about $8,000. It became Purdy's Harbor Inn. Purdy leased the hotel dock to GE for the Claverack, left. It burned at the dock in July 1924. The only thing left at this site from the hotel is the concrete bulkhead on which the two people are sitting.

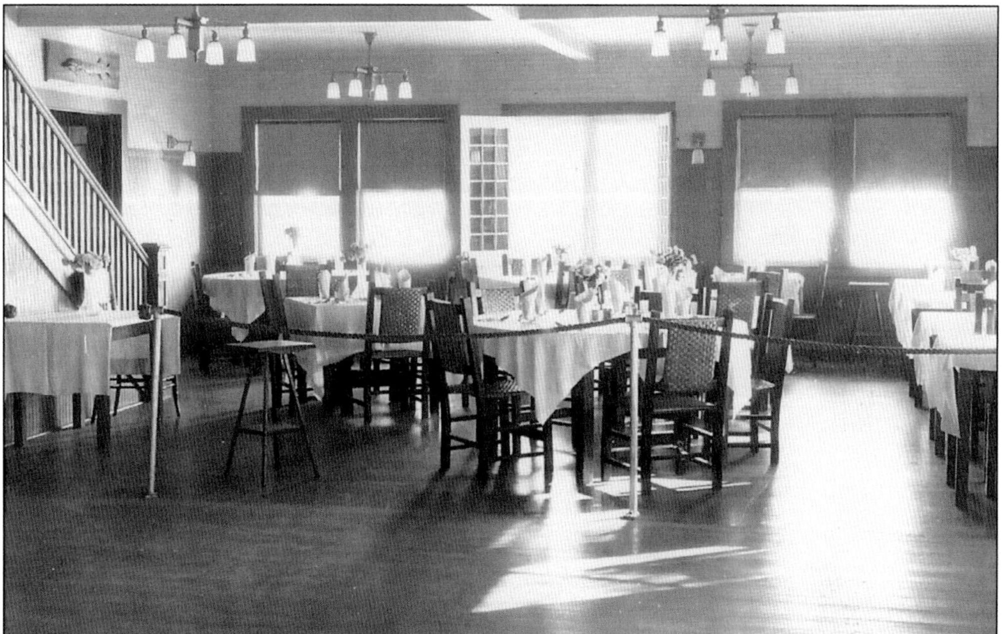

Charles J. Purdy invested nearly $7,000 in the Harbor Inn dining room, kitchen, and guest rooms. By 1917, GE purchased the complex at auction and leased it to James J. Bridgman of Lowville, New York. In December 1932, GE demolished the classic 100-room hotel. GE used the hotel site and docks for the next 25 years for boats shuttling passengers to and from Association Island.

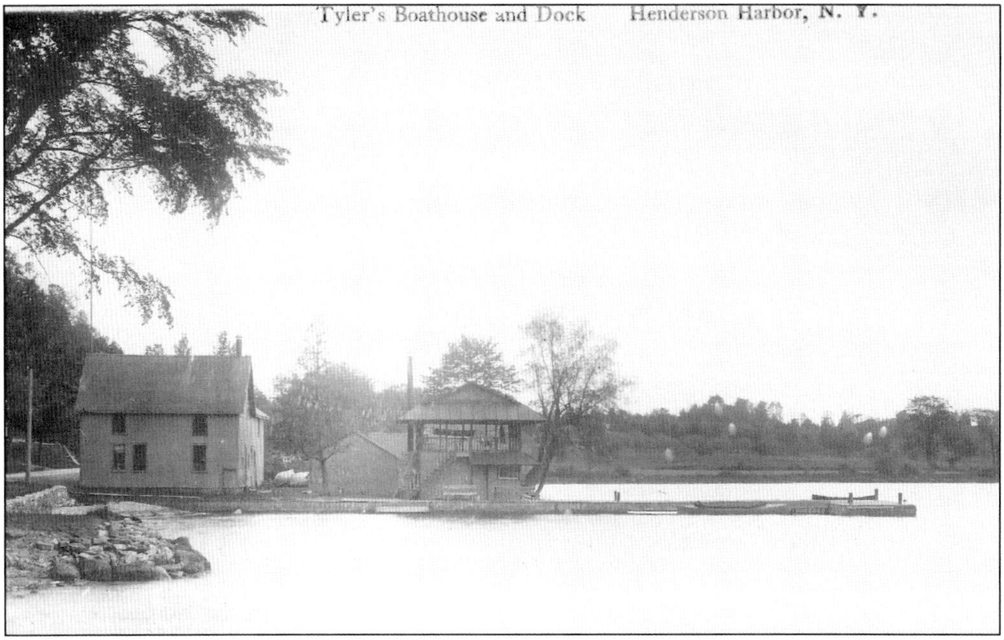

Tyler's Inn and marina were located along Harbor Road on the southeast side of Henderson Harbor. In the photograph above, its long dock extends into the water. In the 1870s, Capt. Elman and Cynthia Tyler took in summer boarders at their waterfront farm. Tyler's cottages and boathouses included several docks and a boat livery.

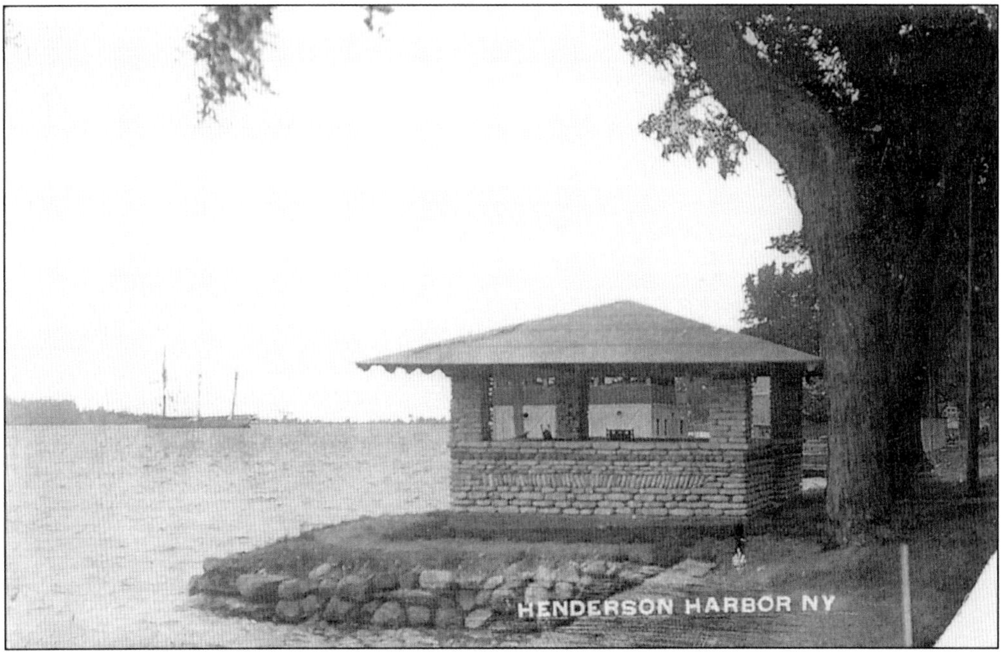

One of the most recognizable landmarks in Henderson Harbor is Tyler's pagoda, or gazebo, which is a stone and concrete waterfront structure used over the years for lunches, sunbathing, and meetings. It is one of the most photographed locations in Henderson Harbor, especially at sunset.

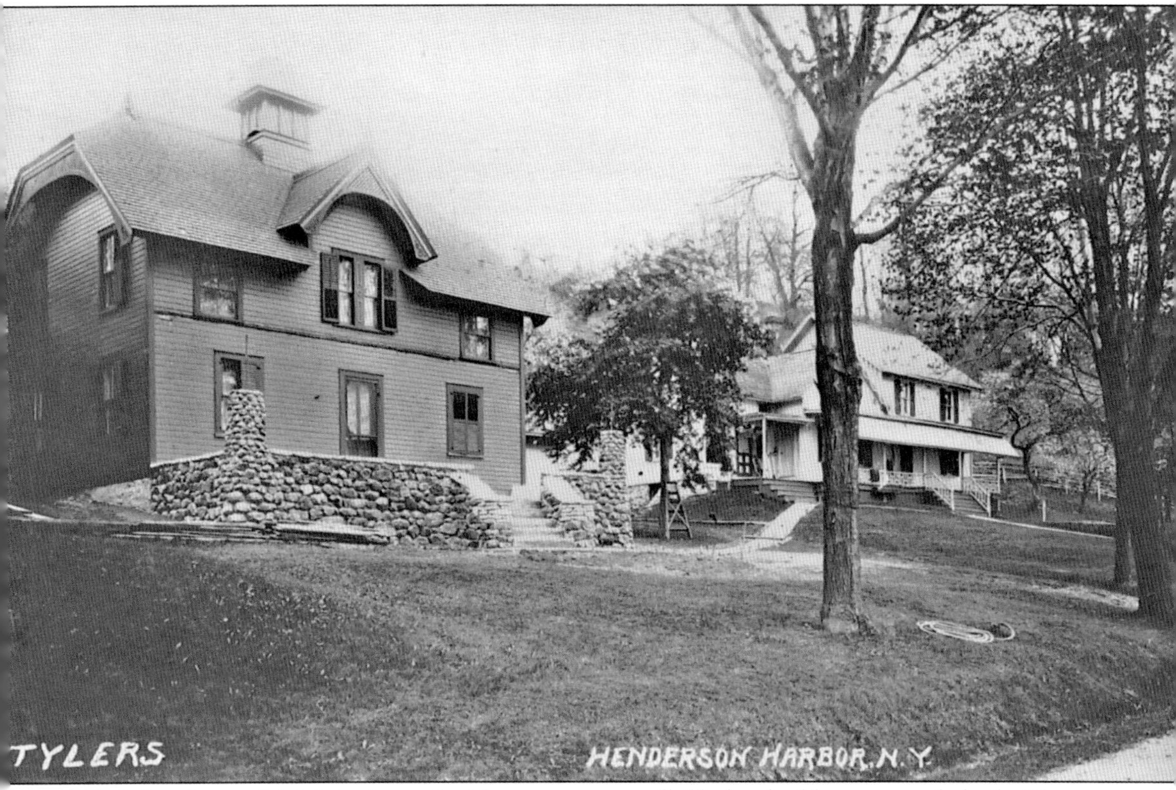

Tyler's farmhouse (right) is pictured with a new cottage (left) that had been recently built. The porch roof on the new cottage was completed in 1910. In 1884, Tyler's Inn was one of just four locations in the town of Henderson with a telephone. Birt and Harriet Moody Tyler ran the inn until Harriet's death in 1946. Claude Dunk purchased a large portion of Tyler's farm in 1945.

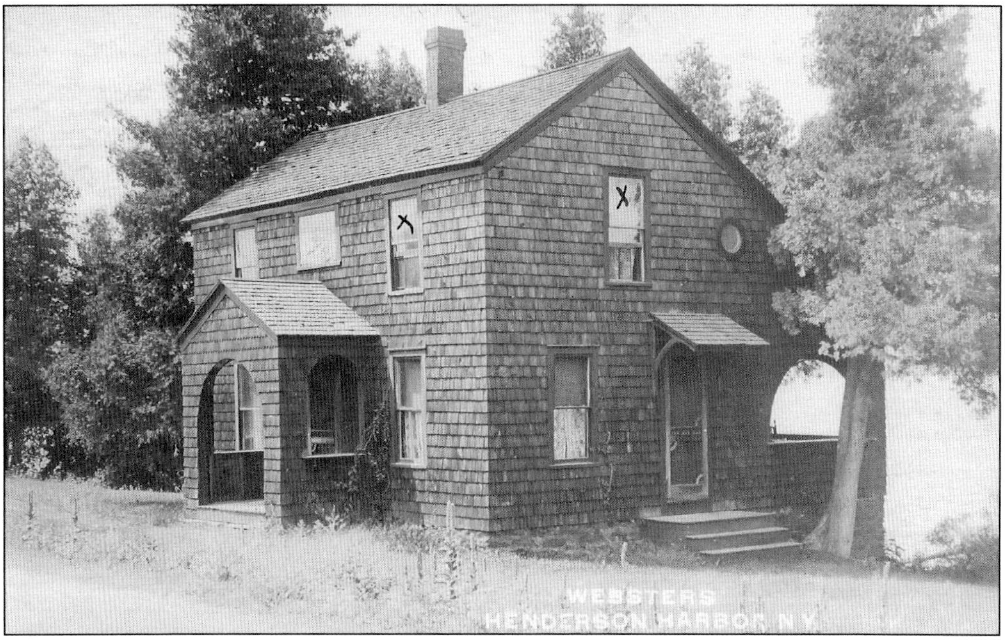

Webster's cottage along Harbor Road was rented as a guesthouse for visitors to Henderson Harbor. Built by Fred L. and Fannie Webster of Adams, New York, it was originally called the Cedars because of the many cedar trees along the water.

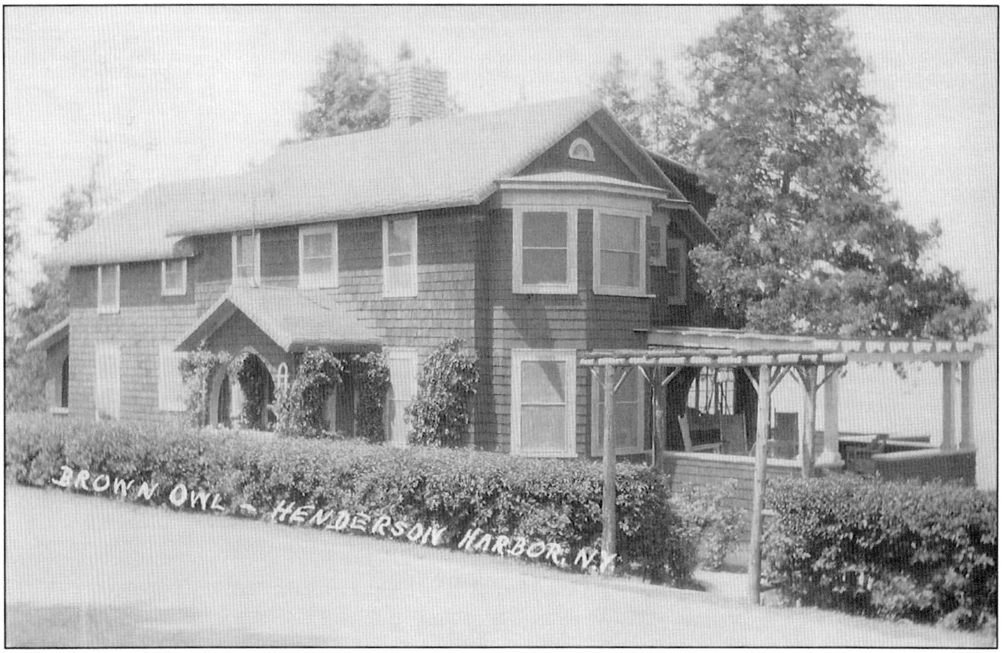

Webster's cottage has been enlarged over the years, including adapting a porch to a large cedar tree. Renamed the Brown Owl, this Harbor Road shingled cottage is a well-known landmark, by car or by boat.

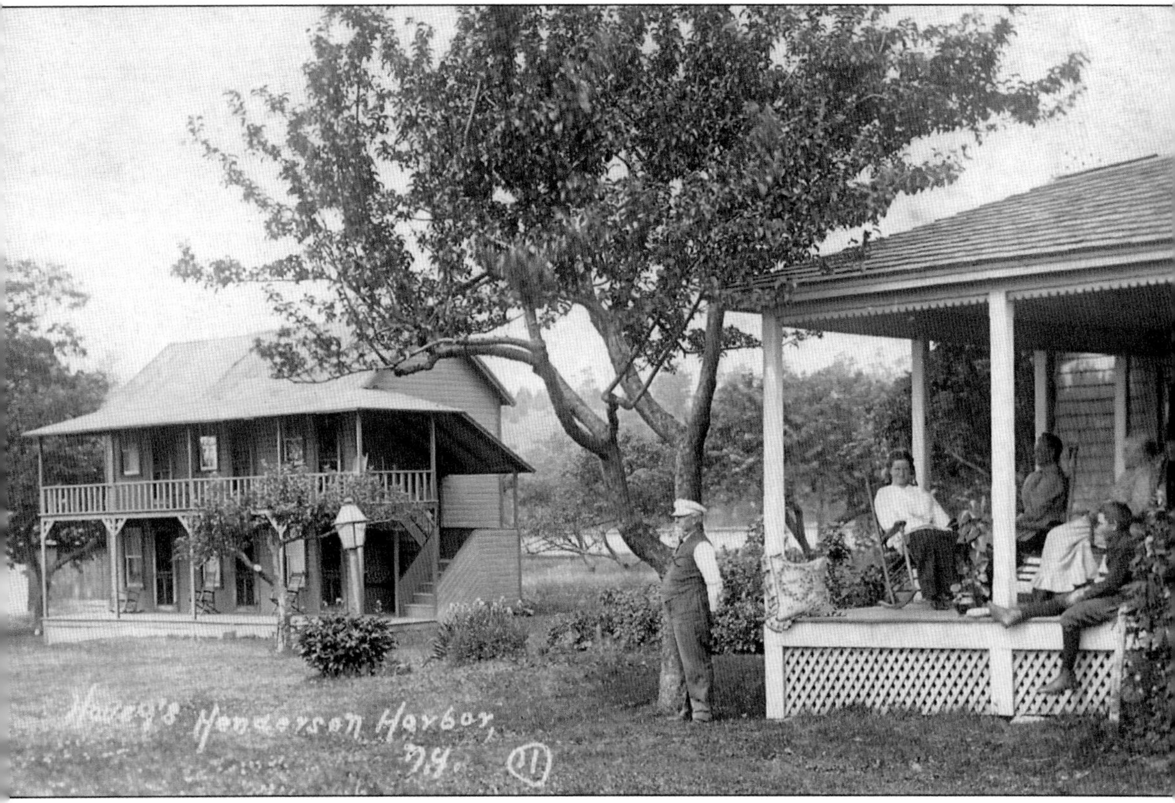

Hovey's Snowshoe Inn was located near the family's farmhouse on Hovey's Island. The six-room fishermen's cottage was built near the boathouse on Snowshoe Bay, where Winnie Hovey could row his clients to the fishing spots on the lake without having to first row across Henderson Harbor. In the background is the end of Snowshoe Bay and the gravel bar that later became the cut.

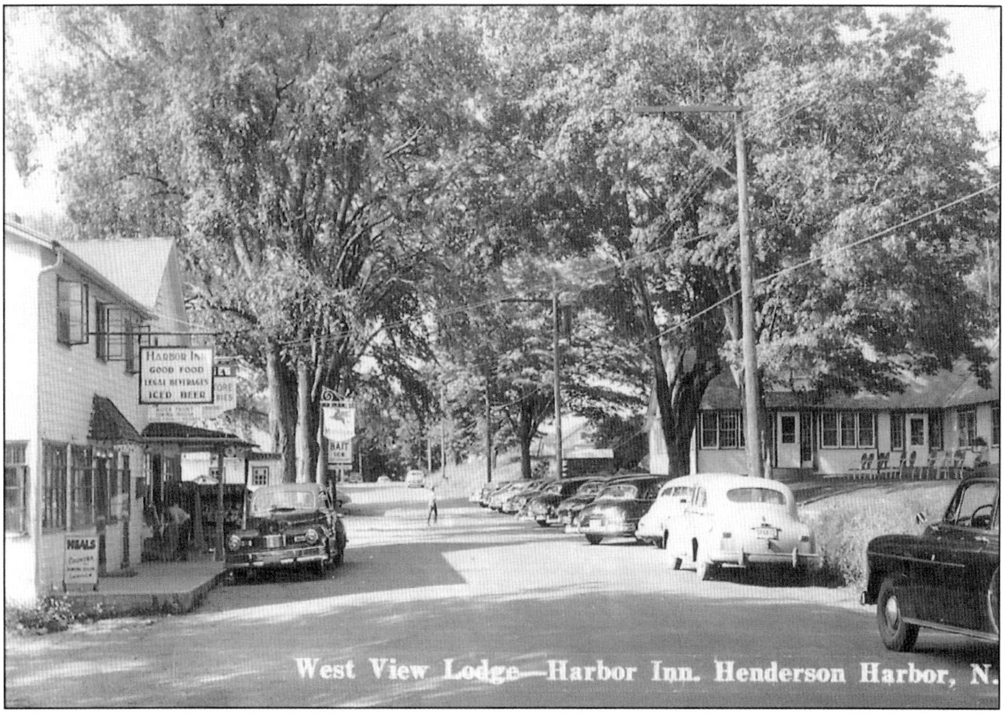

Westview Lodge (right) and the new Harbor Inn are landmarks in the heart of Henderson Harbor. Westview Lodge was originally named Lake Lodge when it was established prior to 1930. The new Harbor Inn (left) was formerly the site of Pilon's garage and dock.

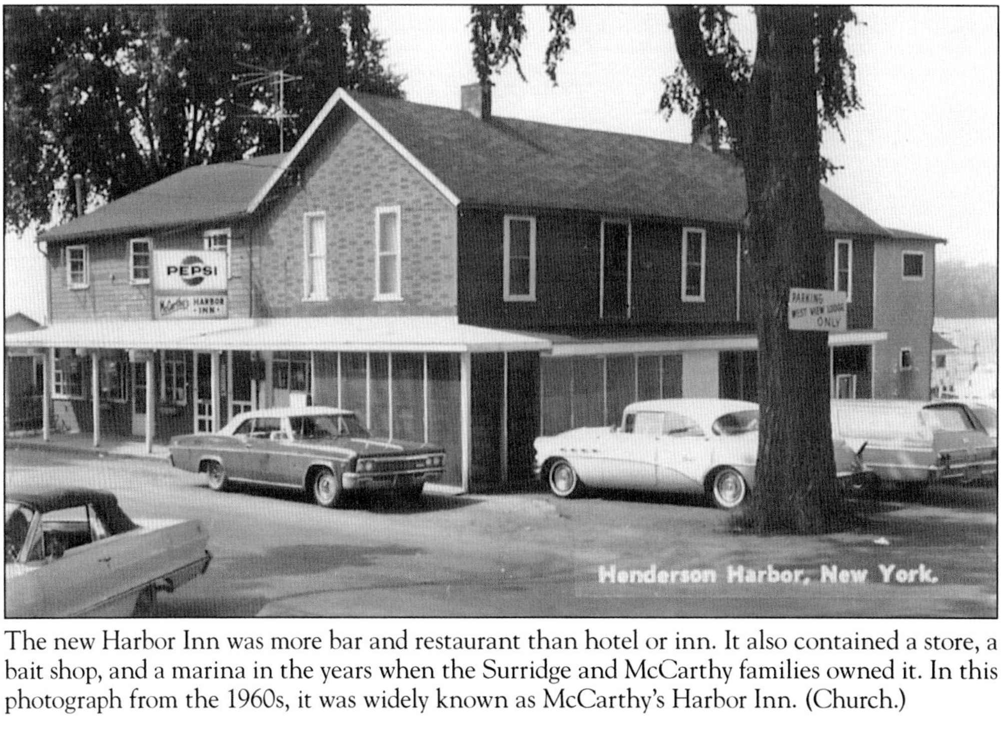

The new Harbor Inn was more bar and restaurant than hotel or inn. It also contained a store, a bait shop, and a marina in the years when the Surridge and McCarthy families owned it. In this photograph from the 1960s, it was widely known as McCarthy's Harbor Inn. (Church.)

Three

Fishing Guides and Families

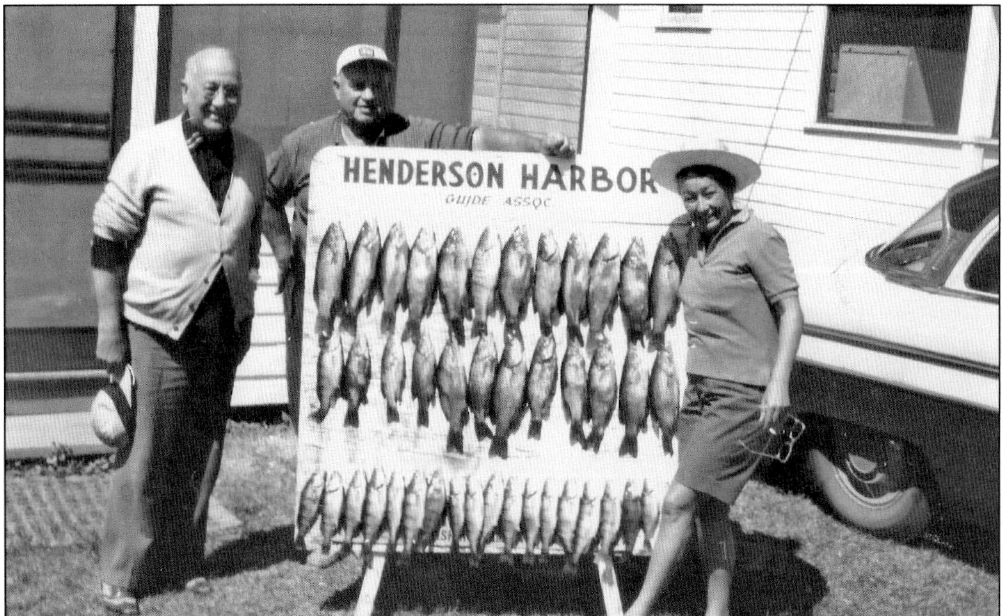

Bass and perch have long been the prized game fish at Henderson Harbor. Well-known Henderson Harbor fishing guides have included Prince, Will, Alden, Albert, Harry, and Melvin Stevens; Myron Barney; J. Aiken Montague; Ross White; Dave Hess; Winnie and Nelson Hovey; Nello Vorce; Gib Gertner; Charlie and George Henchen; Claude Dunk; Bill and Barry Smith; Fremont Powers; Charlie Ragonese; Gene Howard; Lyle, Bob, and Dave McCrae; Ruddy, Ron, and Jack Ditch; Bob Dick; Scott Durant; Grover Moore; Arden Greene; Jim McGowan; Bill Saiff Jr.; and Bill Saiff III.

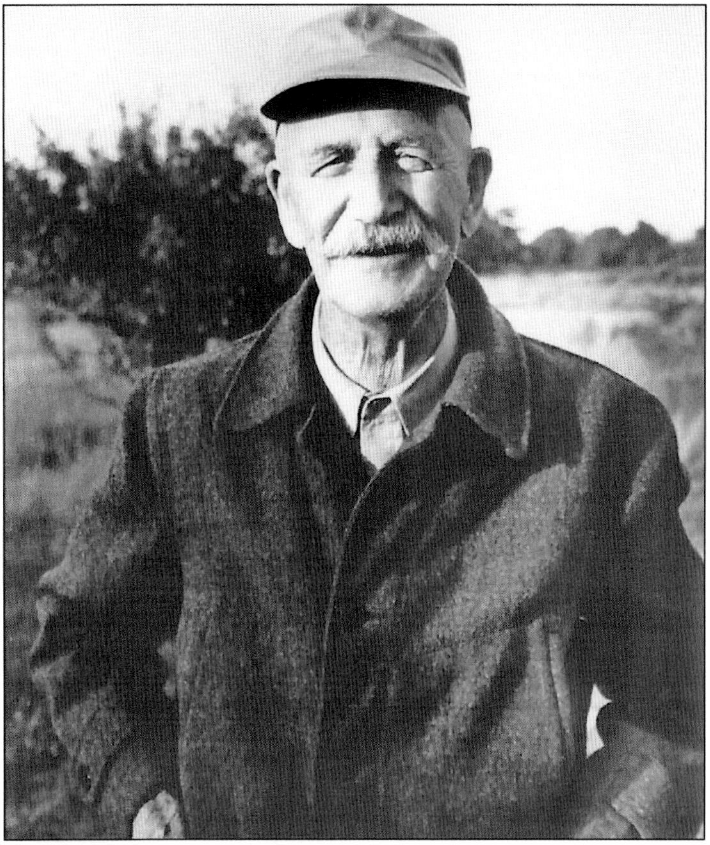

The most revered fishing guide in Henderson Harbor was Willett H. "Will" Stevens, who died in 1958 at the age of 98. As a young man, Stevens was the guide for US Secretary of State John W. Foster and later for secretaries Robert M. Lansing and John Foster Dulles. Stevens's father, Prince, is said to have initiated what is known as the shore dinner. (The Stevens family.)

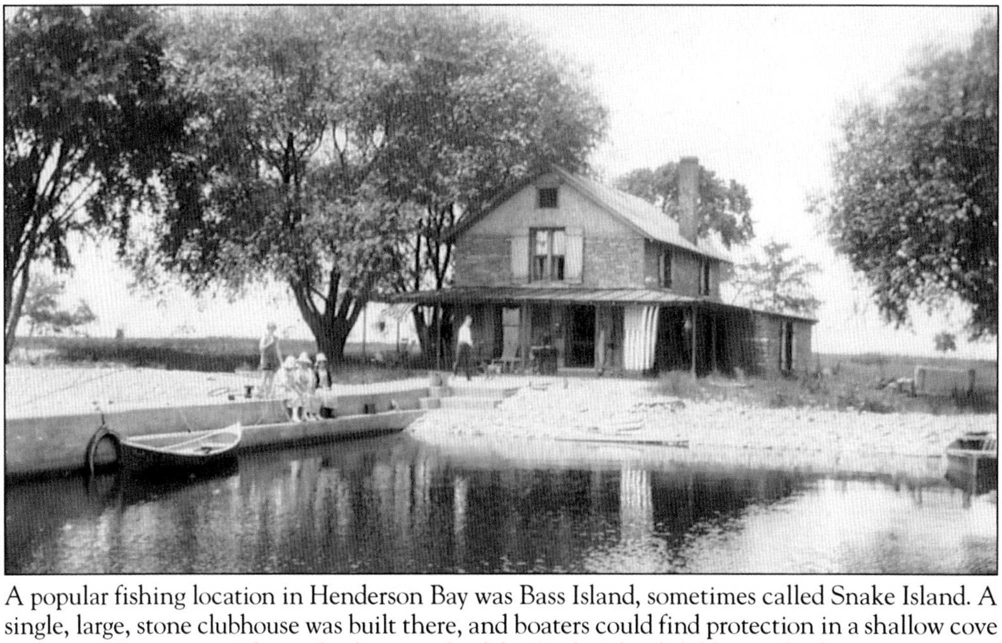

A popular fishing location in Henderson Bay was Bass Island, sometimes called Snake Island. A single, large, stone clubhouse was built there, and boaters could find protection in a shallow cove in front of the cottage. This early photograph of the Snake Island clubhouse displays an American flag, perhaps for an Independence Day celebration. (John D. Marsellus.)

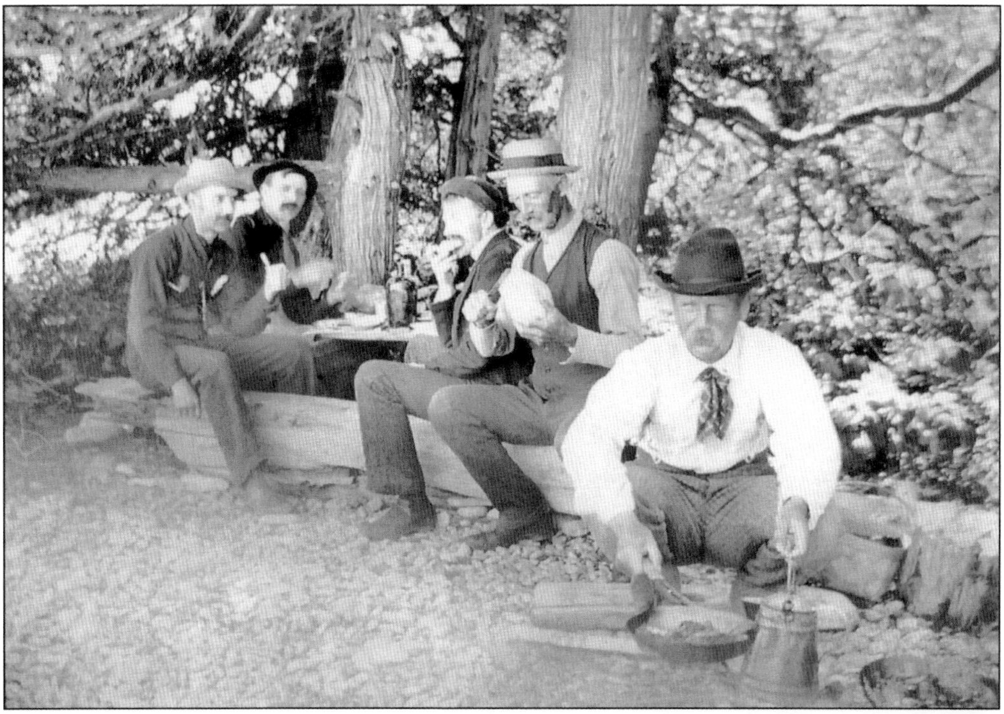

Guiding ran deep in the Stevens family of Henderson Harbor. The first three men in this photograph are unidentified, and at right, the older brothers of Will Stevens, Alden and Albert Stevens, prepare a shore dinner among the large native cedar trees on one of the offshore islands of Lake Ontario. A guide until the very end, Albert Stevens died in his boat while fishing alone on Stony Island pond in August 1924 at the age of 76. He had a fish on his line when his body was found. (The Stevens family.)

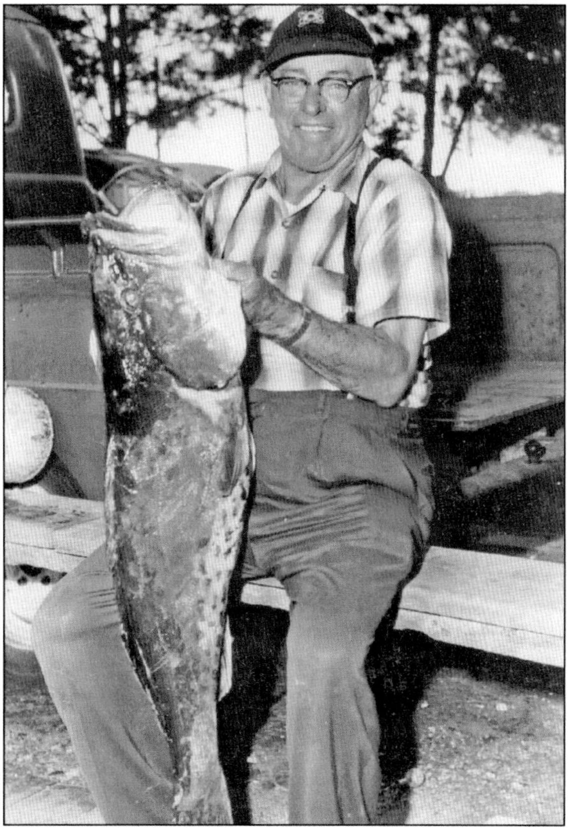

Charles "Charlie" Henchen, founder of Henchen Marina, bares a smile while struggling to hold up this giant catfish. Henchen and his wife, Lottie, purchased the former Oliver J. McConnell boathouse in 1937 and transformed it into the most successful marina in Henderson Harbor. (Diane Henchen Gamble.)

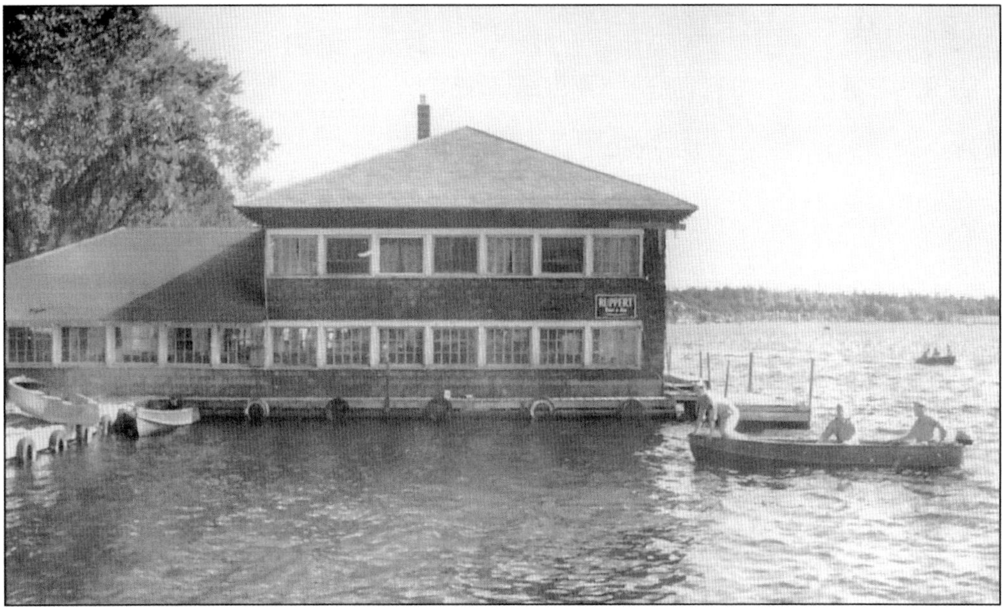

Henchen Marina has always been the place to meet a fishing guide, purchase tackle, or to have fish cleaned. This c. 1945 photograph shows soldiers in uniform approaching Henchen Marina in small outboard motorboats. (Diane Henchen Gamble.)

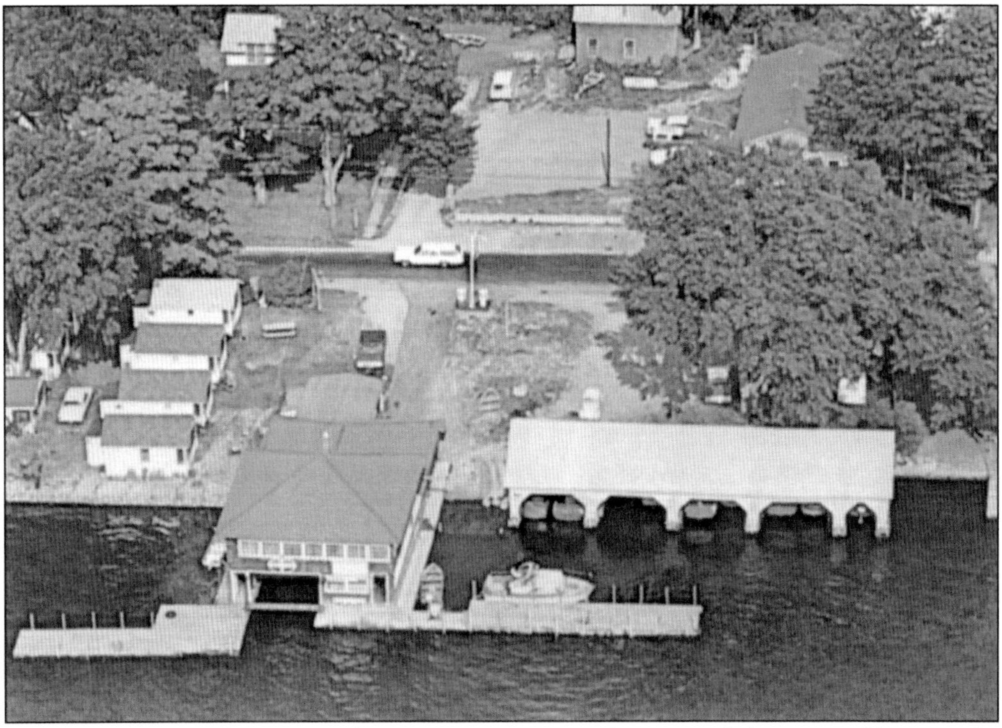

George Henchen took over Henchen Marina in 1962 and continued the seasonal business for many years. By then, the marina consisted of the bait and tackle shop, Henderson Harbor Guides Association headquarters, a boathouse, a gas dock, fish-cleaning services, and rental cabins. (Diane Henchen Gamble.)

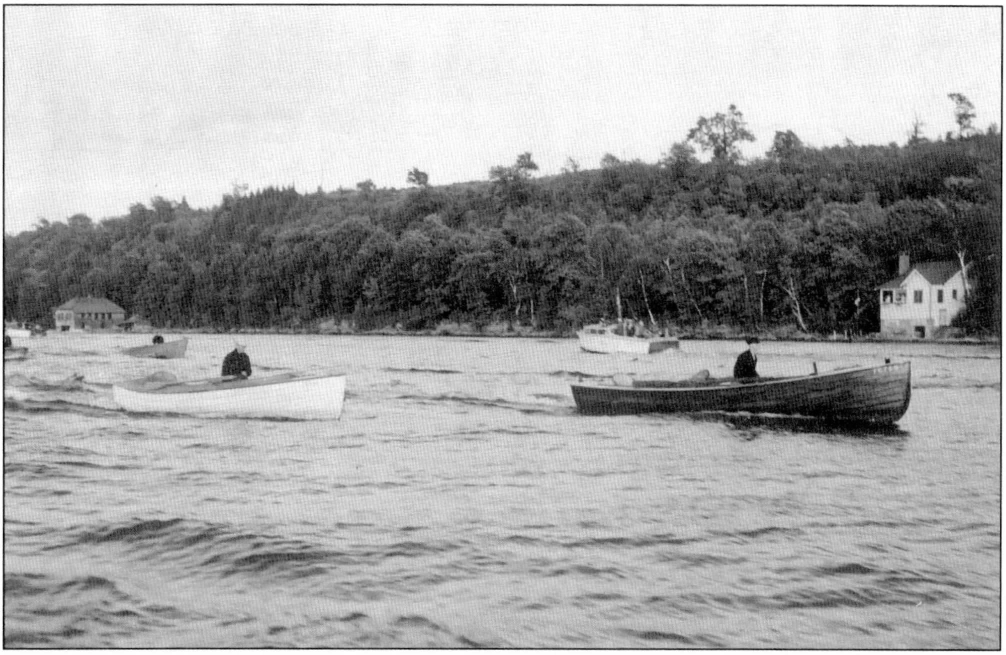

Navigating their guide boats into Henderson Harbor in the 1940s, fishing guide J. Aiken Montague (right) is followed closely by fellow guide Ross E. White. The Montague family owned a sizeable portion of Stony Island. White is from the family for whom White's Bay is named. (Ann Montague Maurer.)

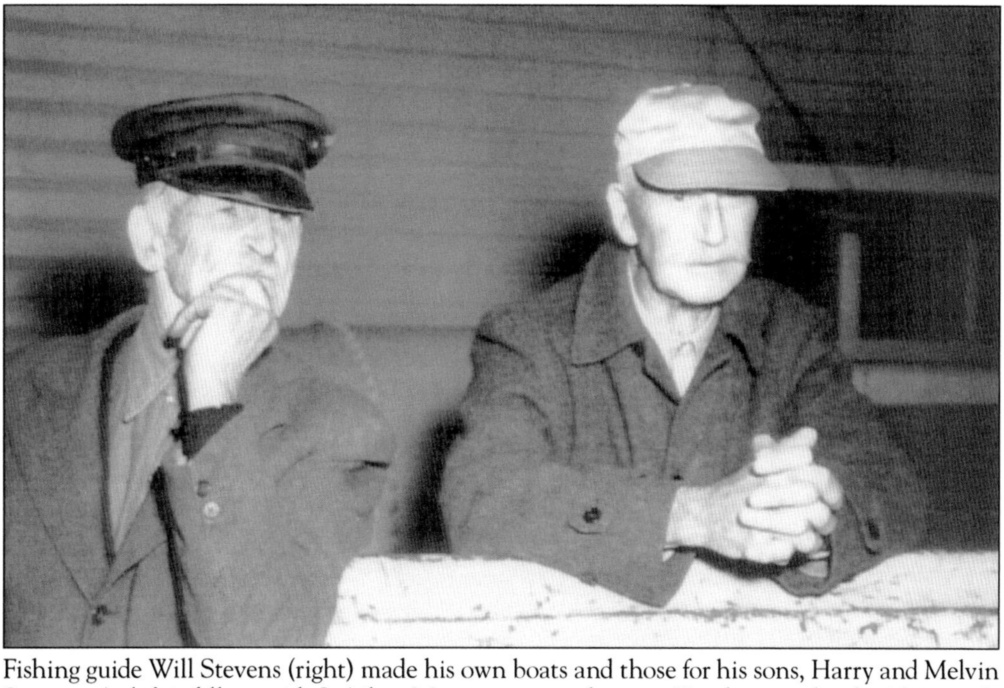

Fishing guide Will Stevens (right) made his own boats and those for his sons, Harry and Melvin Stevens. At left is fellow guide J. Aiken Montague, a professor at Henderson schools. Along with Ross White, these men were the most sought after fishing guides in Henderson Harbor during the first half of the 20th century. (The Stevens family.)

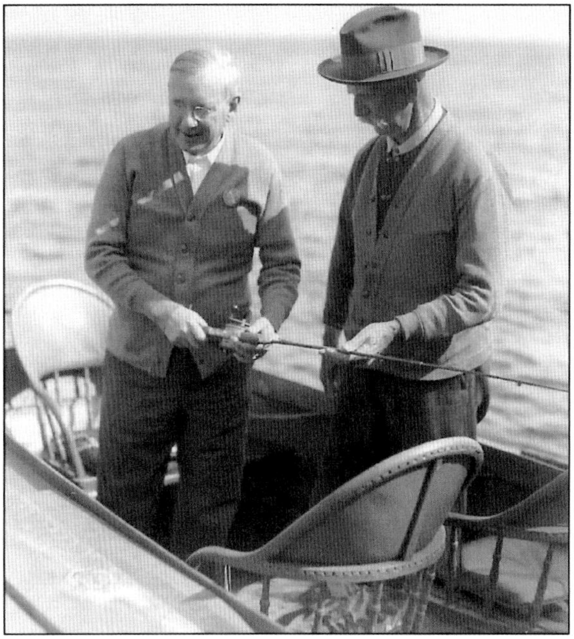

Stevens was such a renowned guide that he was chosen by *Watertown Daily Times* publisher and Henderson Harbor summer resident Harold B. Johnson to guide for a special visitor to Henderson Harbor in May 1938. Stevens, right, is giving fishing tips to 1936 Republican presidential candidate and Kansas governor Alfred M. Landon in Stevens's boat in front of Johnson's cottage, Underbluff. (The Johnson family.)

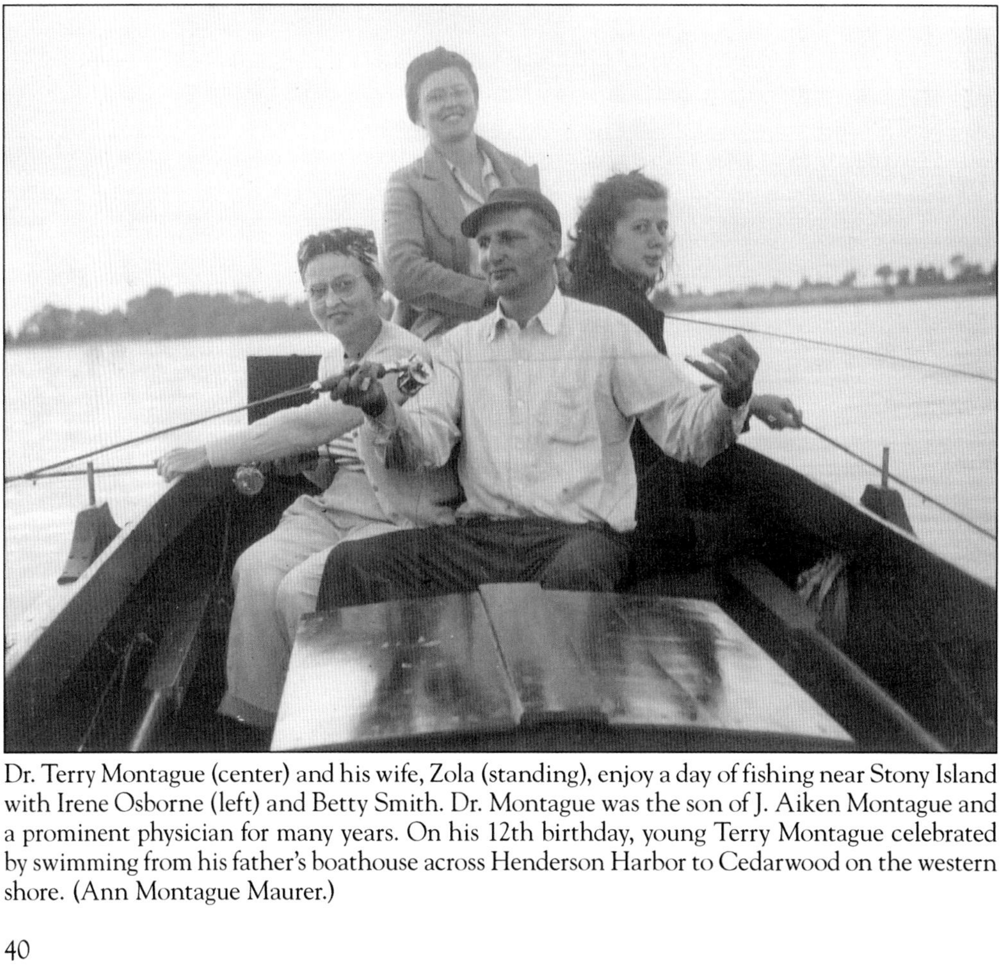

Dr. Terry Montague (center) and his wife, Zola (standing), enjoy a day of fishing near Stony Island with Irene Osborne (left) and Betty Smith. Dr. Montague was the son of J. Aiken Montague and a prominent physician for many years. On his 12th birthday, young Terry Montague celebrated by swimming from his father's boathouse across Henderson Harbor to Cedarwood on the western shore. (Ann Montague Maurer.)

Bass and perch were plentiful in Henderson Harbor. A seasoned fishing guide could easily produce a catch of 17 smallmouth black bass in the summer of 1935. From left to right are Francis Lewis, Ken Hovey, Ernie Lewis, guide Winnie Hovey, and Harold Lewis. (Stan Hovey.)

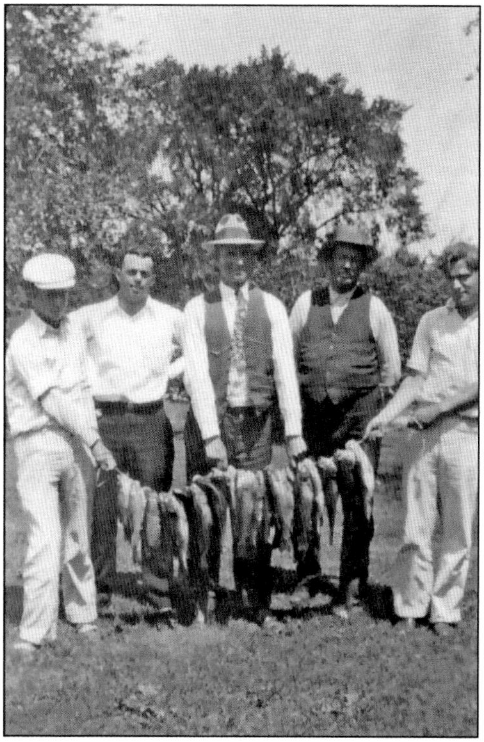

Many fishing guides found their career to be so satisfying they never retired. Fremont "Freem" S. Powers began guiding in the Thousand Island area before moving to Henderson Harbor and settling in the former Tyler's Inn cottages. Powers was a regular guide for insurance executive Erwin Dickey. (Susan Powers Washburn.)

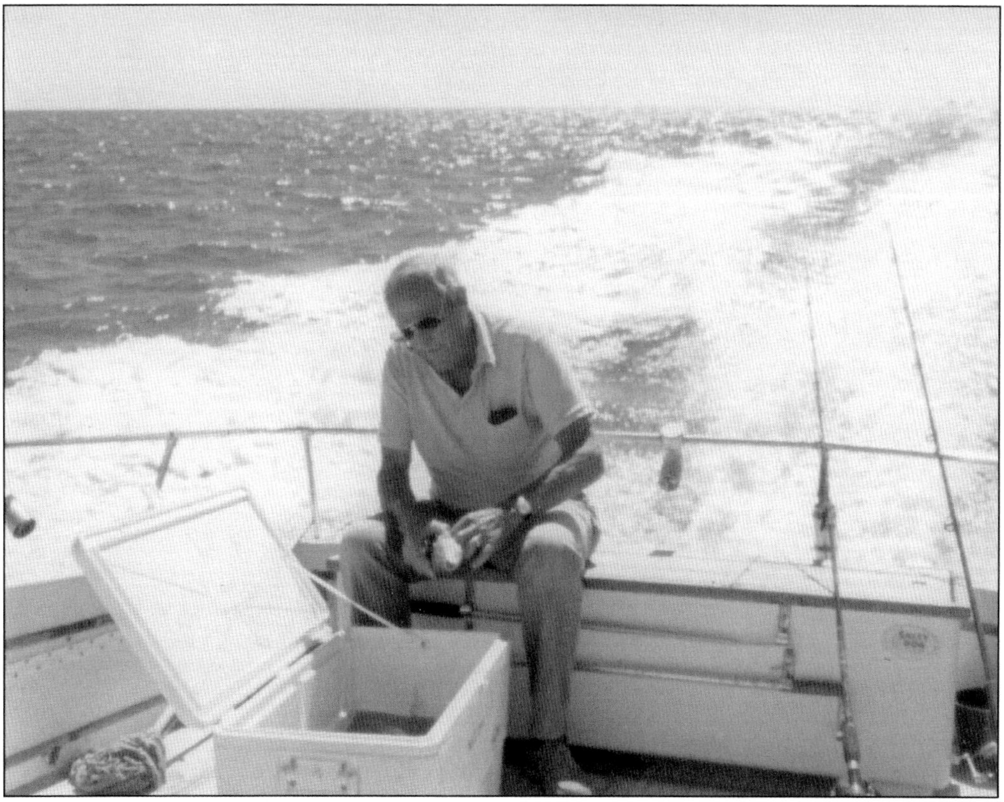

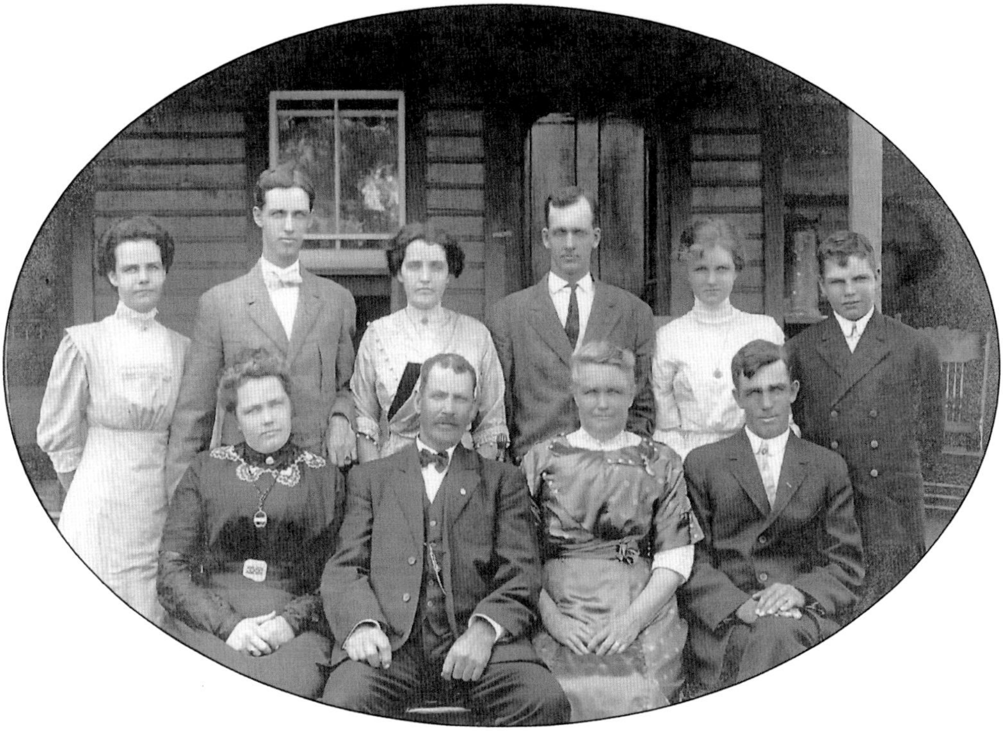

Winnie and Martha Hovey pose for a family portrait just before Martha's death in July 1916 at Snowshoe Inn. Pictured from left to right are (seated) Flora, Winnie, Martha, and Claude Hovey; (standing) Margaret, Ernest, Bernice, Nelson, Thelma, and Harold Hovey. (Stan Hovey.)

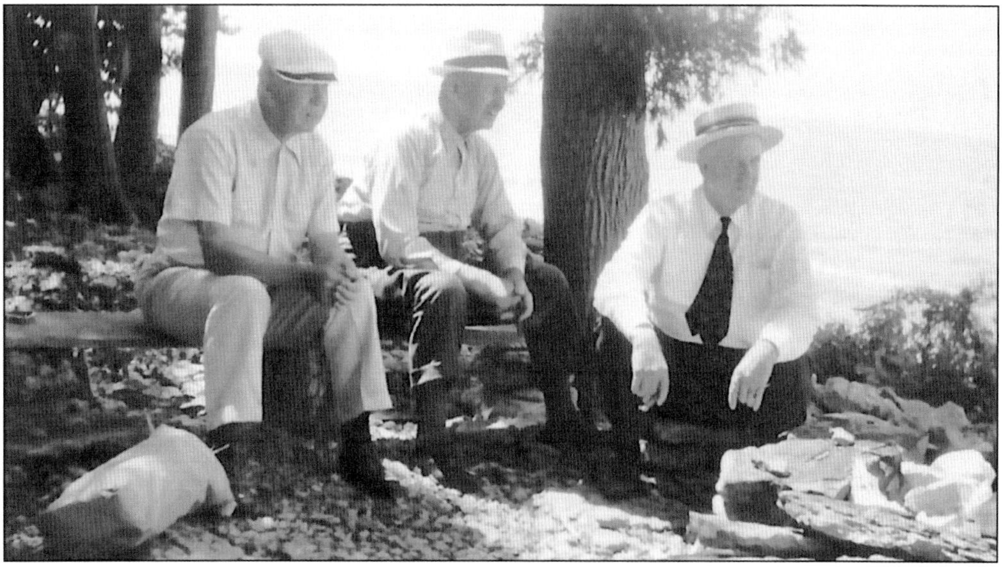

Originally from Galloo Island, the Hovey family was scattered around the country by the 1920s. George S. Hovey (left) was a banker in Kansas City, Missouri. Winnie Hovey (center) ran Snowshoe Inn on Hovey's Island. Ford Hovey was a banker and president of an Omaha, Nebraska, stockyard. This August 1940 photograph shows the Hovey brothers at a Henderson Harbor shore dinner. (Stan Hovey.)

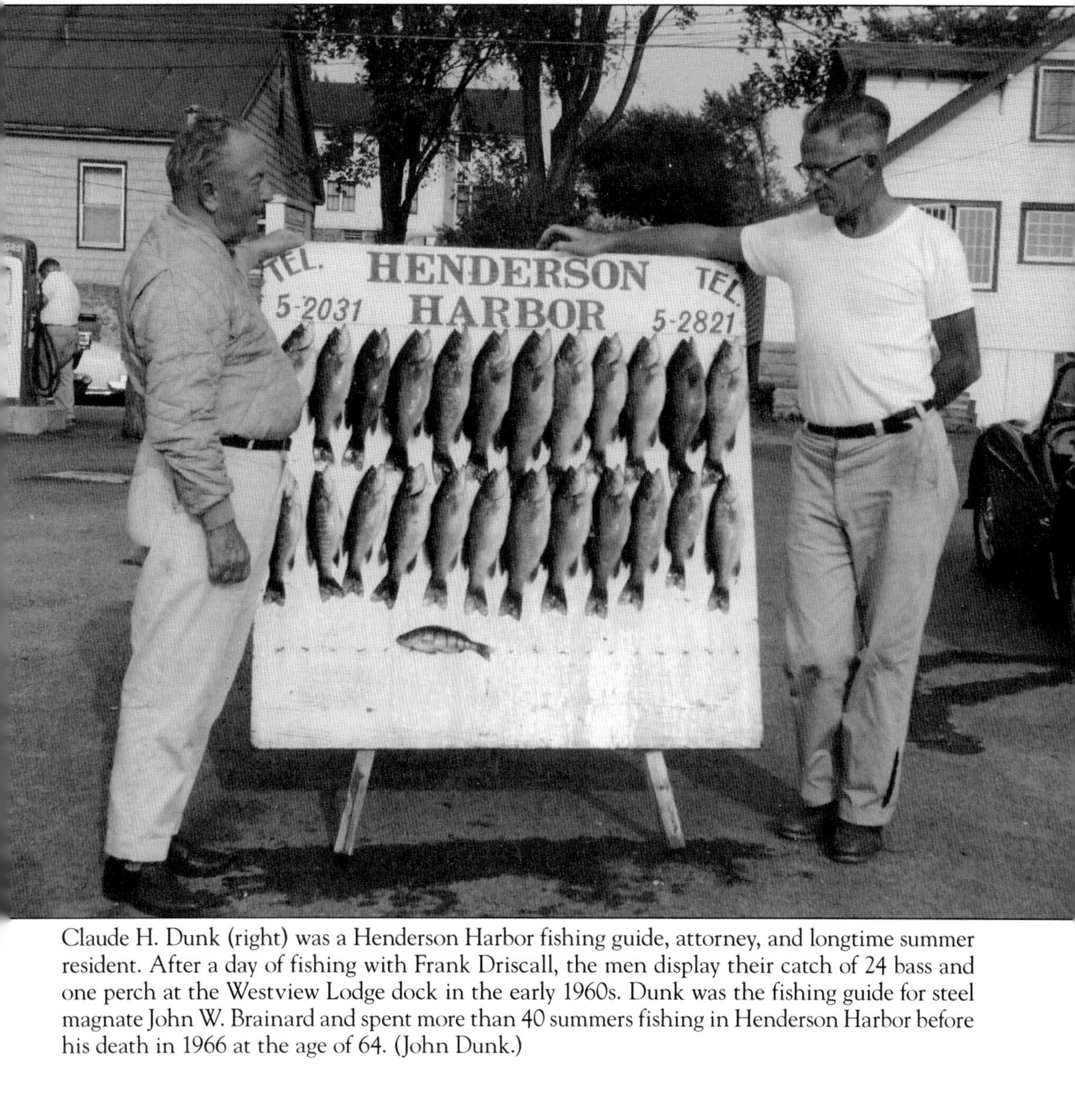

Claude H. Dunk (right) was a Henderson Harbor fishing guide, attorney, and longtime summer resident. After a day of fishing with Frank Driscall, the men display their catch of 24 bass and one perch at the Westview Lodge dock in the early 1960s. Dunk was the fishing guide for steel magnate John W. Brainard and spent more than 40 summers fishing in Henderson Harbor before his death in 1966 at the age of 64. (John Dunk.)

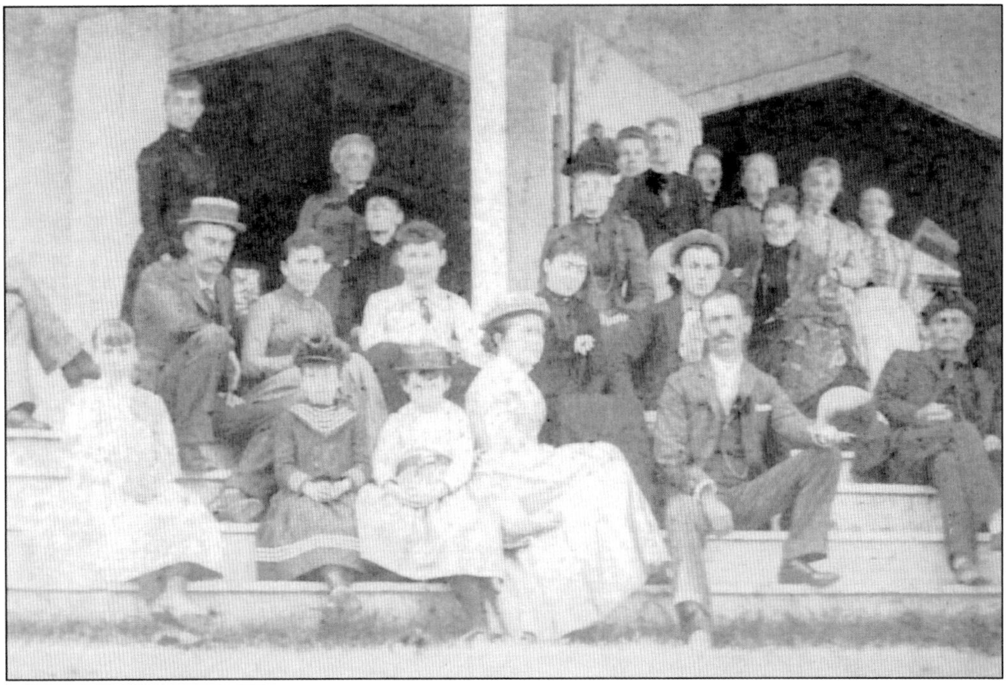

Families from Highland Park spent their summers in Victorian homes on the western shore of Henderson Harbor. They ate together at the Highland Park dining hall, where this group posed for a c. 1900 photograph. (The Averill family.)

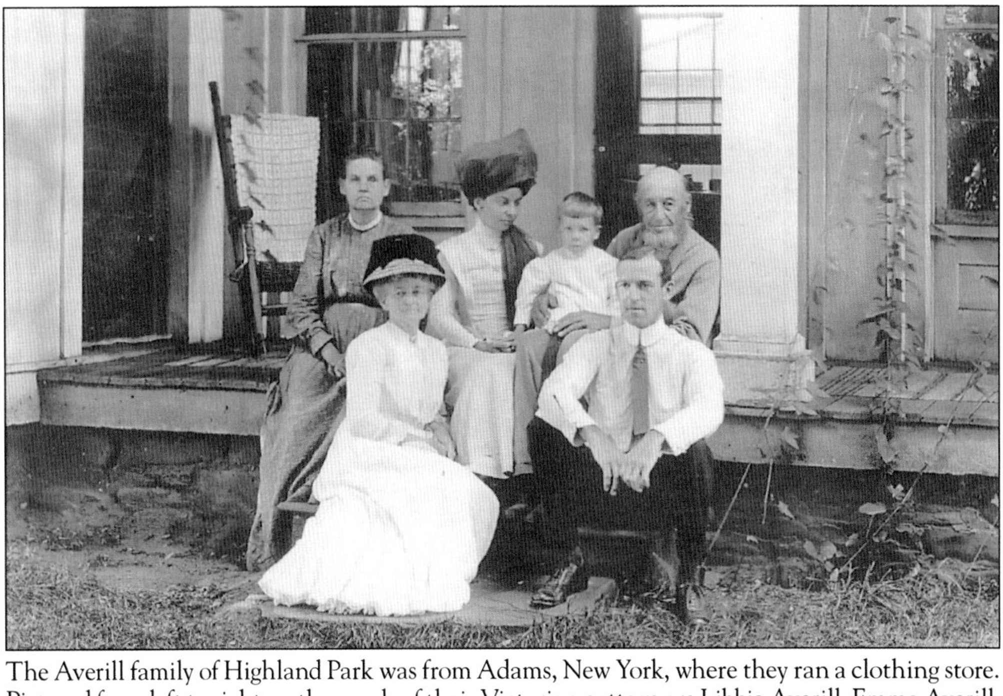

The Averill family of Highland Park was from Adams, New York, where they ran a clothing store. Pictured from left to right on the porch of their Victorian cottage are Libbie Averill, Emma Averill, Bertha Waite Averill, Edgar "Bill" Averill, Earl Amos Averill, and grandfather Asa Averill. (The Averill family.)

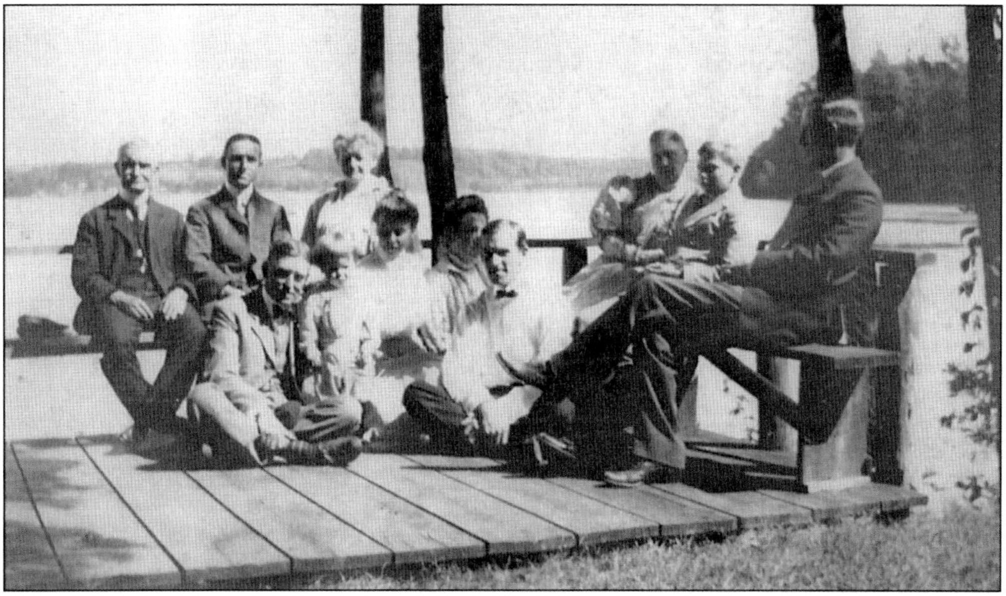

The extended Waite and Averill family is together in 1910 on the Highland Park dock. From left to right are Willis, Robert, and Herbert Waite; Edgar, Emma, and Bertha Waite Averill; Mary Waite; Earl Averill; Ruth Waite; Franklyn Edward Waite; and Edward J. Waite. Willis Waite was one of the eight original partners in the Highland Park Association. The family is now into its sixth generation at Highland Park. (The Averill family.)

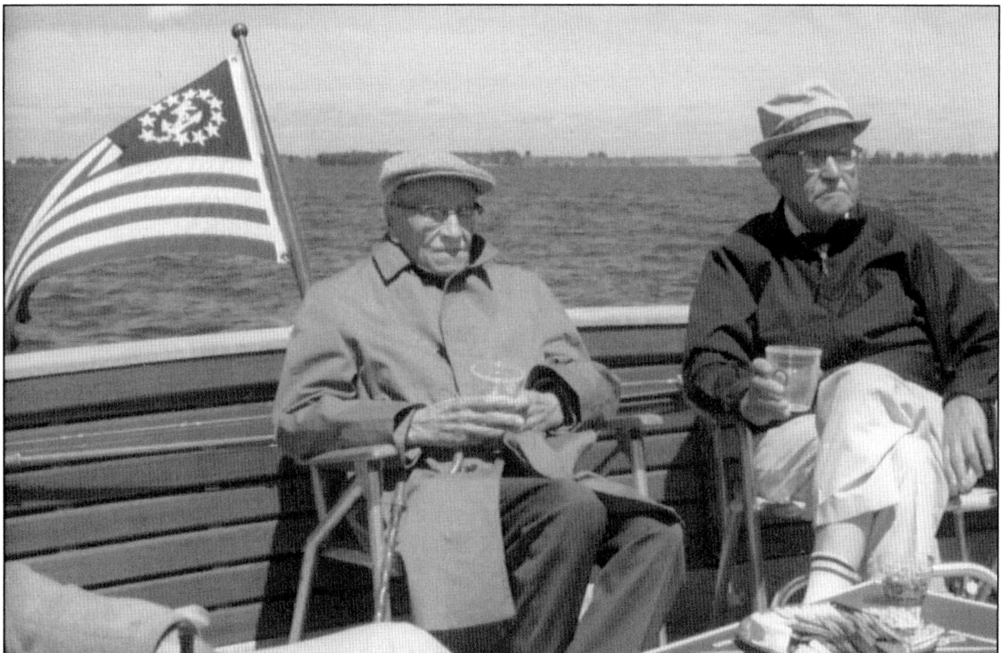

Skipper E. Austin Barnes (left) first sailed into Henderson Harbor on his large yawl, *Themis*, prior to 1920. Barnes settled into the Paradise Park Hotel as his summer cottage with his wife, Eva Snaith Barnes. Pictured here with his good friend Charles B. Cooper, Barnes spent many summers sailing and fishing at Henderson Harbor. (John D. Marsellus.)

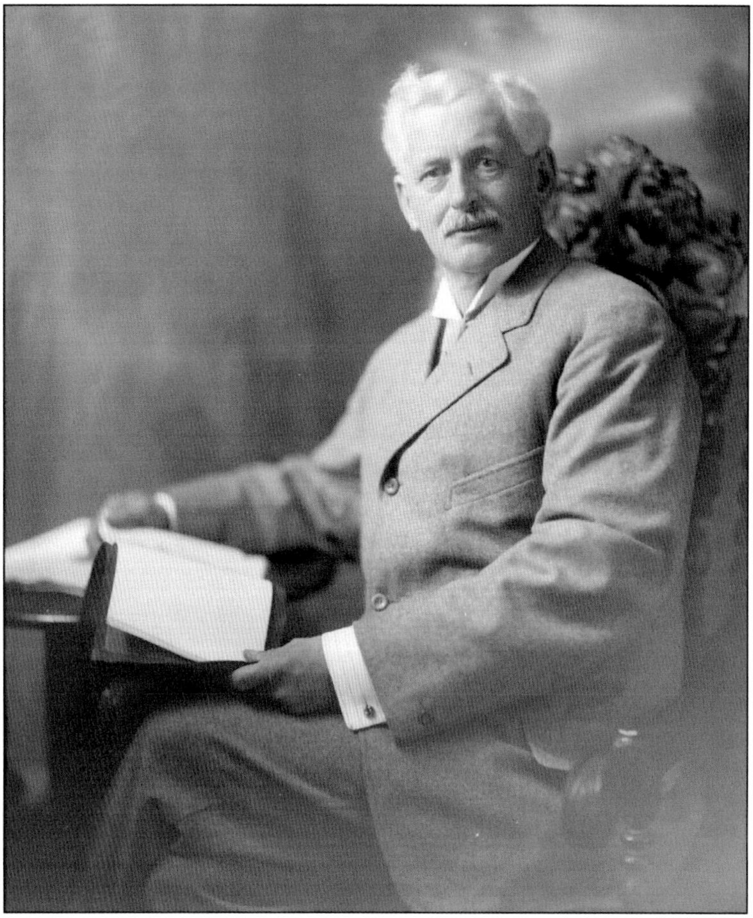

Stephen R. Cleveland was one of the first of several Watertown, New York, business owners to purchase waterfront and boathouse lots along Harbor Road between Warner's Inn and the Gill House. In 1913, Cleveland began construction of his large waterfront cottage but used it for only a few years. (JCHS.)

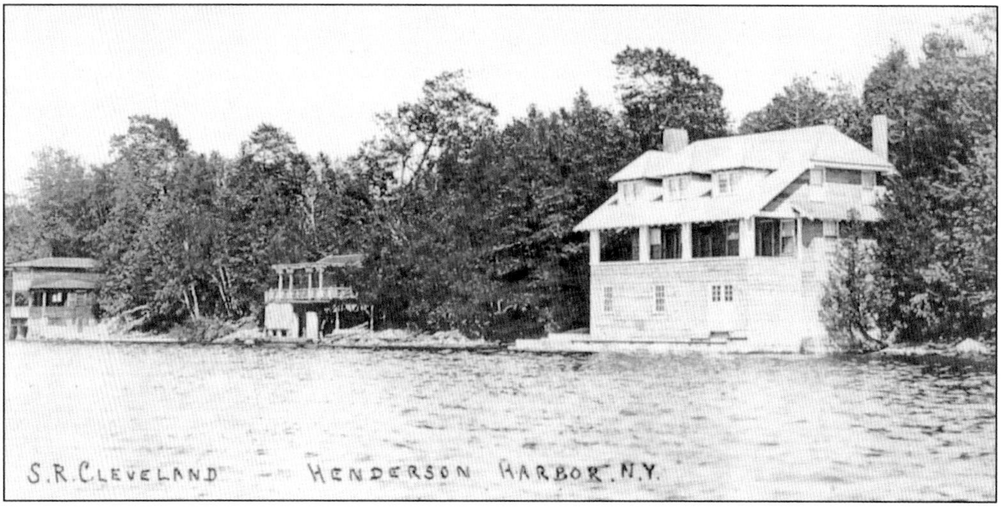

The Cleveland cottage was a large, three-story structure, including the basement, which provided storage for a boat to be drawn under the cottage on tracks. Typical of Harbor Road cottages, which established their foundations in the bay, the original Cleveland cottage burned from a clothes dryer fire in 1976 and was replaced.

Emma Flower-Taylor was the daughter of former New York governor Roswell P. Flower of Watertown, New York. A wealthy woman through inheritance, Flower-Taylor purchased or built cottages along Harbor Road for herself and reportedly for her pastor and chauffeur. She purchased the Cleveland cottage for herself. (JCHS.)

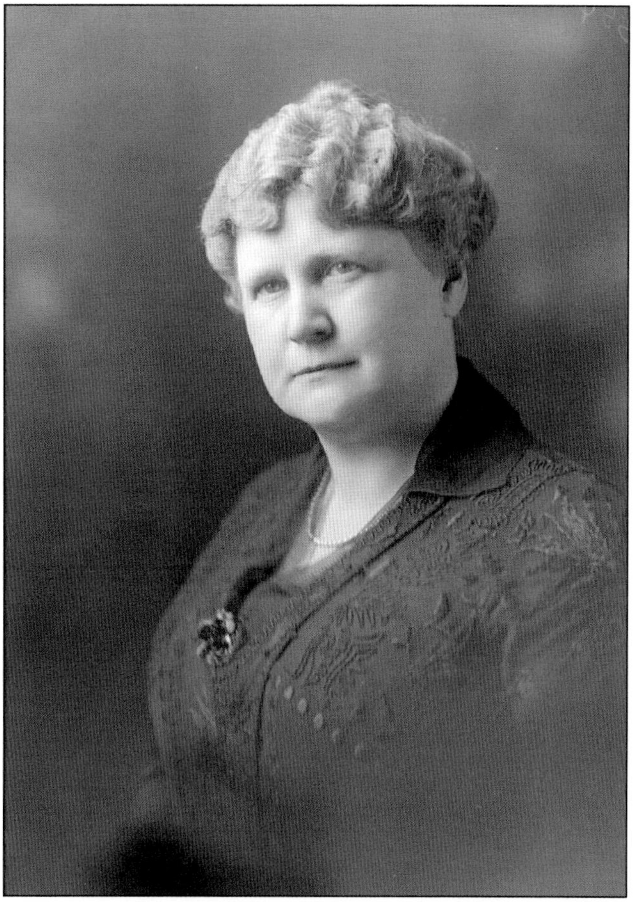

Next door to the Cleveland cottage, Flower-Taylor built Little Chief Lodge, an Adirondack-style cottage of log and twig architecture. Near Little Chief Lodge is where New York State originally planned to build a public dock, pavilion, and parking lot. It was part of the original subdivision for Henderson Harbor Park but was never completed.

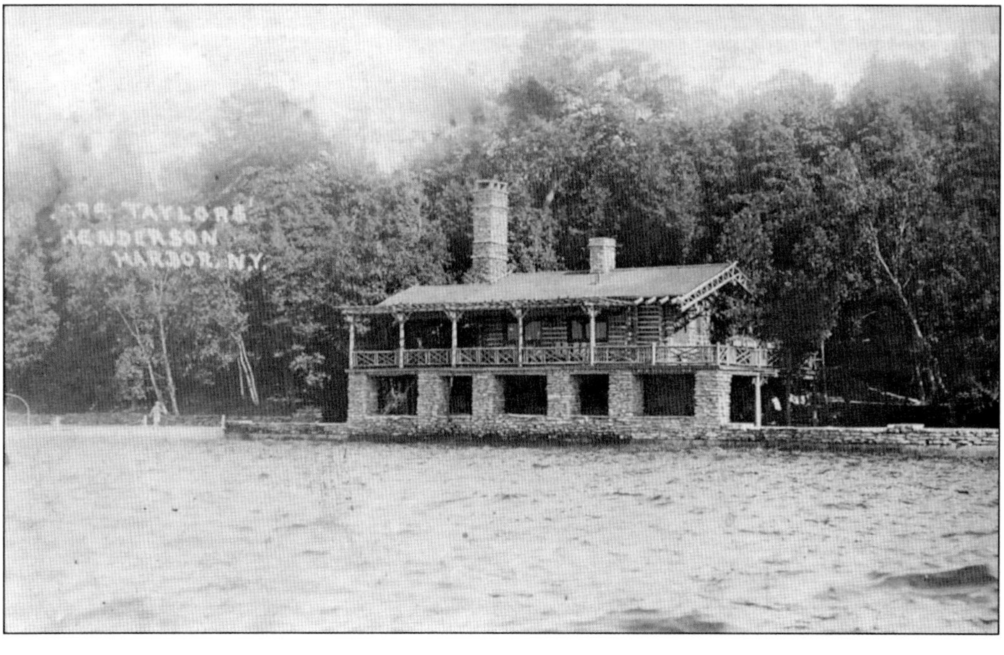

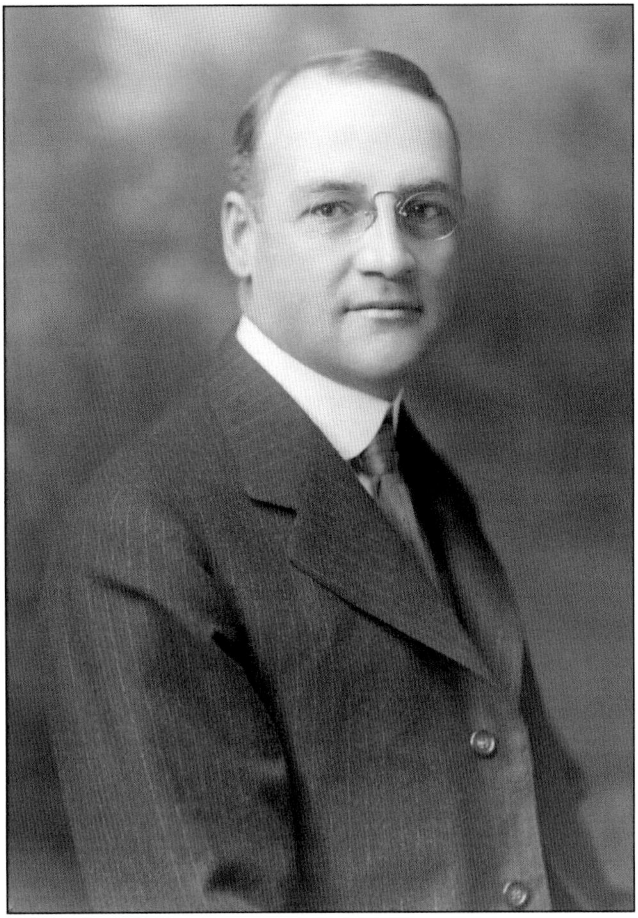

Watertown, New York, businessman Charles W. Valentine was another early cottage builder along Harbor Road. He was also an original member of the PK Club on Galloo Island. (JCHS.)

Charles W. Valentine built a large cottage on the bay with an extended dock for his boat, which was used primarily for trips to the PK Club on Galloo Island. The Valentine cottage has been owned for many years by James and Mary Parke Manning, descendants of the Foster and Dulles families.

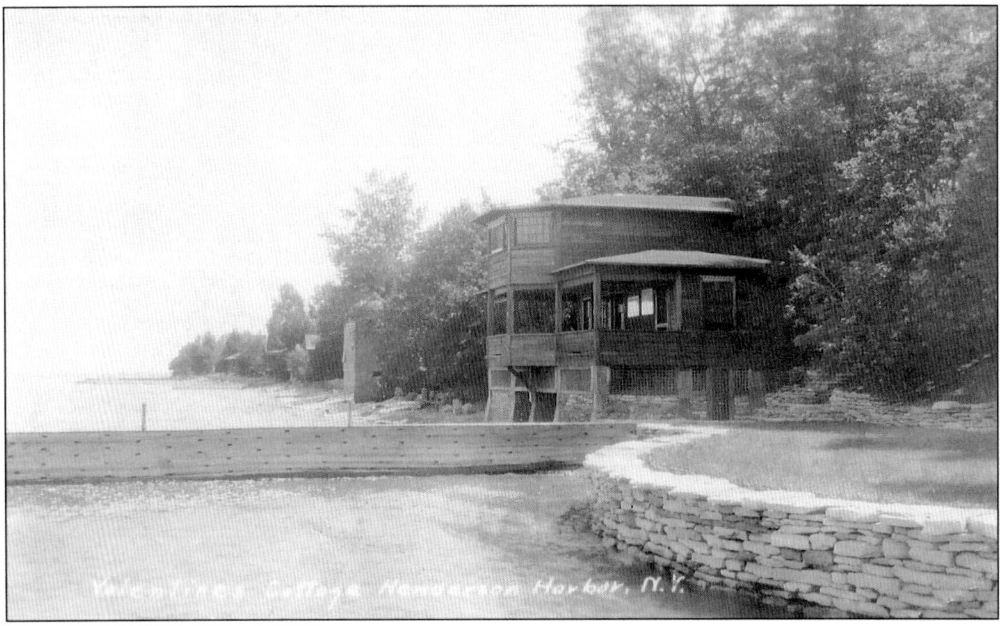

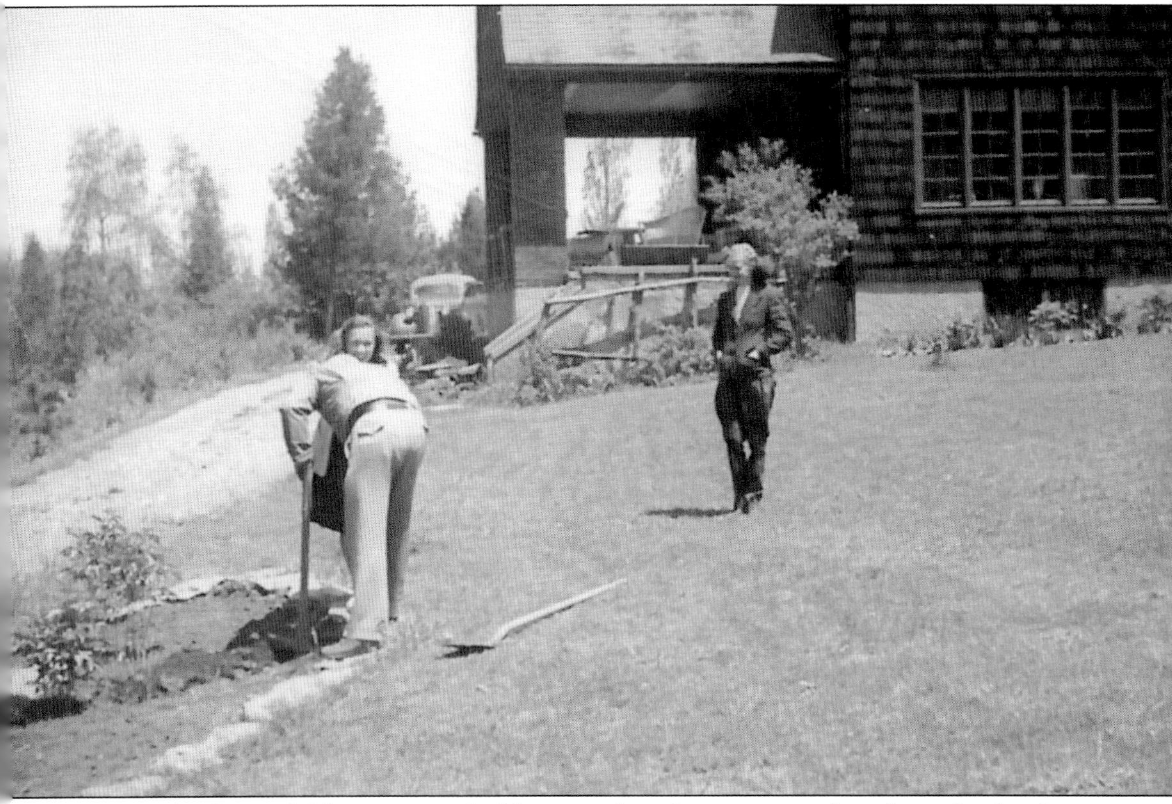

By 1944, the George I. Hovey cottage had been purchased at auction and was being fixed up by the John Riordan family of Drexel Hill, Pennsylvania. Formerly the Hugh and Minnie Gill apple orchard, the property provided one of the best views of Henderson Bay, located to the left of the photograph. (Sue Riordan McKenna.)

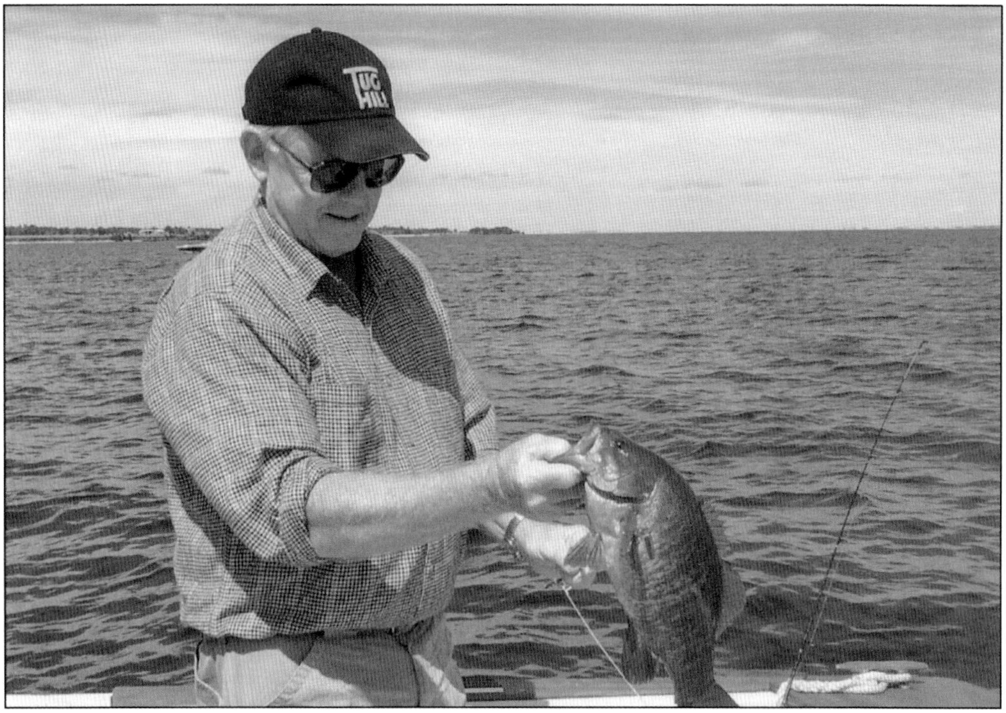

Fishing guides continue the Henderson Harbor tradition today. Some of them, such as Watertown, New York, attorney James H. McGowan III, guided while holding down full-time careers. McGowan is holding a large bass onboard his Bertram fishing boat, *Hobo,* near Stony Island.

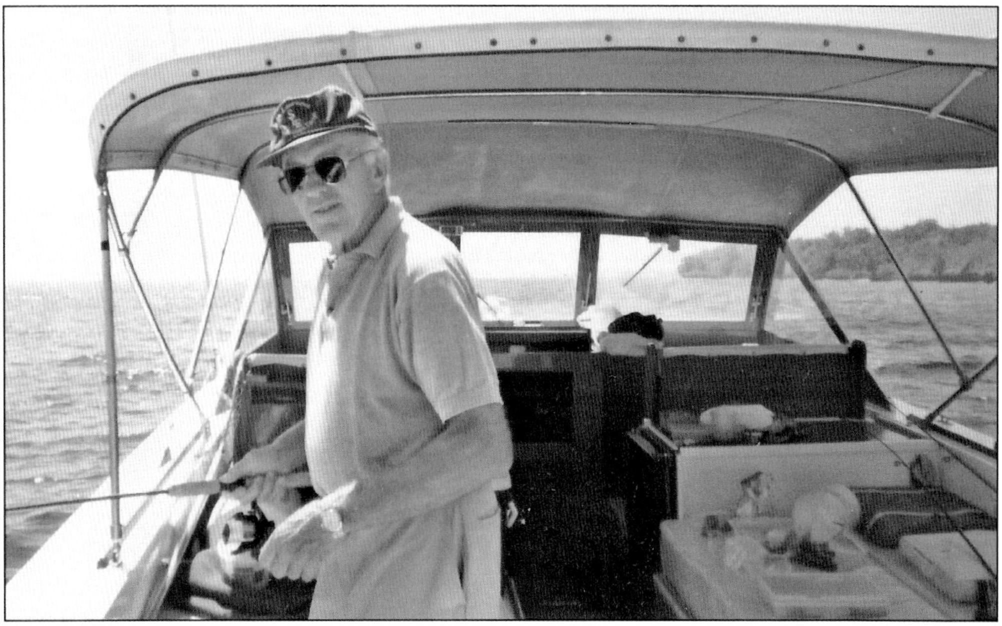

John S. Dunk continues the family tradition of fishing in Henderson Harbor. Successful in the construction explosives business, Dunk owned several properties in Henderson Harbor and, like his father, Claude, fished for many years from his 1966 wooden boat *Boom Boom,* custom-made by Cornell's Marina in Henderson Harbor.

Four

FAMOUS RESIDENTS

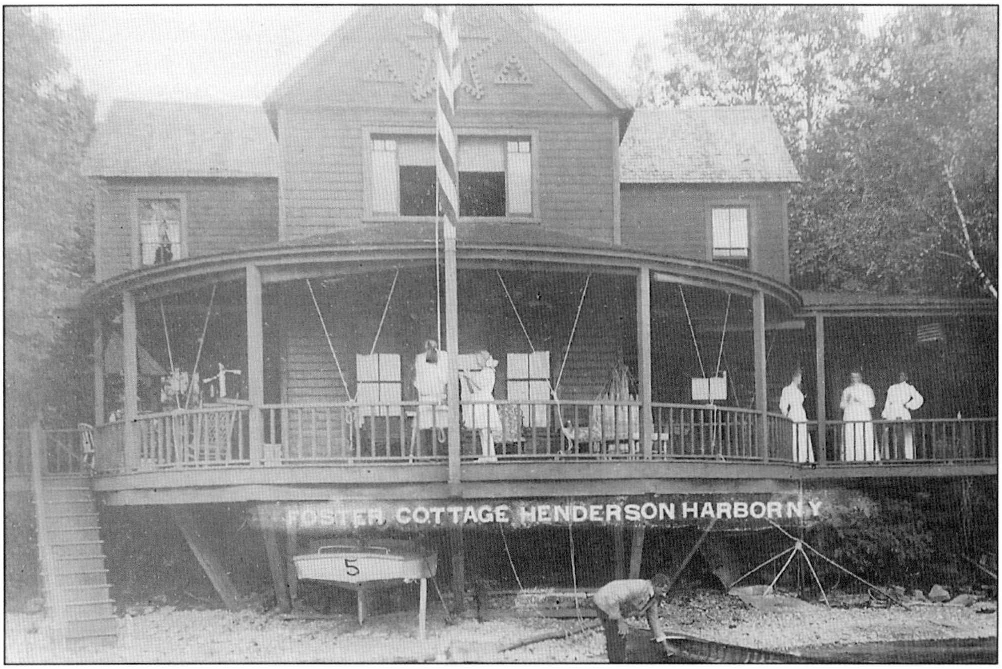

Underbluff was the summer cottage of retired Civil War general and US Secretary of State John W. Foster and his wife, Mary Parke Foster. Built about 1890, they entertained prominent Americans there, such as Pres. William Howard Taft and Andrew Carnegie. The St. Lawrence sailing skiff No. 5 beneath the veranda was General Foster's gift to his young grandson, John Foster Dulles, when a promised trip to the 1901 Pan-American Exposition was cancelled because Dulles had contracted typhoid fever.

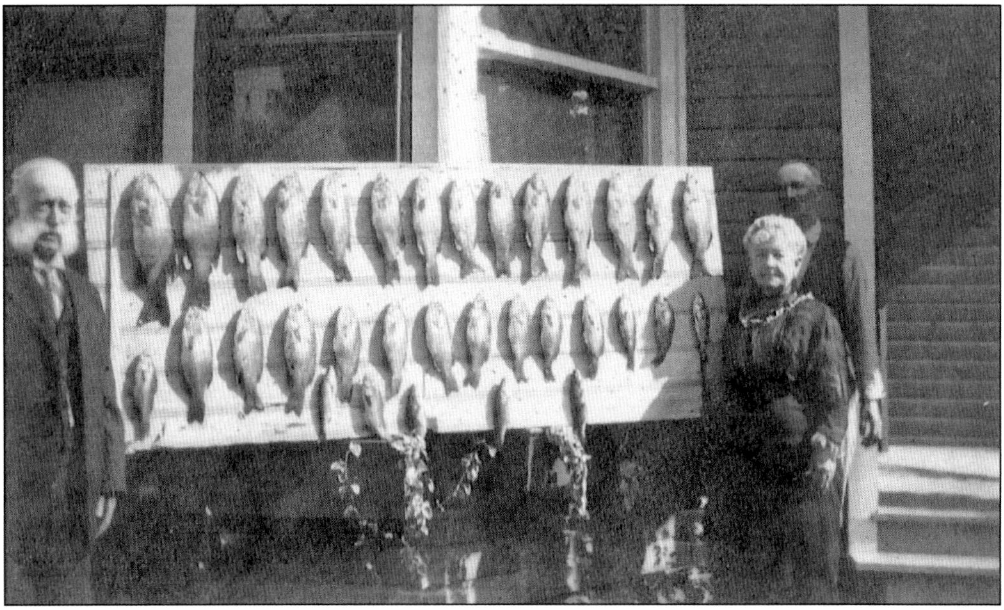

The Fosters loved fishing in Henderson Harbor. This catch of 28 bass and perch is displayed in front of their summer cottage, Underbluff. Looking on is their longtime Henderson Harbor fishing guide and boatman, Willett H. "Will" Stevens. (Mary Parke Manning.)

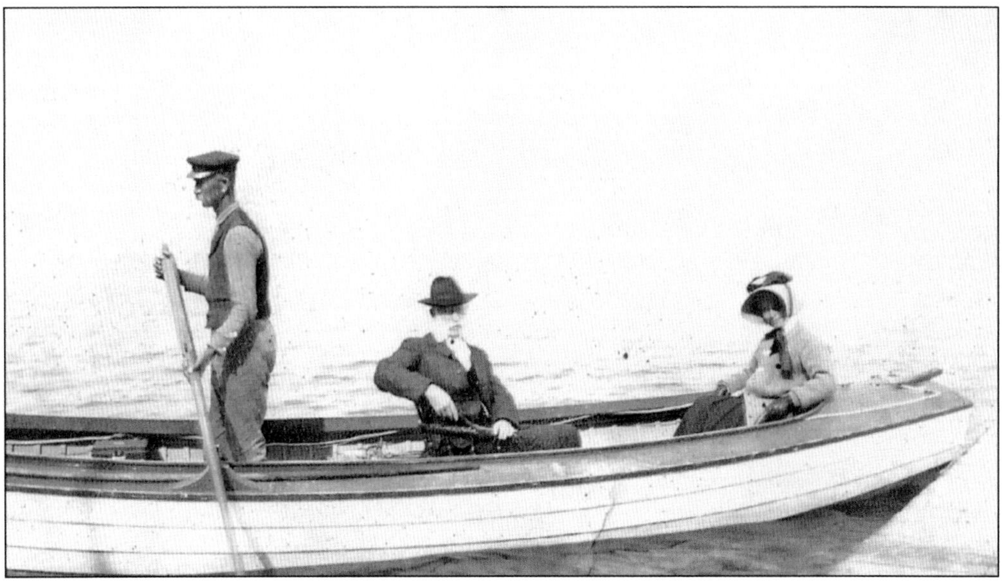

Prior to motorboats, Henderson Harbor fishing guide Will Stevens (standing) transported John W. and Mary Parke Foster to the fishing spots in a double-ended rowing skiff. Rowing to the offshore islands could take more than half a day. Stevens built his own boats. (Mary Parke Manning.)

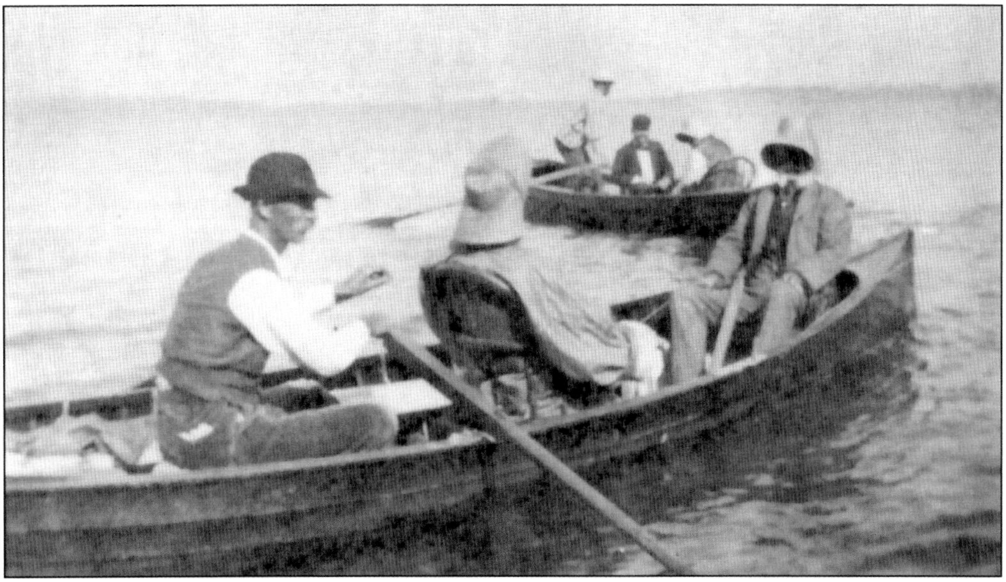

On August 14, 1897, fishing guide Will Stevens rowed Chinese ambassador Chang Yen Hoon (center) to Davis Island, located on the edge of Henderson Harbor, for fishing and a shore dinner. In the bow is retired Secretary of State John W. Foster. A second boat filled out the party of six that made the fishing trip. (Mary Parke Manning.)

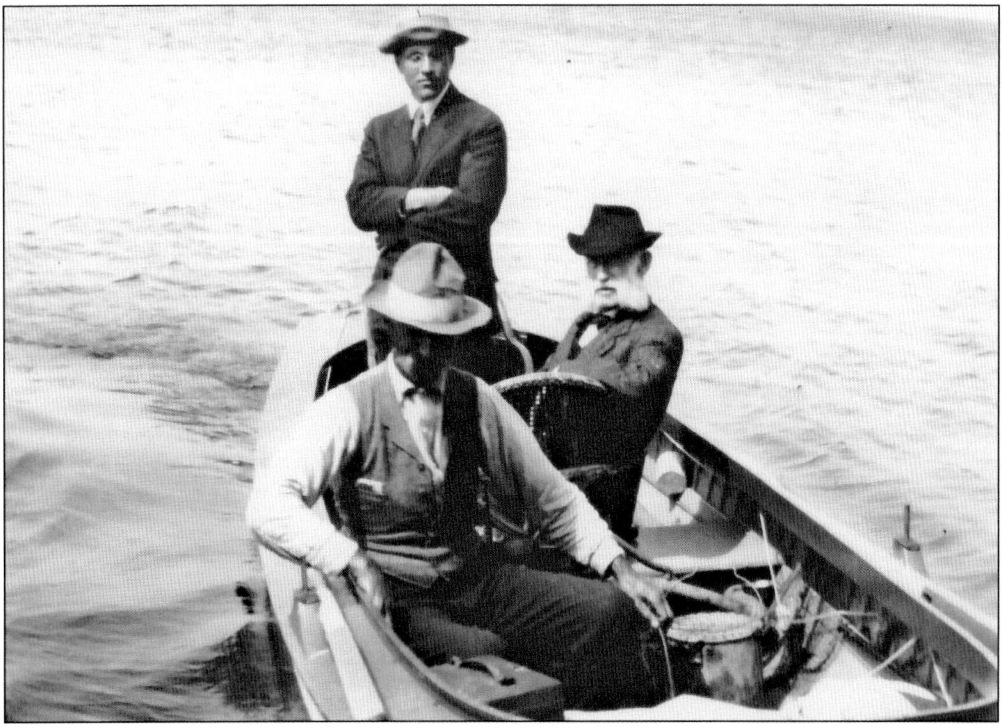

Naphtha- and gasoline-powered motors eventually replaced oars in the Henderson Harbor guide boats. Guide Will Stevens is in the foreground in his custom-made boat with his left hand on the engine throttle and his right hand on the rope for steering. Secretary John W. Foster is also seated, while the man standing in the stern is unidentified. (Mary Parke Manning.)

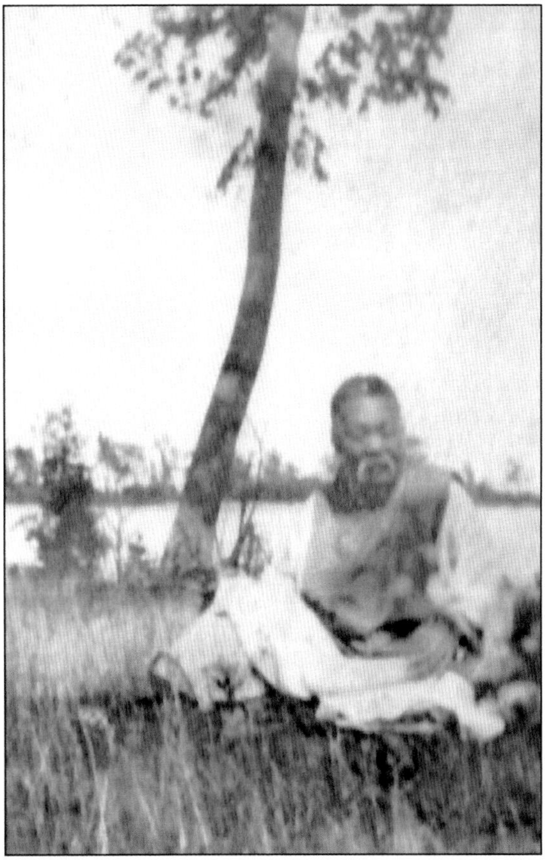

Ambassador Chang was entertained at a shore dinner on Davis Island, which is between what was then Warner's Island (Association Island) and Sixtown Island. Chang was one of several Chinese diplomats who visited Henderson Harbor. Retired Secretary of State John W. Foster helped draft the 1895 Treaty of Shimonoseki for the Qing Dynasty. The treaty ended the Sino-Japanese War of 1894–1895. Foster reportedly received a $250,000 fee for his negotiating skills. (Mary Parke Manning.)

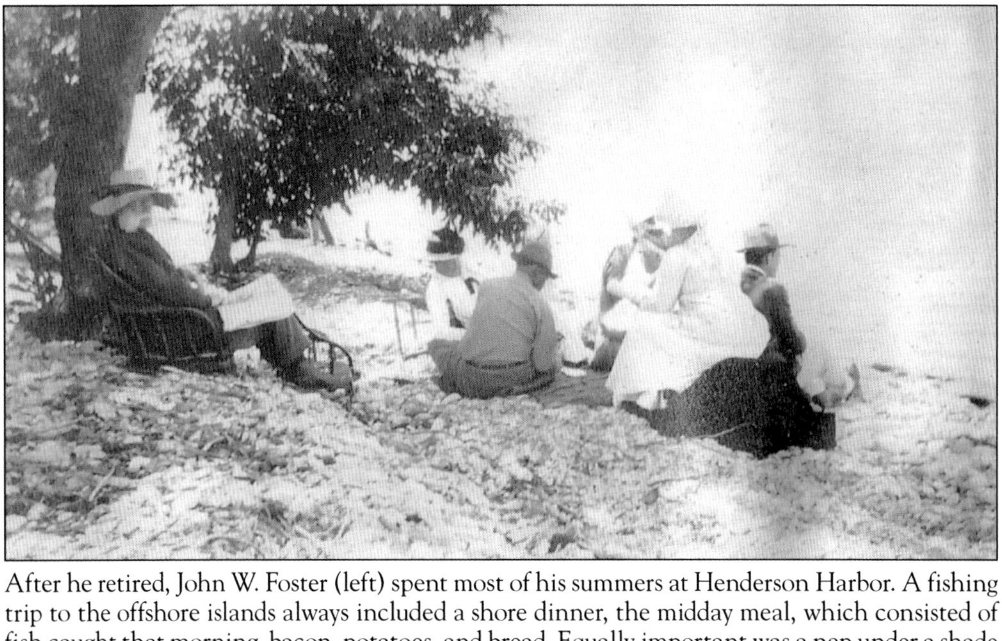

After he retired, John W. Foster (left) spent most of his summers at Henderson Harbor. A fishing trip to the offshore islands always included a shore dinner, the midday meal, which consisted of fish caught that morning, bacon, potatoes, and bread. Equally important was a nap under a shade tree along the shoreline. (Mary Parke Manning.)

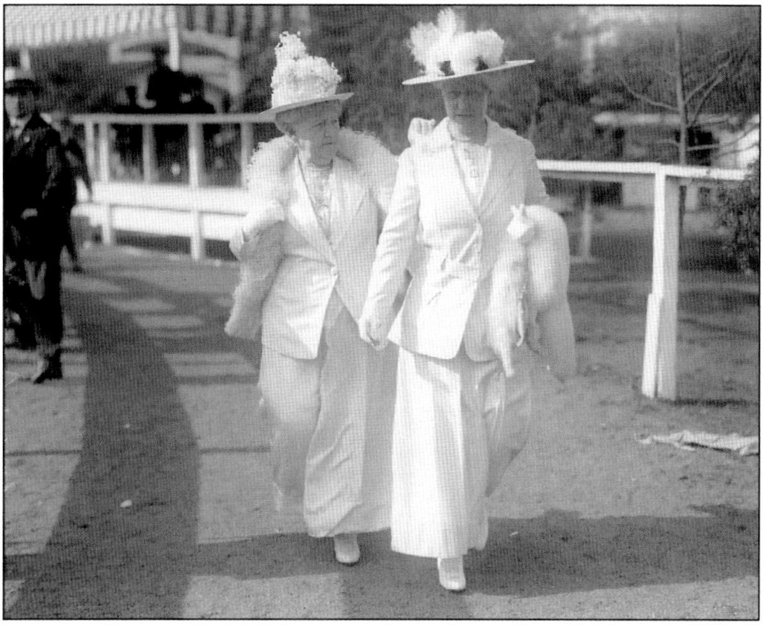

Mary Parke Foster (left) and John W. Foster's daughter Eleanor (right) married Robert M. Lansing, who was the US secretary of state in the Woodrow Wilson administration. Pictured at a horse track on Long Island, the family travelled extensively between their home in Washington and their cottage in Henderson Harbor.

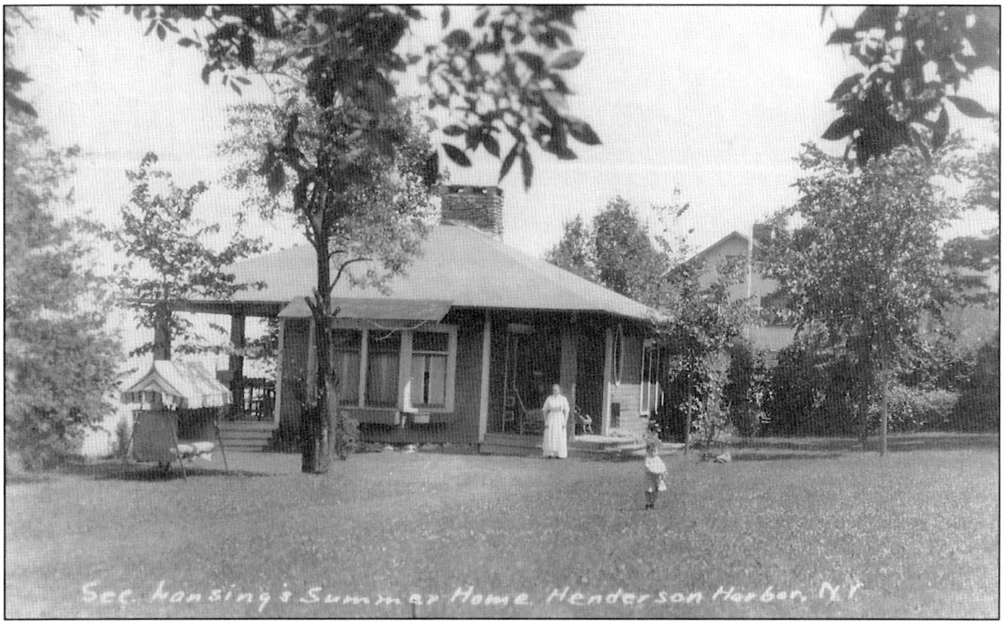

The Lansing cottage was modest, but its location on the edge of Henderson Bay offered a view of the sunset, which was spectacular. Originally a one-bedroom cottage when it was built on the north side of Underbluff around 1903, guests would stay at the nearby Warner's Inn where a direct telephone connection to Washington, DC, had been established. Linden Lodge has since been expanded but still retains its original cottage charm.

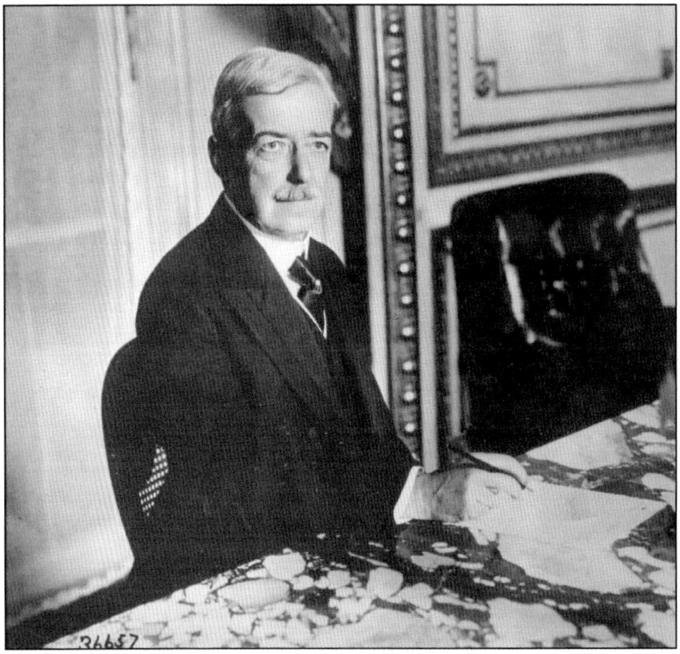

Secretary of State Robert M. Lansing spent months at the Hotel de Crillon during the 1919 Paris Peace Conference. A lawyer from Watertown and cofounder of the Fortnightly Club fishing lodge on Galloo Island, Lansing distinguished himself by founding the *Journal of International Law.* His role in Paris was diminished by Pres. Woodrow Wilson. Lansing resigned from the US Department of State in 1920, continued practicing law in Washington, DC, and spent long summers at Henderson Harbor and Galloo Island until his death in 1928.

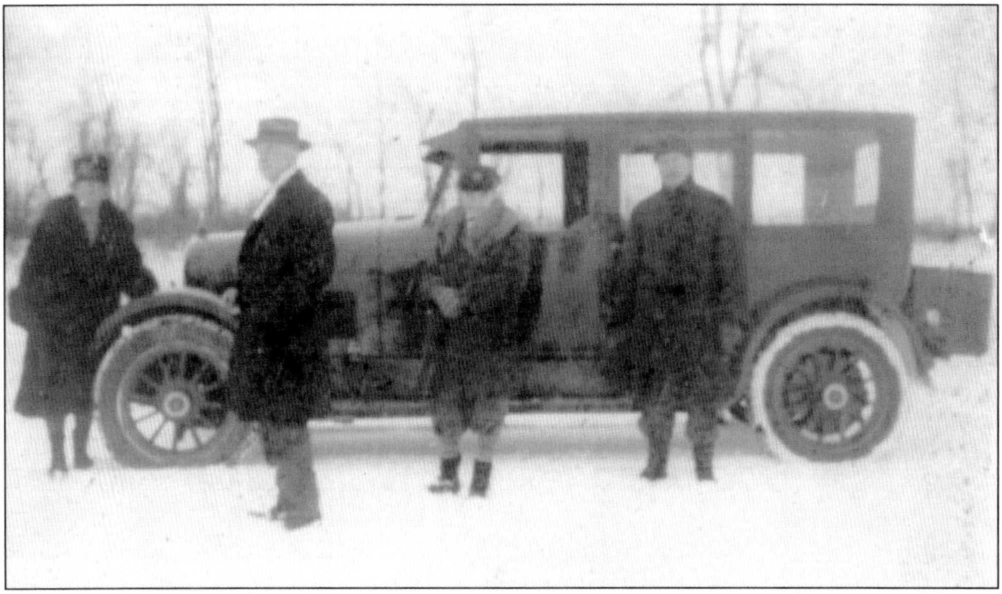

The Foster's other daughter, Edith, married Allen Macy Dulles, a Presbyterian minister from Watertown. Pictured is their car on the ice at Sixtown Point on February 13, 1923. From left to right they are Edith Foster Dulles, Rev. Allen Macy Dulles, their son John Foster Dulles, a future secretary of state, and unidentified. The Dulleses built their cottage, Greyledge, in 1916 on the south side of Underbluff.

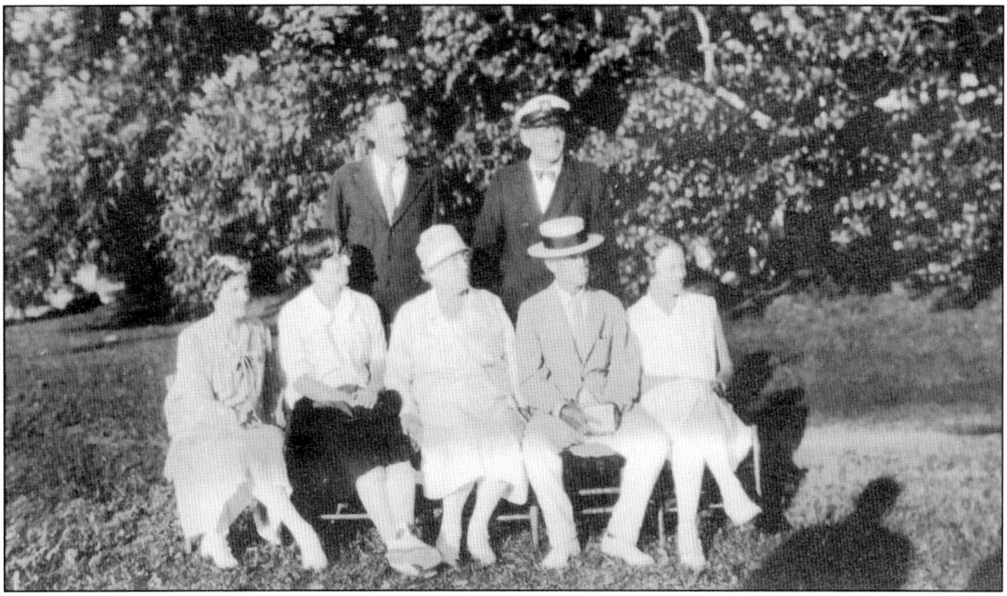

Henderson Harbor's most famous family is pictured on the lawn at their summer cottage, Greyledge, in 1928. From left to right they are (seated) Margaret Josephine Dulles, Eleanor Lansing Dulles, Edith Foster Dulles, Rev. Allen Macy Dulles, and Nataline Dulles; (standing) Allen Welsh Dulles and John Foster Dulles. (Ann Dulles Joor.)

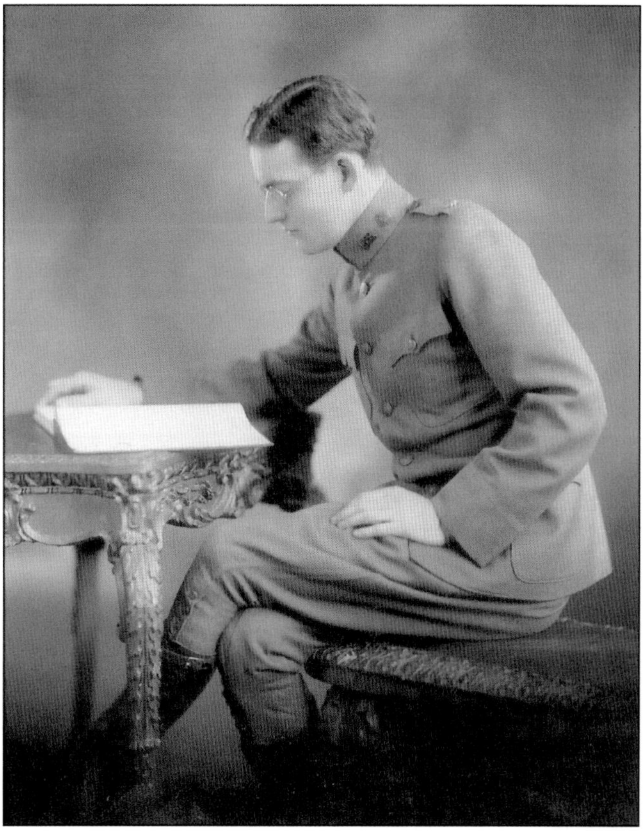

John Foster Dulles was the third member of the family to become US secretary of state, serving during the Dwight D. Eisenhower administration. Rejected from the Army during World War I for poor vision, Dulles served as a major on the War Industries Board. He distinguished himself as a state department staff attorney during the 1919 Paris Peace Conference with his uncle "Bert" Lansing. It led to Dulles's career in the US Department of State.

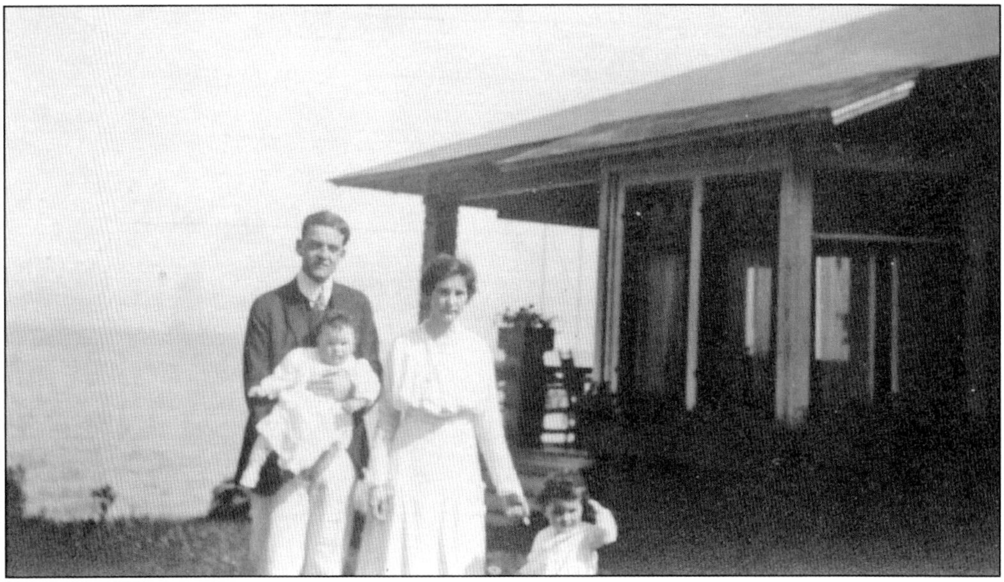

An athletic sailor and fisherman, John Foster Dulles reportedly swam across Henderson Harbor and later spent many summers sailing the Great Lakes and St. Lawrence River. He and his wife, Janet Avery Dulles, are pictured with their children in front of Linden Lodge in 1915. They purchased Main Duck Island in Lake Ontario from fish merchant and one-time bootlegger Claude "King" Cole for a vacation retreat. They also purchased Sixtown Island in Henderson Bay, and it was still owned by the family in 2012. (Ann Dulles Joor.)

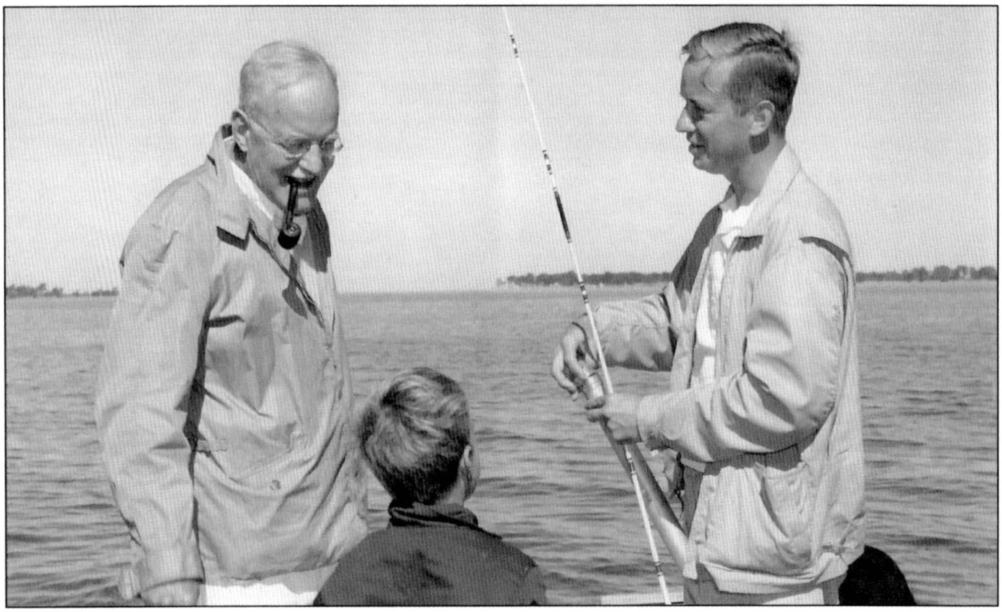

Allen Welsh Dulles (left) was often described by the family as being a romantic. He rose to become director of the Central Intelligence Agency (CIA) during the Eisenhower and Kennedy administrations but retired after the failed Cuban Bay of Pigs invasion. After Pres. John F. Kennedy's assassination, Dulles served on the Warren Commission. In this photograph, Dulles is going fishing with his nephew James A. Manning (right) and Thomas A. Manning (center) at Henderson Harbor. (Mary Parke Manning.)

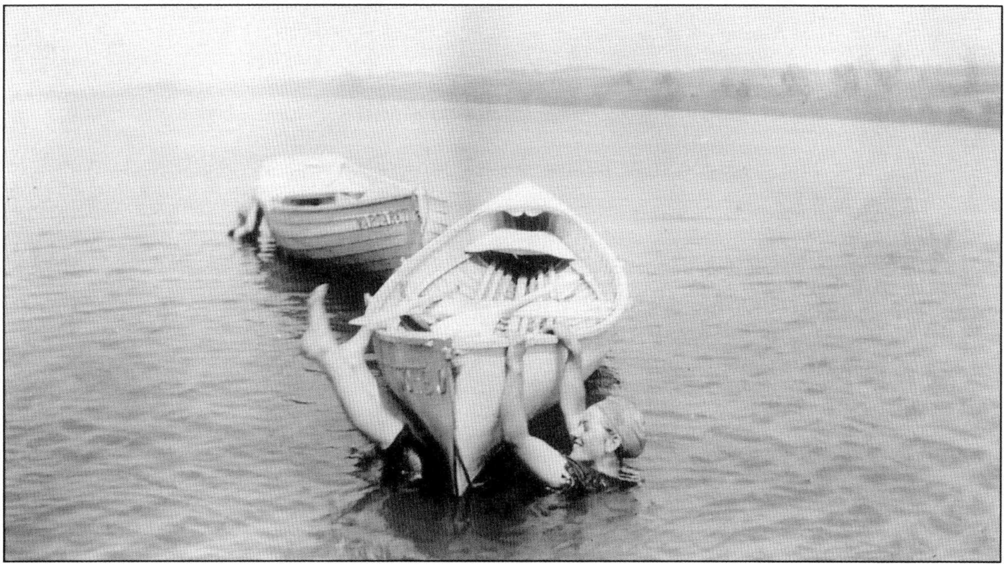

Eleanor Lansing Dulles kept a competitive pace with her brothers while swimming and boating in Henderson Harbor. Later, as an economic specialist and head of the state department's West German desk, Dr. Dulles was called "the Mother of Berlin" for her work to revitalize the German economy after World War II. (David Joor.)

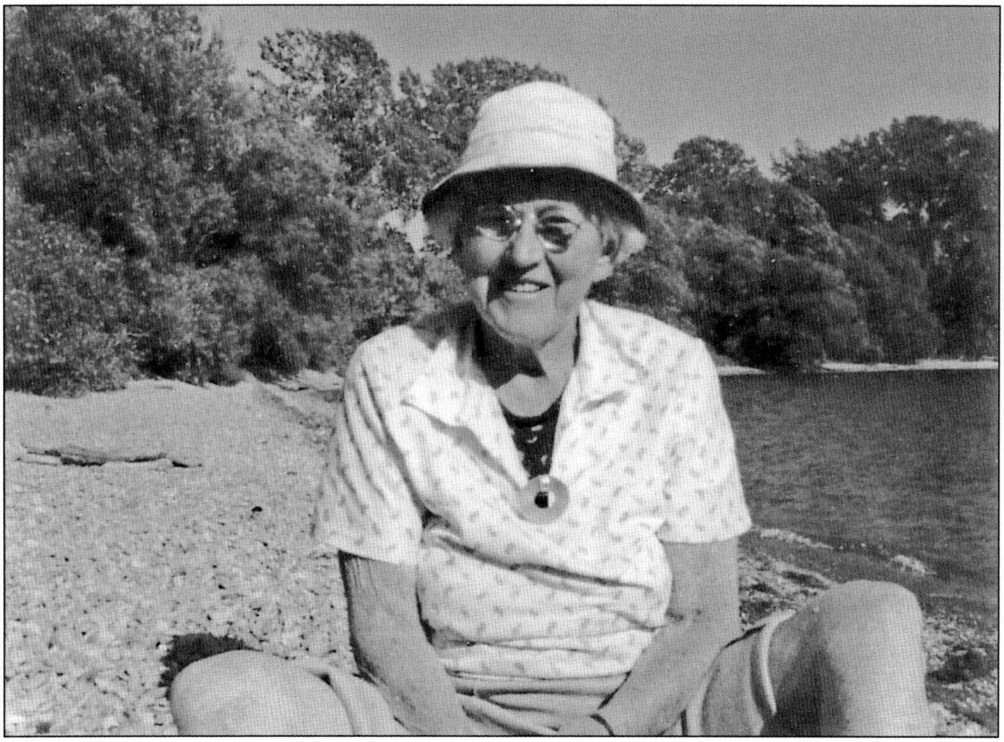

Dr. Eleanor Lansing Dulles promoted environmental conservation on Lake Ontario and the islands near Henderson Harbor. Pictured on the stony beach of the family's Sixtown Island in 1986, Dr. Dulles advocated support for clean air and water as well as preservation of the historic homes around Henderson Bay. She died at the age of 101 in 1996. (Mary Parke Manning.)

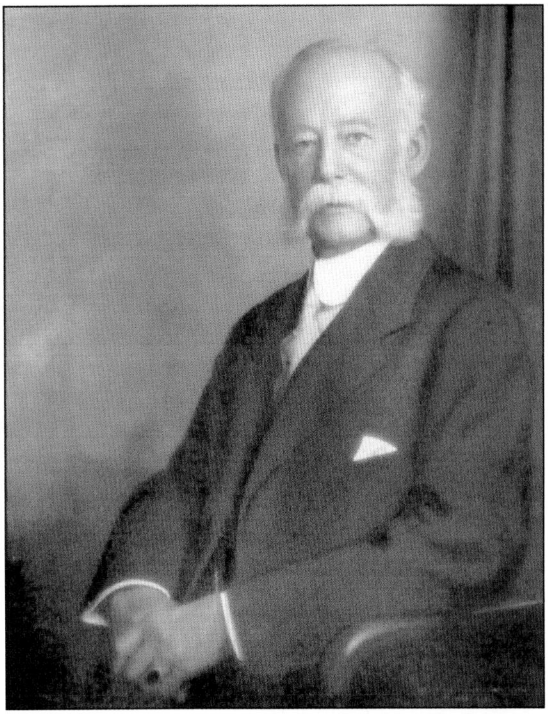

John Marsellus, founder of the Marsellus Casket Company of Syracuse in 1872, made Henderson Harbor his summer home late in life, staying first at Warner's Inn. The family nicknamed him "Whiskers" because of his mutton chop sideburns. The Marsellus Casket Company was renowned for high-quality craftsmanship and prominent clients, including presidents Truman, Kennedy (and Jackie Kennedy Onassis), Nixon, and Reagan as well as sports stars Mickey Mantle, Vince Lombardi, and Arthur Ashe and composer Leonard Bernstein. (Sandy Conde.)

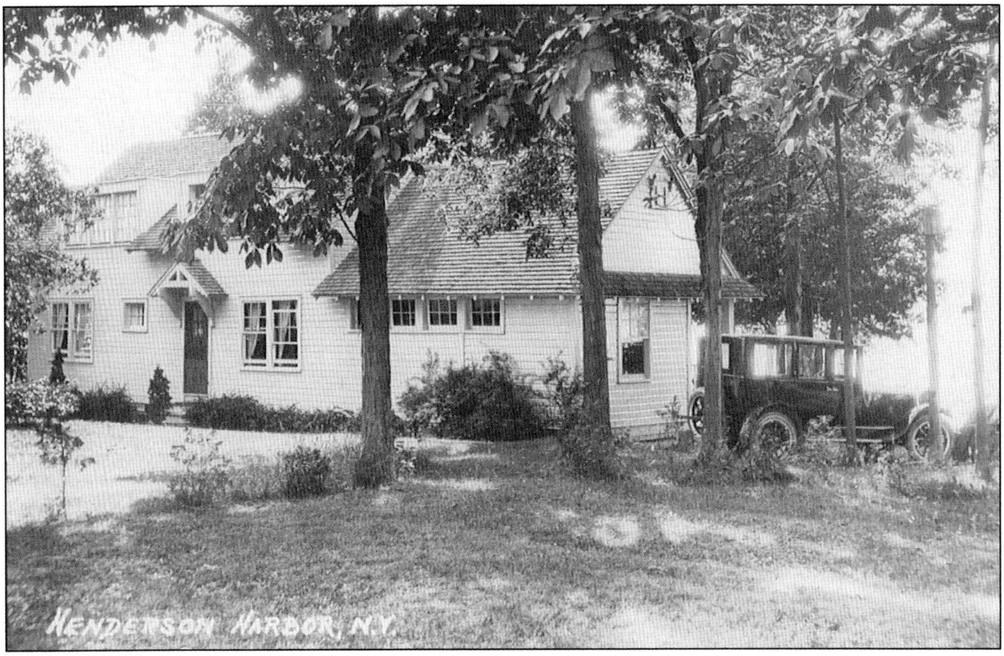

John Marsellus's son John C. Marsellus began his visits to Henderson Harbor by working at the Warner's Inn farm and sleeping in the barn. Around 1922, he purchased a cottage nearly across Harbor Road from Warner's Inn. This early photograph of the Marsellus cottage, Cedarbrook, was taken before the additions and the boathouse were built. It was named for the large stand of cedar trees and the brook that flowed through the property and into Henderson Bay. (John D. Marsellus.)

John C. Marsellus loved fishing at Henderson Harbor. With Melvin Stevens as his guide and boatman, Marsellus could often be found on Calf Island for a shore dinner. He owned several fine lake fishing boats over his many summers on the water. He became one of the most prominent leaders in the early development of Henderson Harbor as a fishing destination. He was a key proponent in building the cut and locating NYS Route 3 on Chestnut Ridge instead of going through the heart of Henderson Harbor. (John D. Marsellus.)

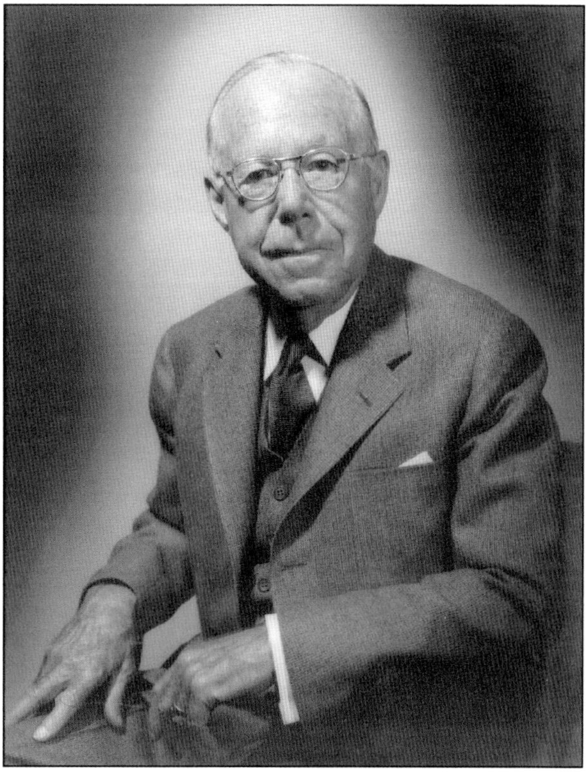

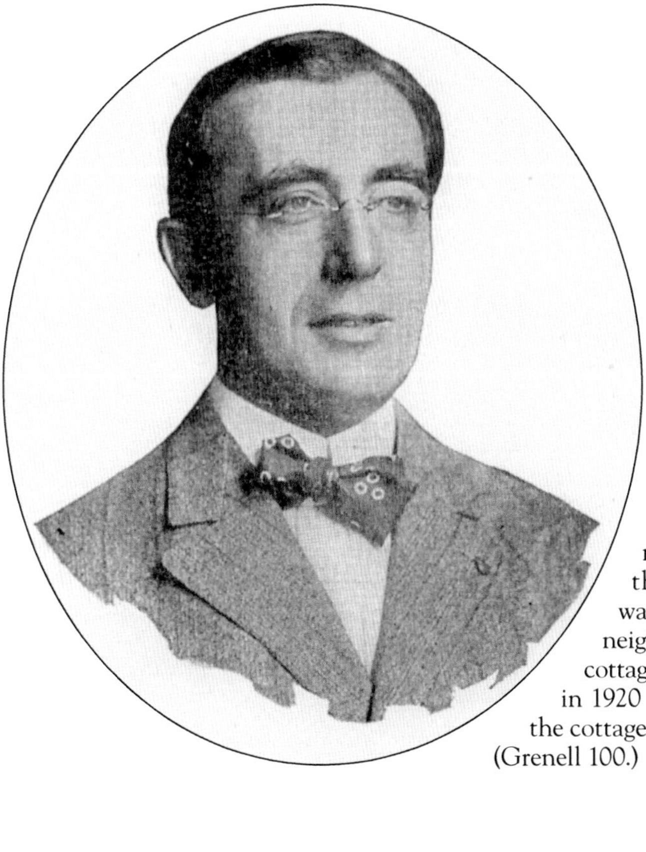

Bernard H. "Ben" Janssen and his wife, Gertrude "Gertie" Janssen, of New York City, built the Marsellus cottage. Owners of the renowned Janssen Piano Company, they purchased the Harbor Road waterfront lot from boat builder and neighbor James Bassett. They built the cottage in 1910. Gertie Janssen died there in 1920 and soon afterward, Janssen sold the cottage to John C. and Beulah Marsellus. (Grenell 100.)

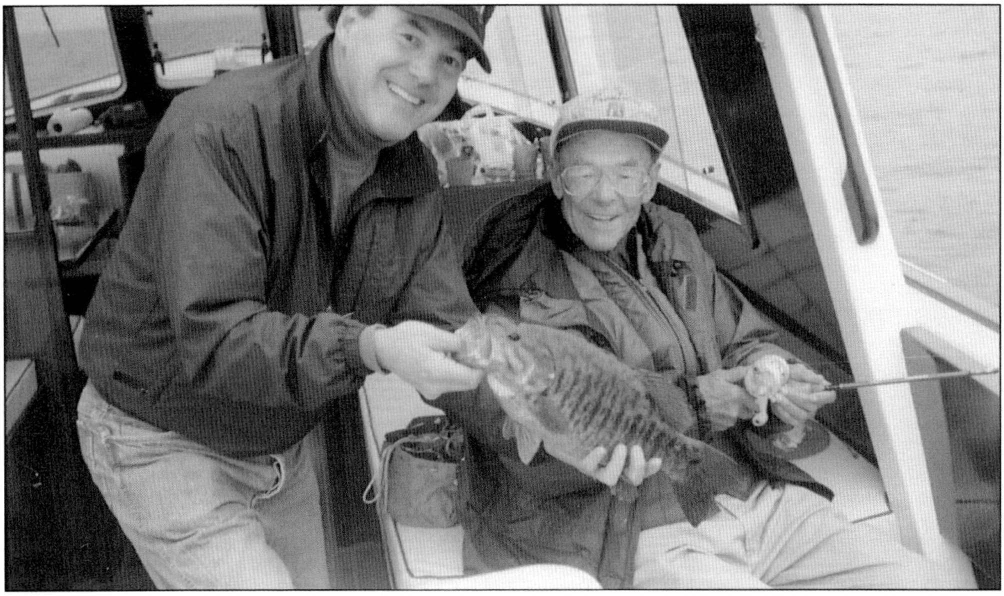

The son and grandson of John C. and Beulah Marsellus, John F. Marsellus (right) and John D. Marsellus, show a large bass caught in Lake Ontario on board the Marsellus boat, *The Fox*. John F. Marsellus maintained the family's summer home in Henderson Harbor and purchased Fox Island, the former fishing and hunting retreat of New York governor Horace White, located offshore from Henderson Harbor. Marsellus kept his lake fishing boats in his large boathouse near Henchen Marina. (John D. Marsellus.)

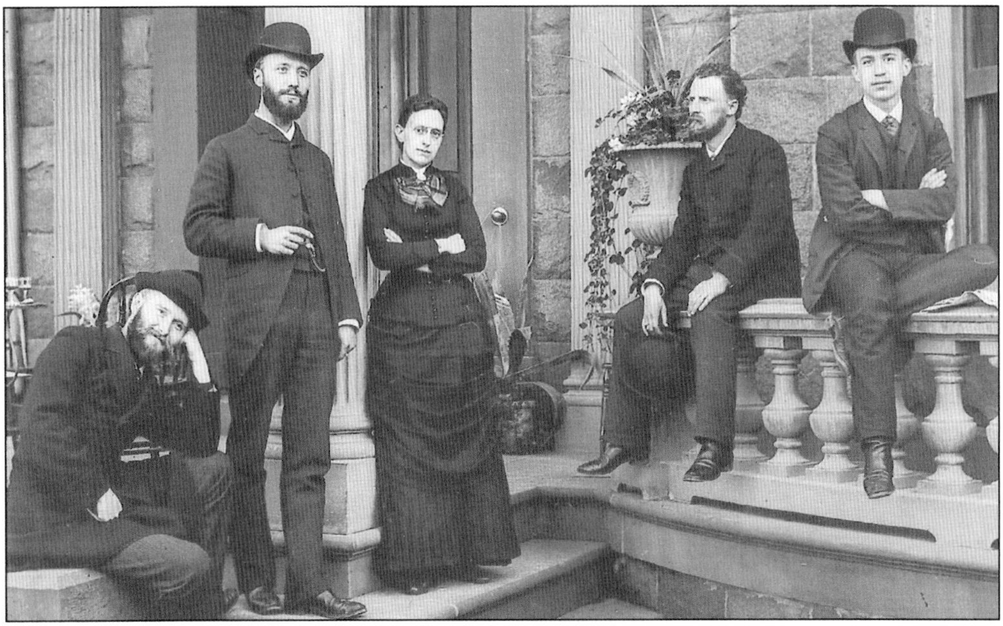

Henderson Harbor was the summer home of Henry W.T. Steinway. He is pictured (second from left) with his siblings at the Steinway mansion in New York. The grandson of the founder of the Steinway and Sons Piano Company, Henry was estranged from the family business. He spent almost every summer for 50 years fishing at Henderson Harbor. He died at the age of 83 in 1939 at the W.S. Rice cottage after a day of fishing with guide Will Stevens. (LCC.)

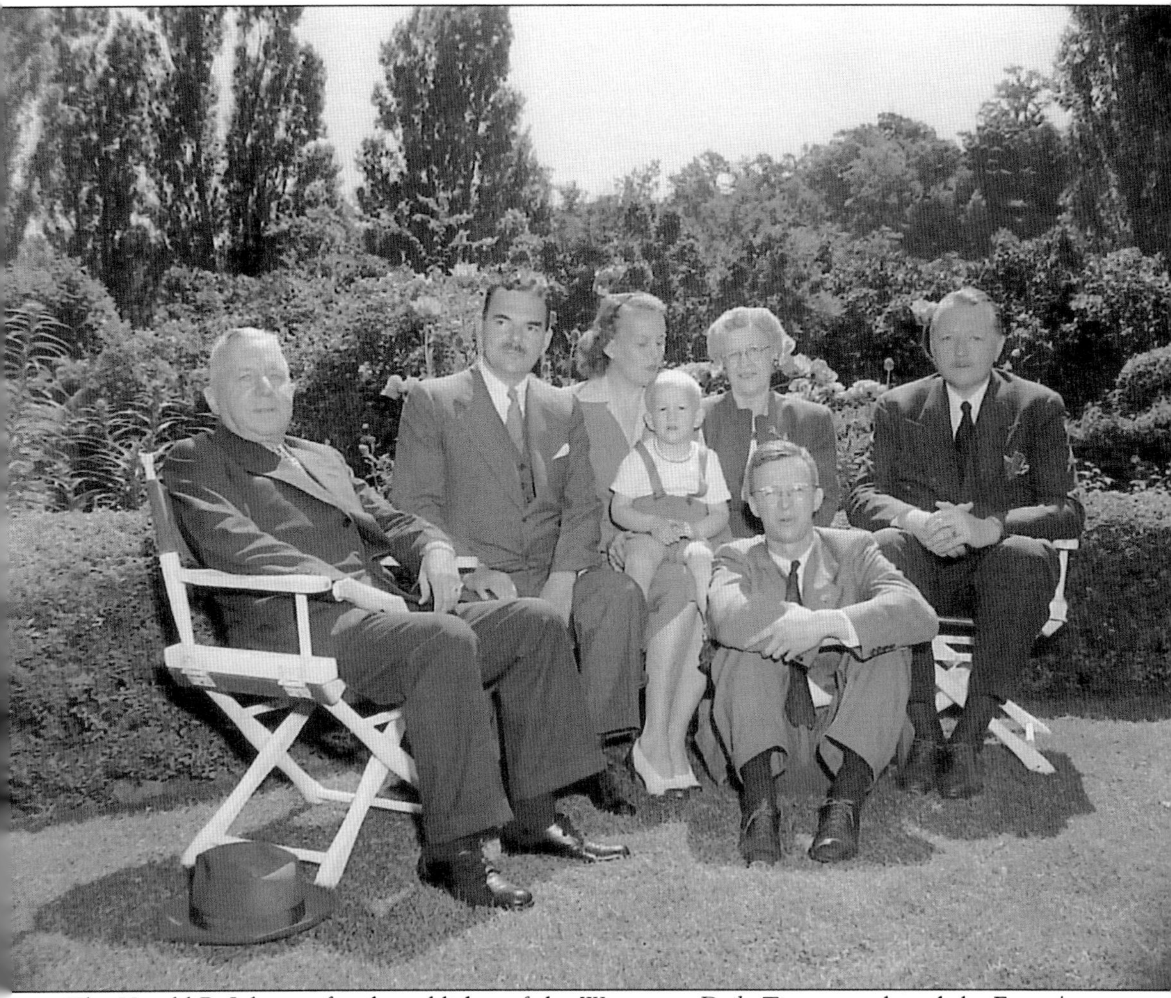

The Harold B. Johnson family, publisher of the *Watertown Daily Times*, purchased the Foster/Lansing cottage, Underbluff, from the estate of Eleanor Foster Lansing in 1937. Soon afterward, Johnson joined with other Watertown and Syracuse residents to purchase the neighboring Warner's Inn farm. Pictured in the garden at Underbluff on June 15, 1946, are, from left to right, Harold B. Johnson, Gov. Thomas E. Dewey, Catherine C. Johnson holding her son John B. Johnson Jr., Mrs. Harold B. Jessie Parsons Johnson, Governor Dewey's assistant James C. Haggerty, and John B. Johnson (sitting in front). (John B. Johnson Jr.)

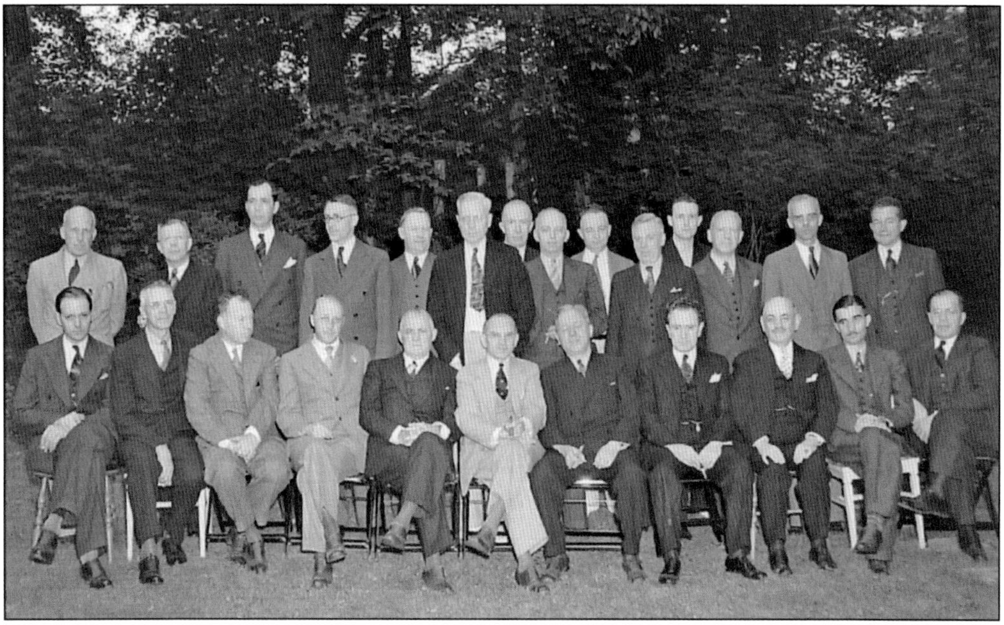

Harold Bowtell Johnson helped organize the New York State Society of Newspaper Editors. They met at Underbluff in June 1938. They included Johnson (seated, seventh from left) and Gannett Company founder Frank E. Gannett (seated, fifth from left). Gannett's parents had lived on Galloo Island, and he often visited Henderson Harbor. (John B. Johnson Jr.)

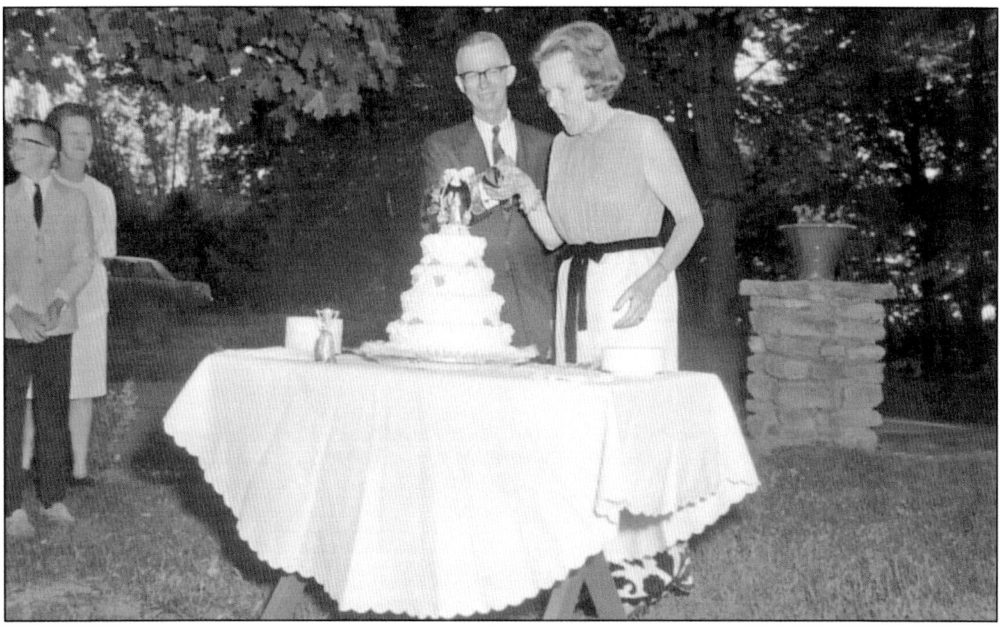

When Harold B. Johnson died at Underbluff in 1949, his son and only child, John Brayton Johnson, became editor and publisher of the *Watertown Daily Times*. John B. Johnson expanded the newspaper's printing plant and the company's broadcasting facilities into television. John B. and Catherine C. Johnson celebrated their 25th wedding anniversary at Underbluff in 1966. Catherine Johnson was a member of the Thousand Islands State Park Commission. (John B. Johnson Jr.)

Louis A. Wehle, chairman of the Genesee Brewing Company of Rochester, often piloted his large cruiser across Lake Ontario from Rochester to Henderson Harbor. Wehle, and Rochester car dealer Thomas Nagle, purchased the former Stony Point Rifle Range for a Hereford cattle ranch. Wehle served as New York State Conservation commissioner under Gov. Averill Harriman and organized a statewide fishing contest that became popular for its $5,000 prize and printing the location of winning catches. (Gatra Wehle.)

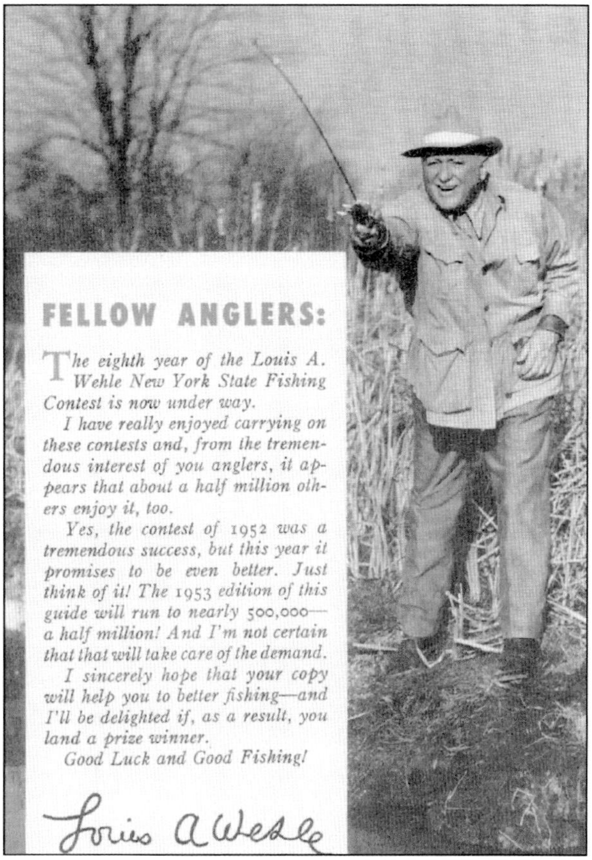

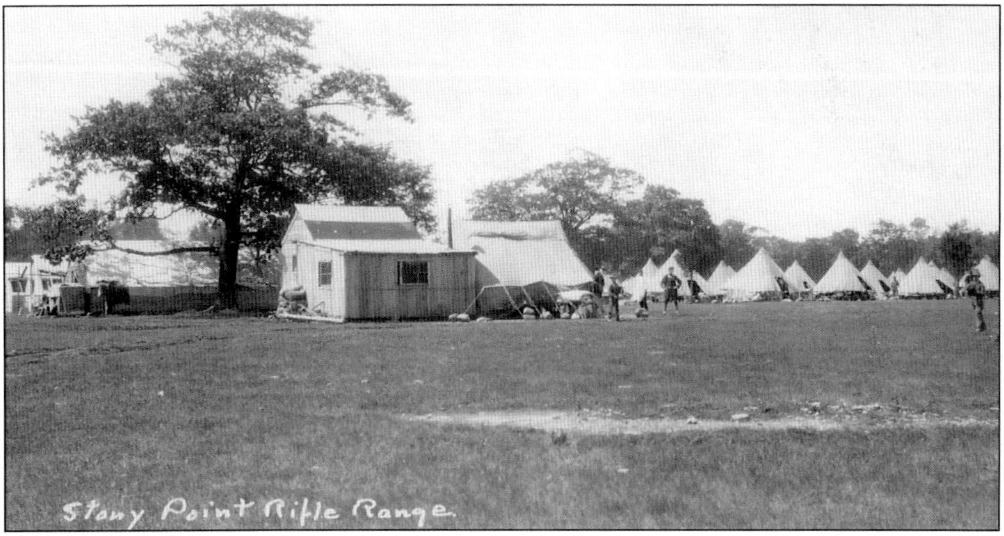

The Stony Point Rifle Range was used by state and federal troops from about 1900 until the late 1940s. Soldiers often marched to Henderson Harbor from as far away as Syracuse and Oswego. They stayed in tents and practiced firing at targets pulled by boats in Lake Ontario. The concrete Military Road from Henderson Harbor to Stony Point was constructed in 1941 as part of the war effort.

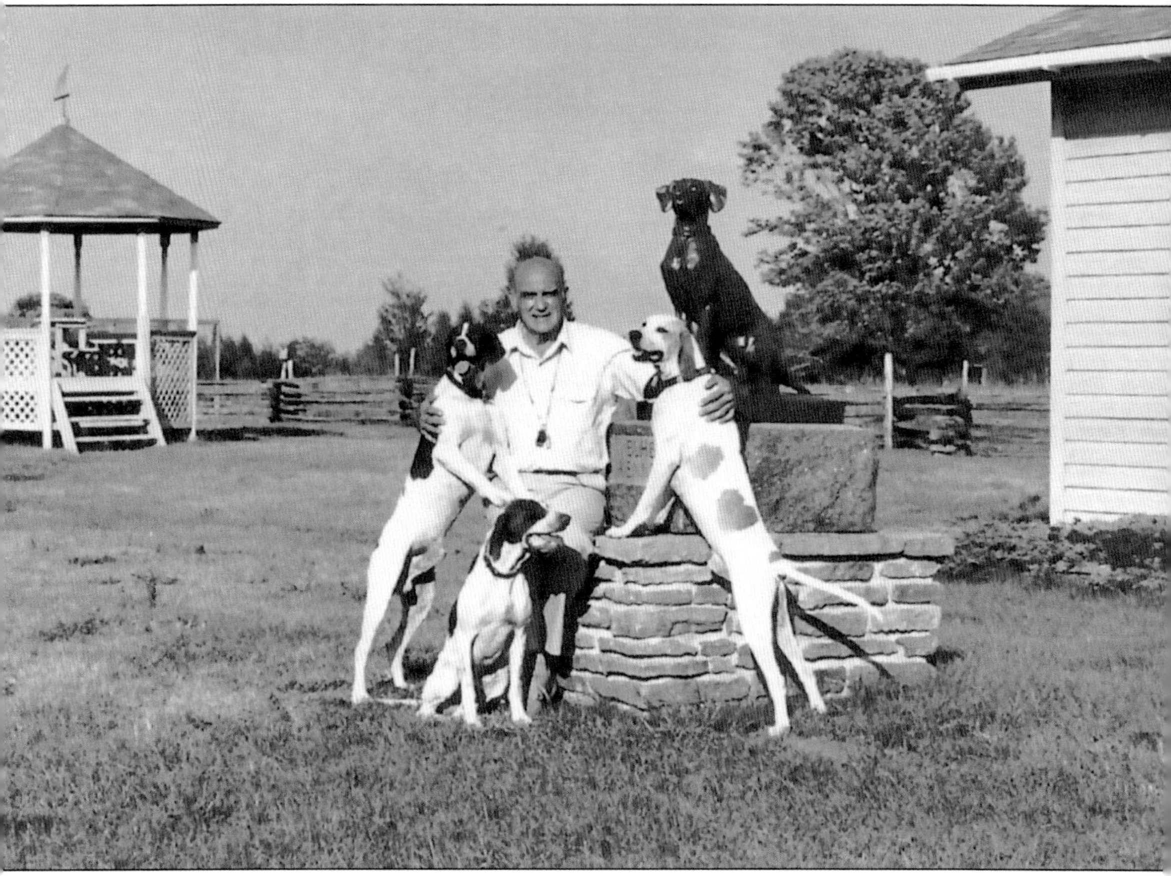

Wehle's son Robert G. Wehle inherited the Stony Point property in the 1960s. He was a world-renowned breeder and trainer of English pointers at his Stony Point Elhew ("Wehle" spelled backwards) Kennels. Some of his dogs are buried in a cemetery near the site of this photograph. Wehle arranged for his Stony Point property to be donated to the state of New York upon his death, and Robert G. Wehle State Park will forever be open to the public. (Gatra Wehle.)

Five

Stony and Galloo

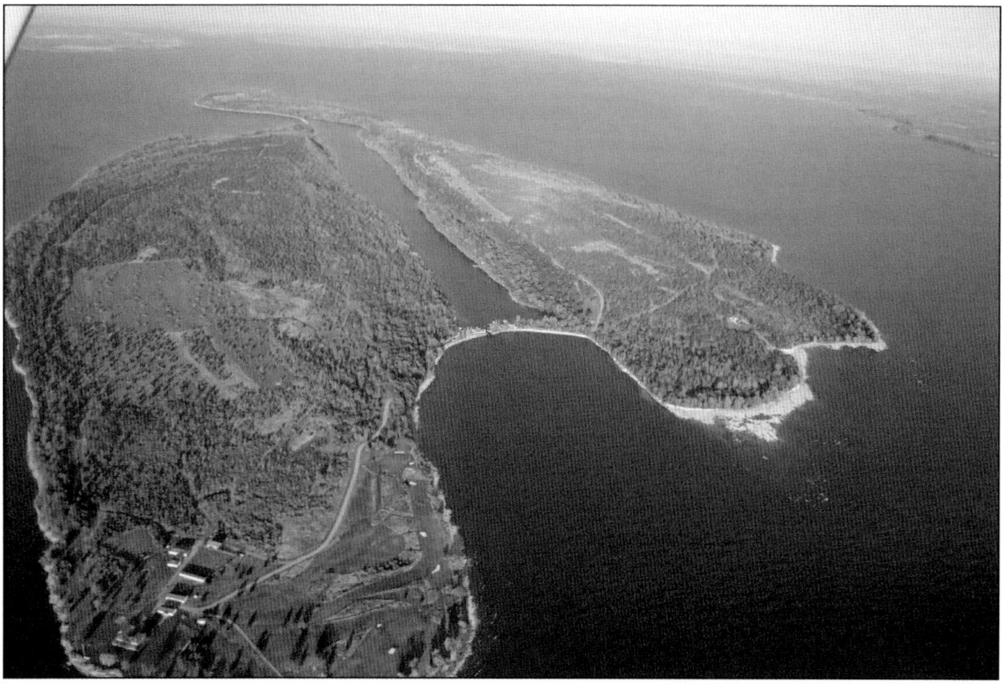

Stony Island was 1,536 acres of giant cedar trees when farm families first settled there in 1806. Lumbering and cattle farming gave way to hosting vacationers from as far away as New York City. Early family names on Stony Island included Camp, Wilkinson, "Dutch" John Bates, Brodie, Benoit, Eveleigh, Luff, Jackson, and Wescott. The Benoit farm became the Stony Island Inn in 1897, but it burned in 1898.

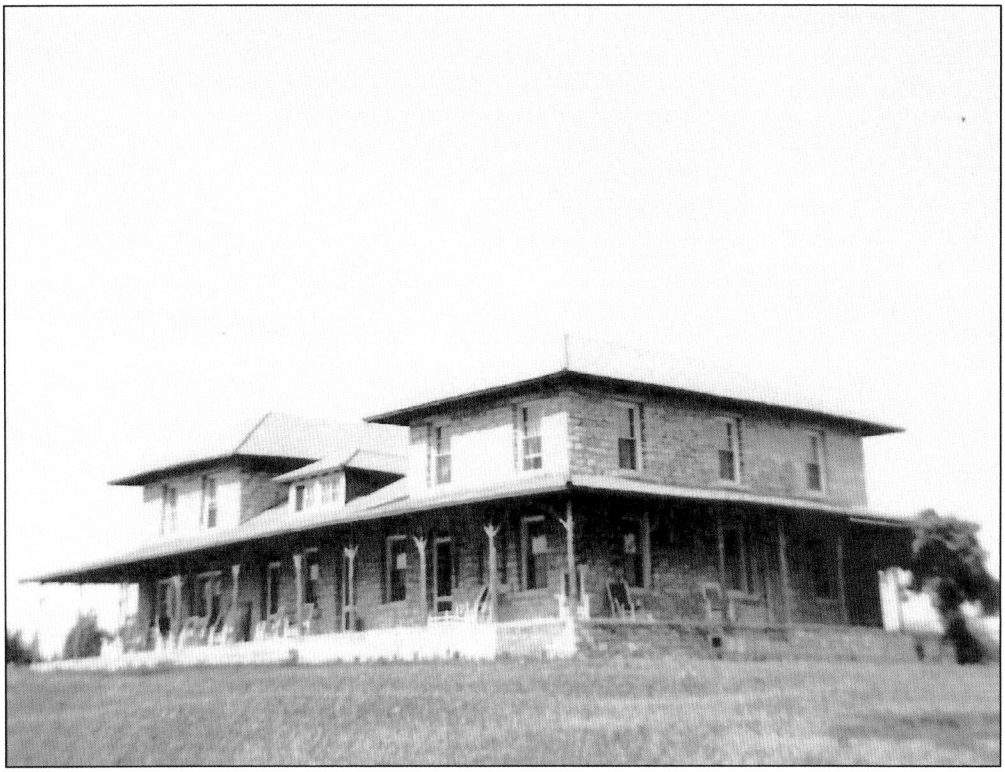

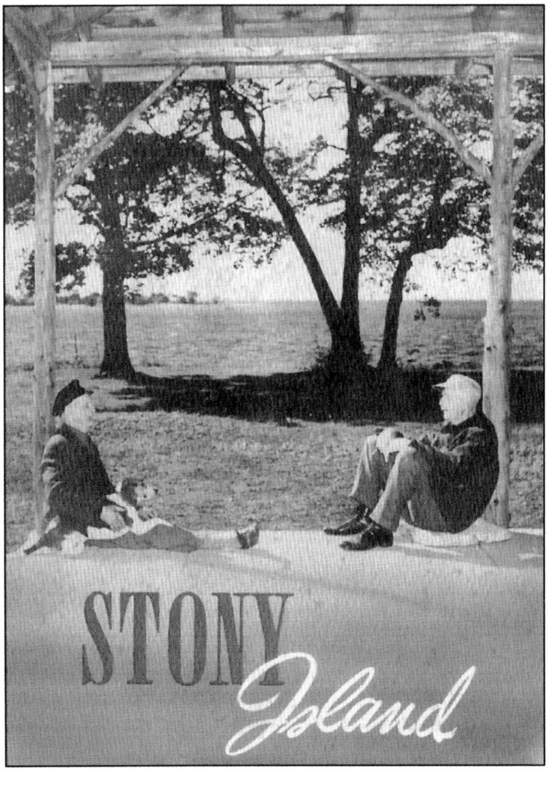

Stony Island Lodge was built in 1901 by members of the Stony Island Club, who enjoyed fishing for bass and perch in Lake Ontario. They included William Cowie, former mayor of Syracuse and postmaster. Designed by architect and club member Archimedes Russell and built by the Delmonico family construction company of Syracuse, the clubhouse's stone was shipped across Henderson Bay from Chaumont, New York. (Janine Smith.)

Stony Island Club required fishing guides and boatmen. J. Aiken Montague (left) and Willett "Will" Stevens were both guides renowned for their skill at finding fish in the shoals around the island. This photograph is from a 1950s brochure that was published by Stony Island steward Frank C. Ash. The Terry and Montague families of Henderson acquired a large tract of Stony Island, which has long been leased to the Stony Island Lodge. (John Ash Clark.)

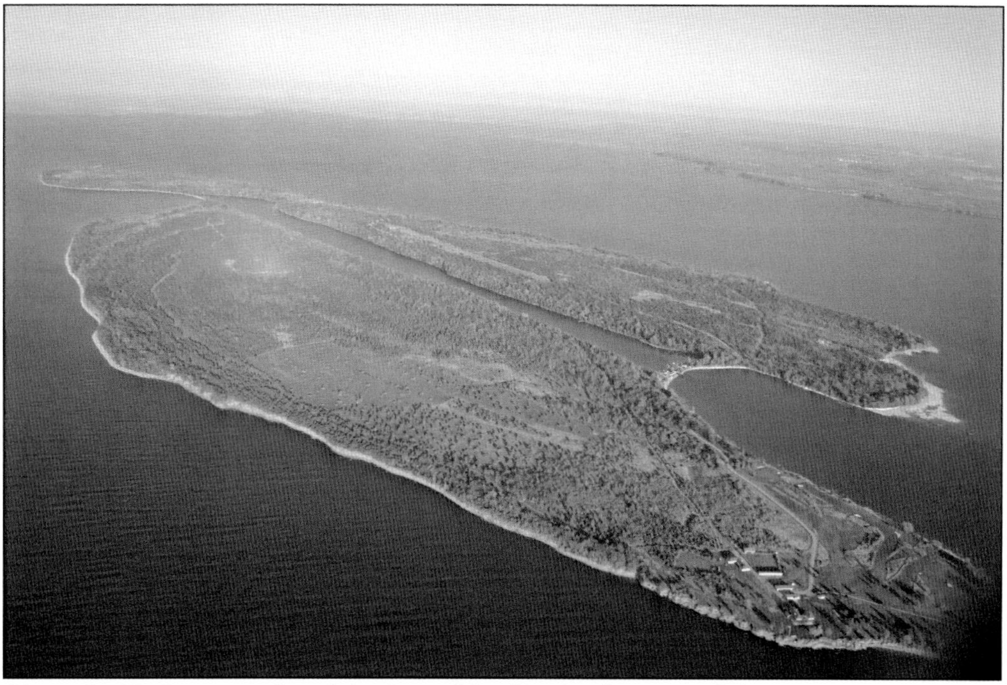

Alexander H. Cowie purchased the Stony Island Lodge (bottom right) in 1924. Cowie was the attorney for the Oswego Falls-Sealright Corporation, a dairy packaging company. Upon Cowie's death in 1948, Sealright acquired Cowie's island holdings in 1949. A distinct and somewhat secretive feature of Stony Island is the pond that splits it into two islands. Once open at both ends, the pond is closed at Dutch John Bay (top left) but open at a constructed channel at Brodie's Bay (right).

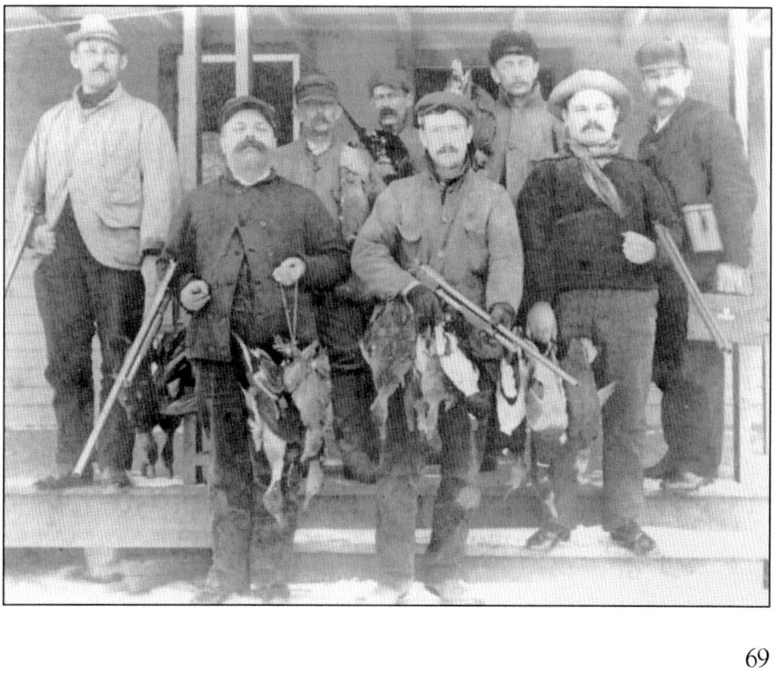

Stony Island was renowned for duck hunting on the shores of the pond. This duck hunting party consists of, from left to right, (first row) Arthur Hicks, Byron Southwick, and W.S. Overton; (second row) Arthur Hicks Jr., Hiram McGrath, Ferd Smith, and two unidentified men. (Janine Smith.)

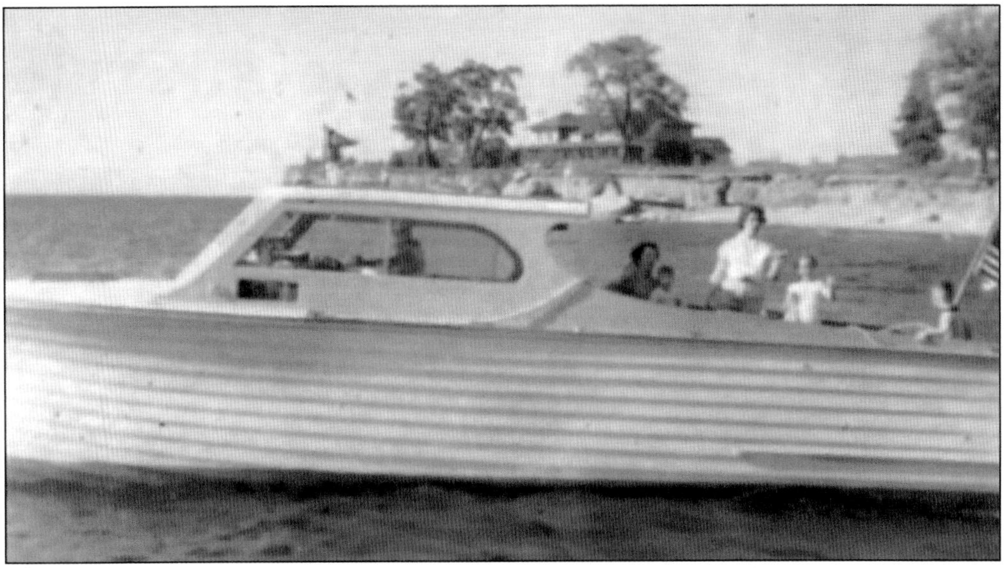

William G. "Bill" Smith of Belleville, New York, was the longtime caretaker and manager of Stony Island Lodge for Frank C. Ash and the Sealright Corporation. Smith is pictured here at the helm of the fishing boat, *Stony*, with his family; they are offshore from Stony Island Lodge in the early 1960s. This location is a well-known shoal that has consistently produced bass and perch. An accomplished hunting and fishing guide, Smith would often pilot his single-engine plane to Stony Island, landing on a grass strip. His mother, Laura May Smith, was the head cook and attendant at Stony Island Lodge for about 30 years. (Janine Smith.)

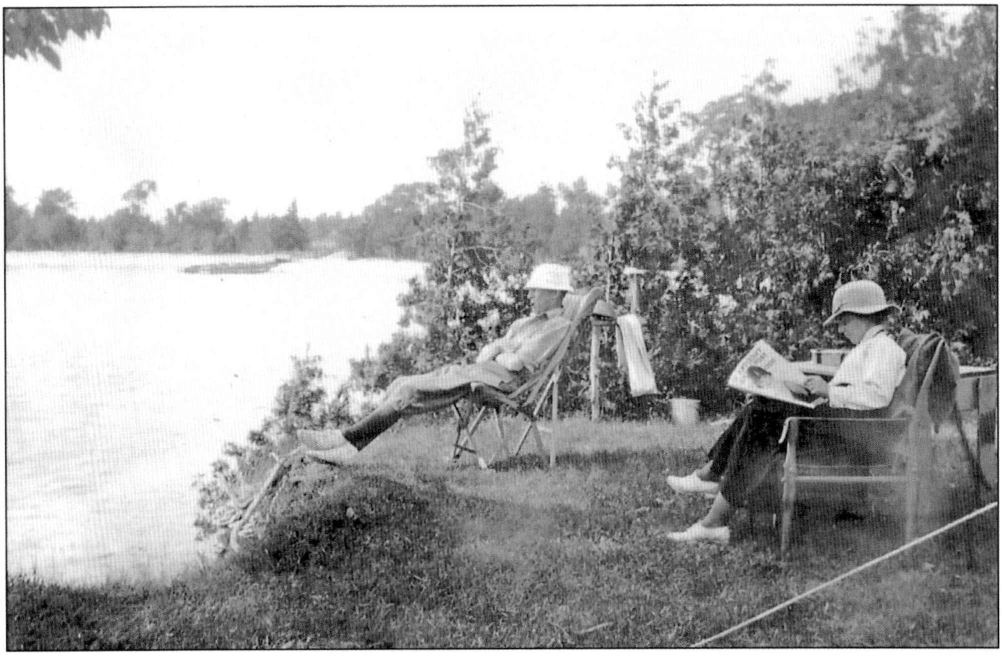

Henderson Harbor summer residents Earl and Bertha Waite Averill also owned a waterfront property on Stony Island. Arriving in their naphtha launch, *Bluebird*, they spent many summer weeks at their northwest island camp. This photograph is dated by the July 24, 1920, *Saturday Evening Post* that Bertha Averill is reading. (The Averill family.)

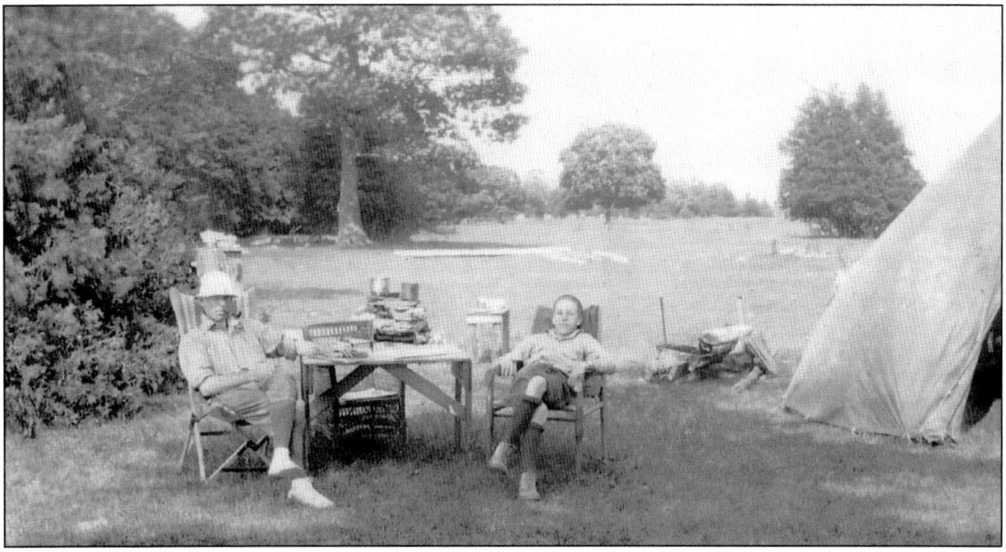

The Averill camp on Stony Island included comforts such as a wicker chair from the *Bluebird*, a handmade table, and a large canvas tent. In this 1920 photograph, Earl Averill and his son Edgar "Bill" Averill enjoy some time together at their Stony Island campsite. (The Averill family.)

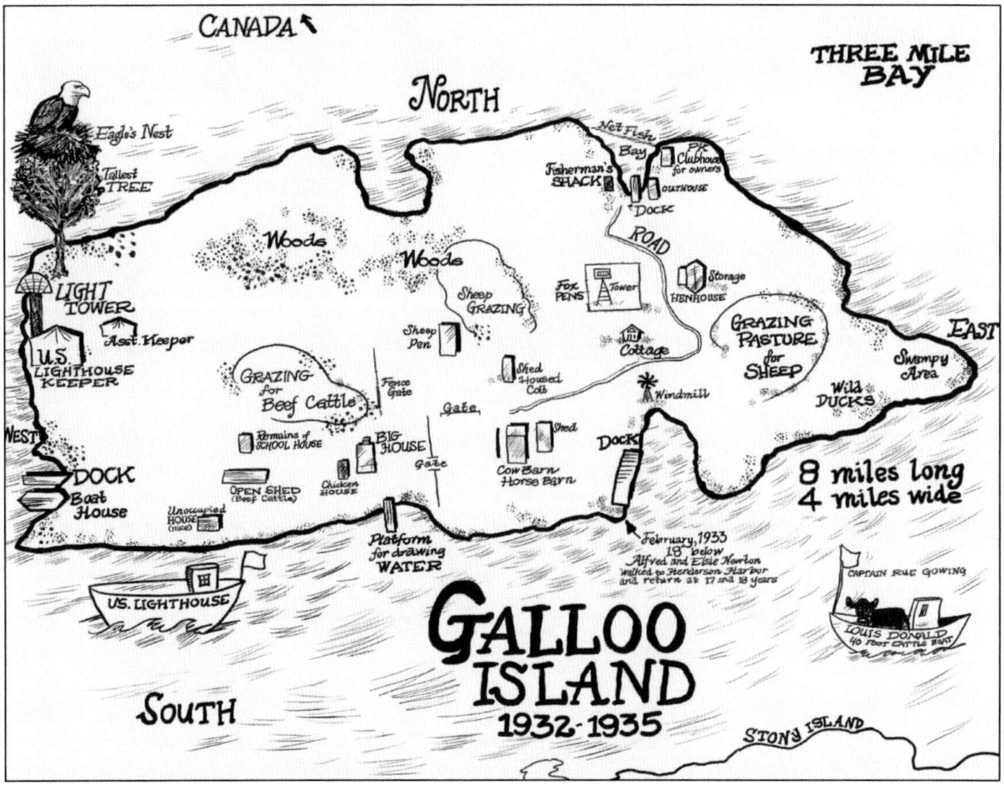

Galloo Island is the largest of Henderson Harbor's offshore islands. Emily Anthony redrew this map of Galloo Island from 1932 to 1935 from a drawing made by Elsie Coit, a resident of Galloo Island in the early 1930s. The map includes locations of the lighthouse, PK Clubhouse at North Pond, and the south bay where the Coast Guard station would be built in 1936.

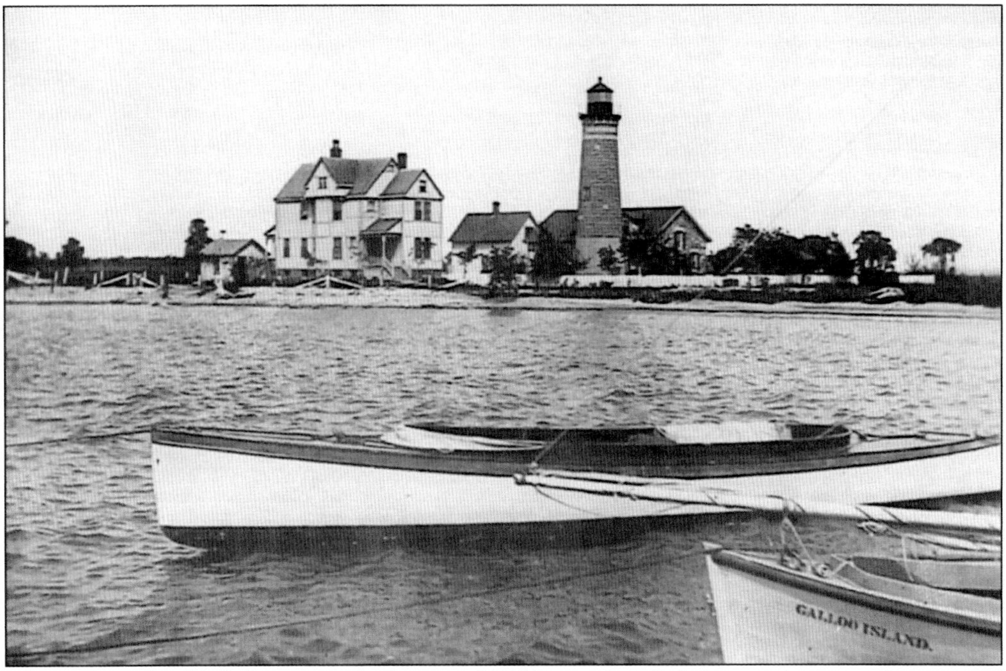

The Galloo Island lighthouse was built around 1857 to replace lighthouses that were first erected in 1820. Despite its size and grandeur, the white house to the left of the light tower is described as the assistant keeper's house; however, only the foundation remains. Although badly deteriorated, the lighthouse and tower are still standing as of 2012.

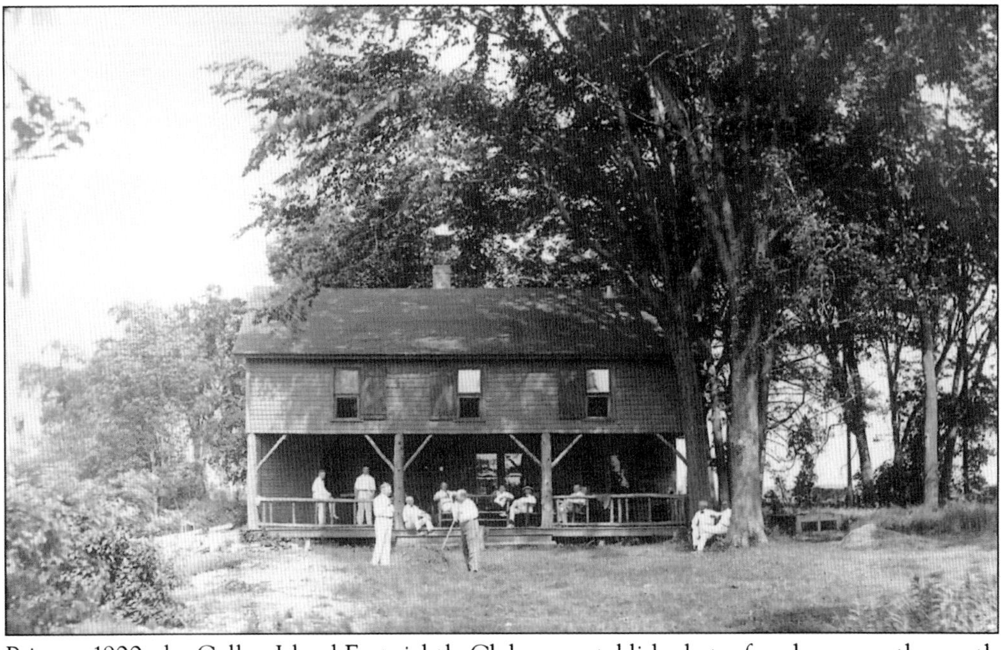

Prior to 1900, the Galloo Island Fortnightly Club was established at a farmhouse on the north end of the island. Within a few years, a large clubhouse, pictured here, was built on the shore at North Pond, a cove that provided protection for boats. The club was organized for fishing, boating, and other activities common to gentlemen professionals of the era. (JCHS.)

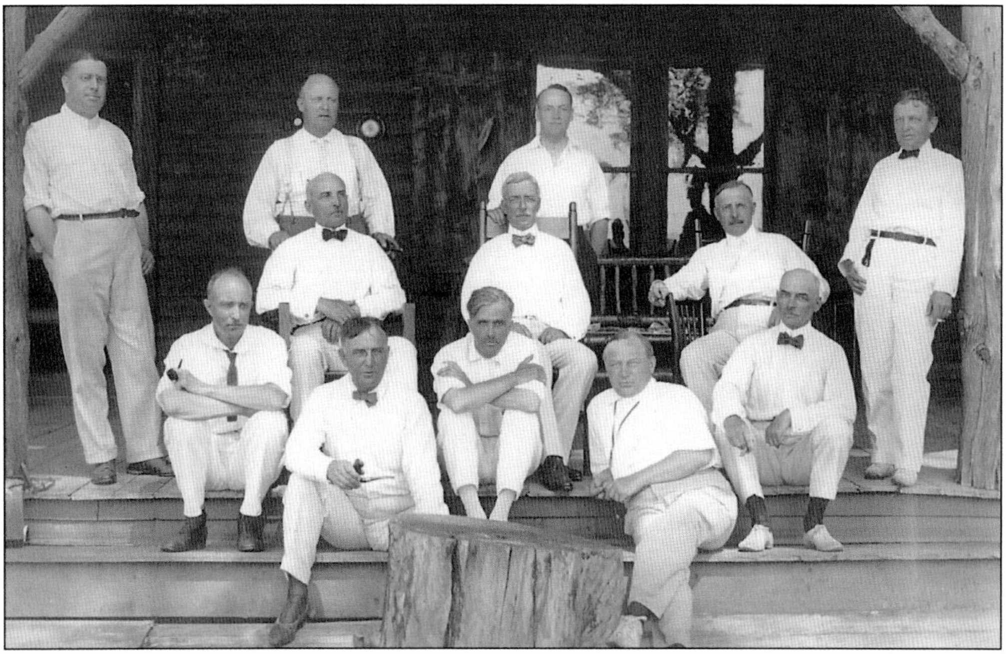

Members of the Fortnightly Club—nicknamed the "PK Club"—in 1924 included cofounder and Secretary of State Robert M. Lansing (center with bow tie), Edward N. Smith, Robert J. Buck, Gary M. Jones, Frederick H. Boyer, Charles W. Valentine, S.A. Upham, Stuart D. Lansing, and Charles L. Parmelee. (JCHS.)

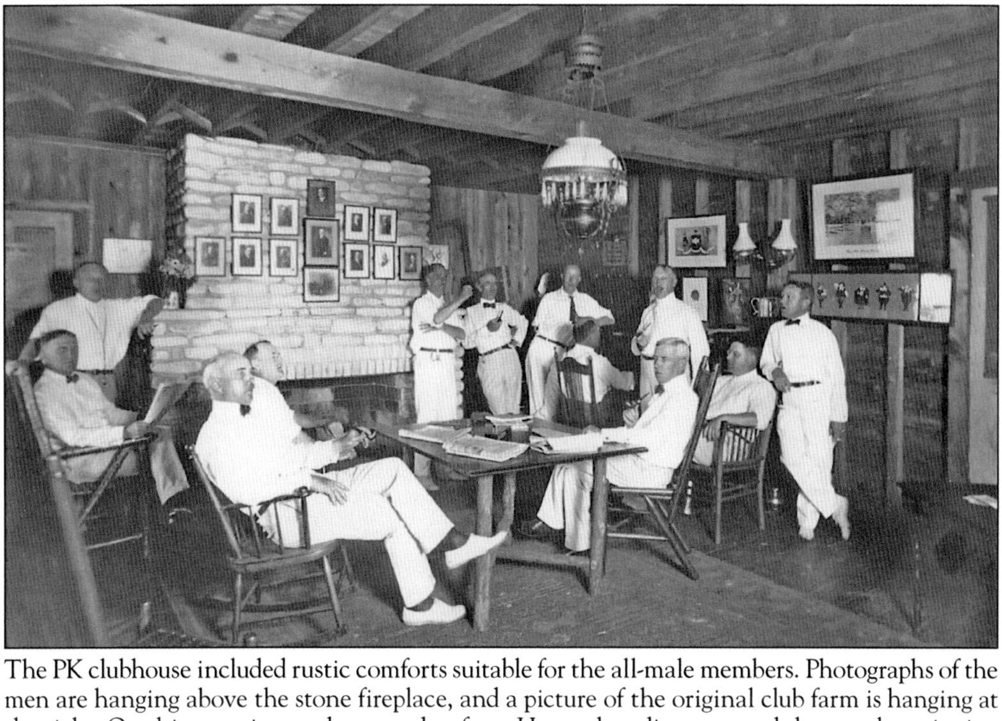

The PK clubhouse included rustic comforts suitable for the all-male members. Photographs of the men are hanging above the stone fireplace, and a picture of the original club farm is hanging at the right. On this occasion, a photographer from Huested studios captured the members singing around the piano. They slept, dormitory style, upstairs. (JCHS.)

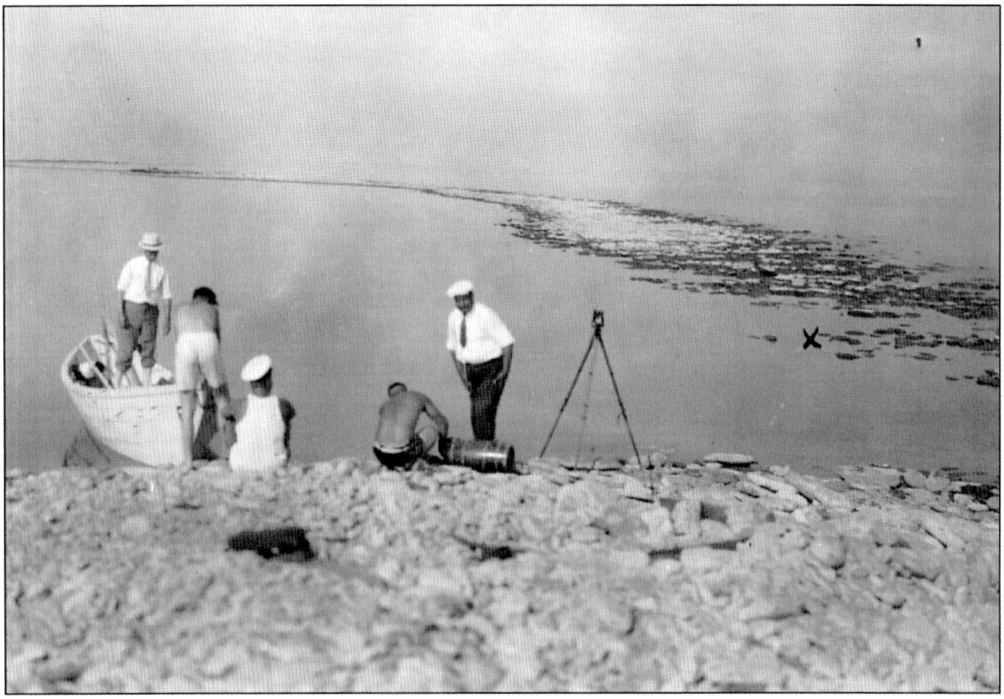

In 1934, a survey party was sent to Galloo Island to plot the location for a boat channel into Gill Harbor for relocation of the Big Sandy Coast Guard base. The reef extending into the water in this photograph would be fortified to form a better protected harbor for Coast Guard boats. (USCG.)

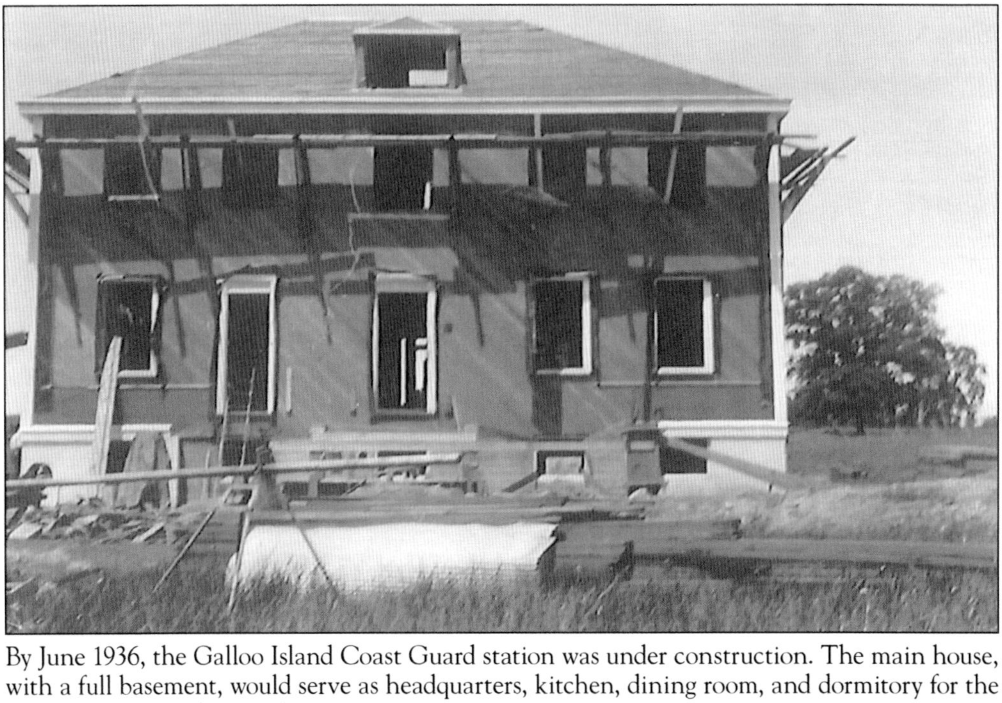

By June 1936, the Galloo Island Coast Guard station was under construction. The main house, with a full basement, would serve as headquarters, kitchen, dining room, and dormitory for the captain and crew. (USCG.)

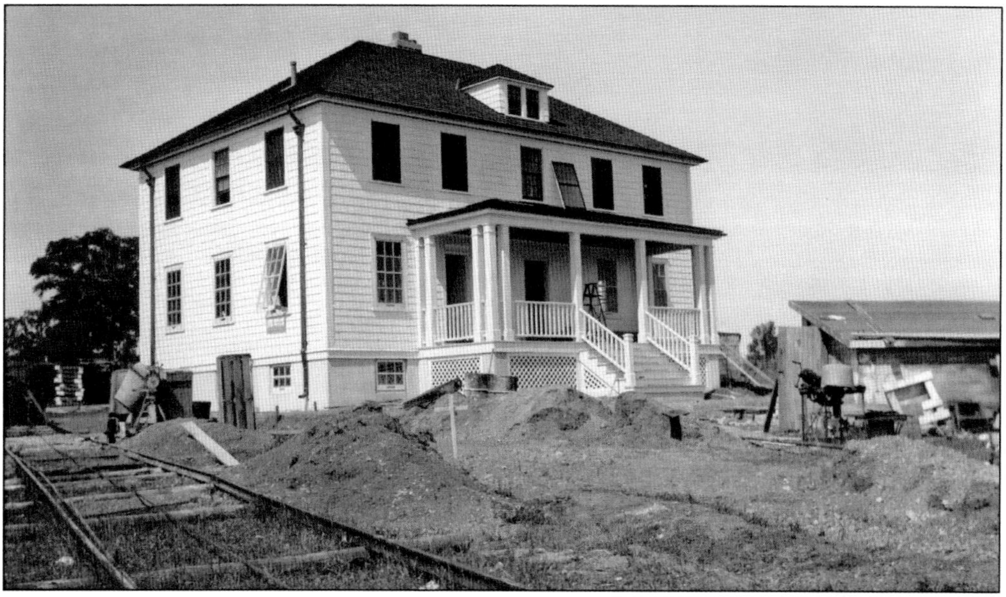

Upon its completion in August 1936, the Galloo Island station house was immediately opened, but it was not fully staffed until 1937. Note the temporary track and cable used to pull boats out of the lake prior to construction of a new boathouse. (USCG.)

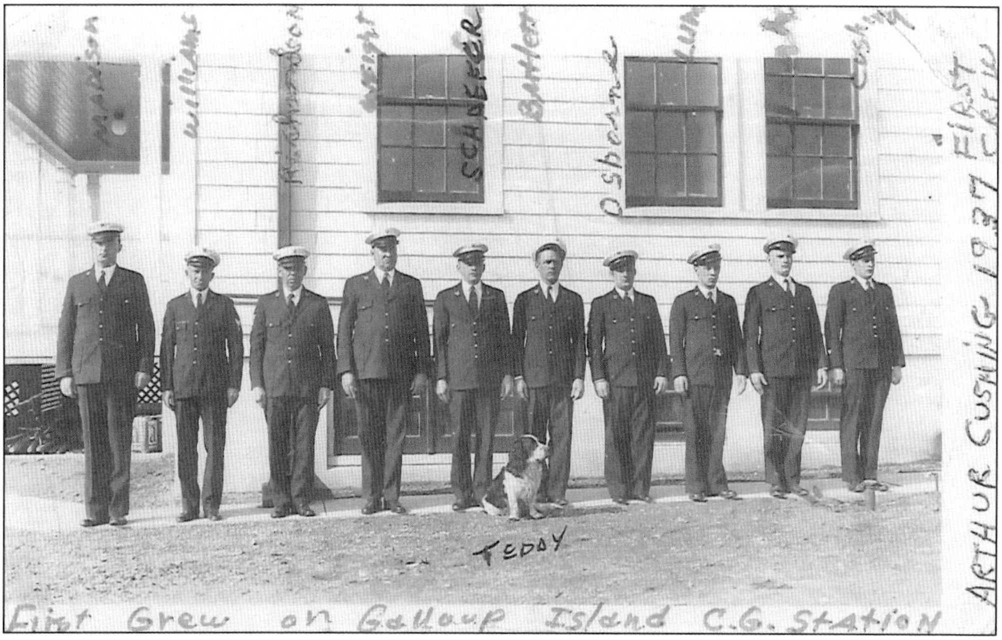

The first full crew at Galloo Island Coast Guard base in 1937 included Capt. Ralph M. Matteson (far left), Harvey E. Richardson (third from left), and Isaac H. "Ike" Wright (fourth from left). These men had been transferred to Galloo Island from Big Sandy or Oswego. (NCNYCGA.)

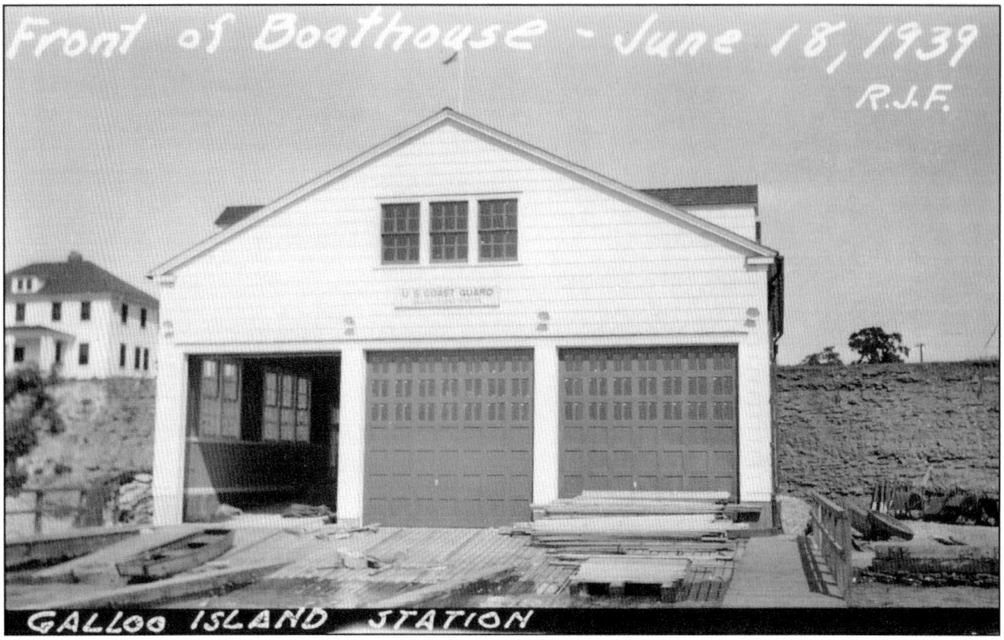

The new Galloo Island Coast Guard base was completed by June 1939 with the opening of the three-bay boathouse. Designed with a ramp and tracks to pull the boats into their bays for the winter, the new boathouse gave the crew rapid access to the water with their powerboats, a feature that was lacking at Big Sandy. The station house is in the left background. (USCG.)

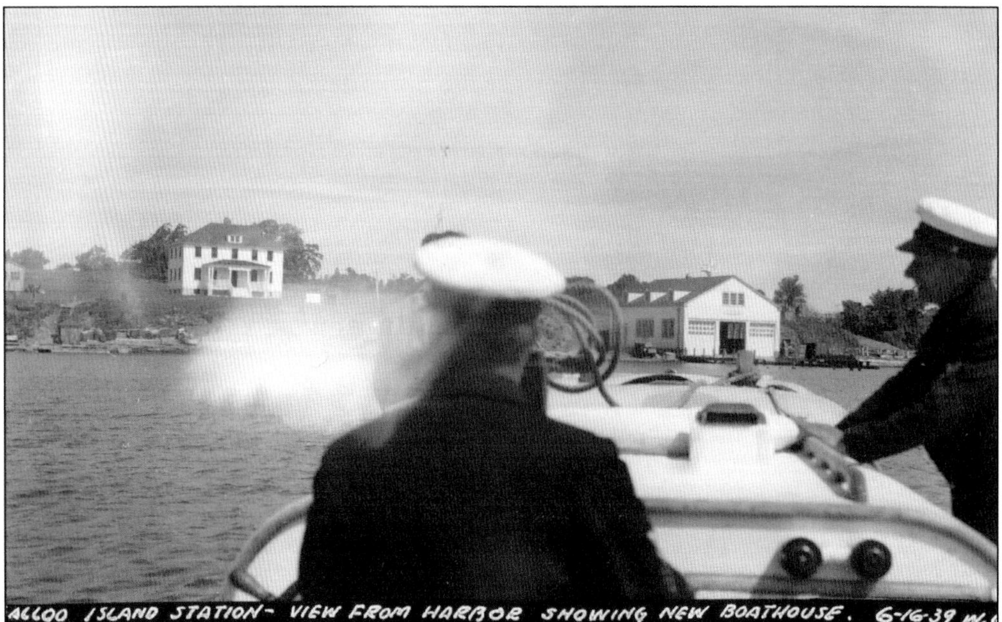

In this June 1939 photograph, a motorized patrol boat with guardsmen in full dress uniform arrives at the newly completed Galloo Island Coast Guard station. By this time, all boats, material, and personnel had been transferred from Big Sandy, and that station had been closed. (USCG.)

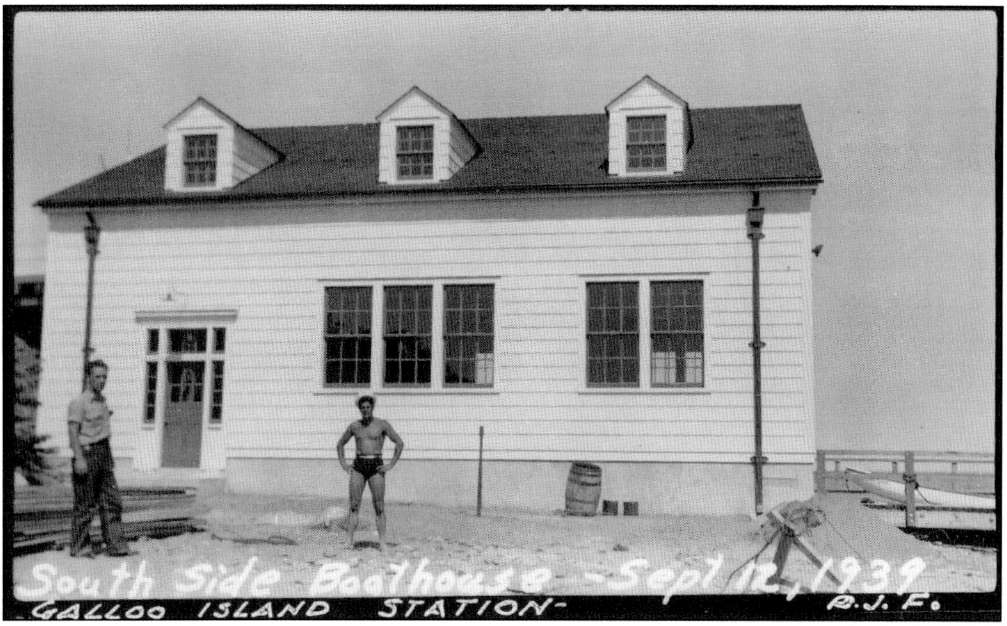

A side view of the newly constructed Galloo Island Coast Guard boathouse shows two of the early guardsmen enjoying a warm day in September 1939. The large six-over-six windows are designed to use natural light to flood the interior of the boathouse. (USCG.)

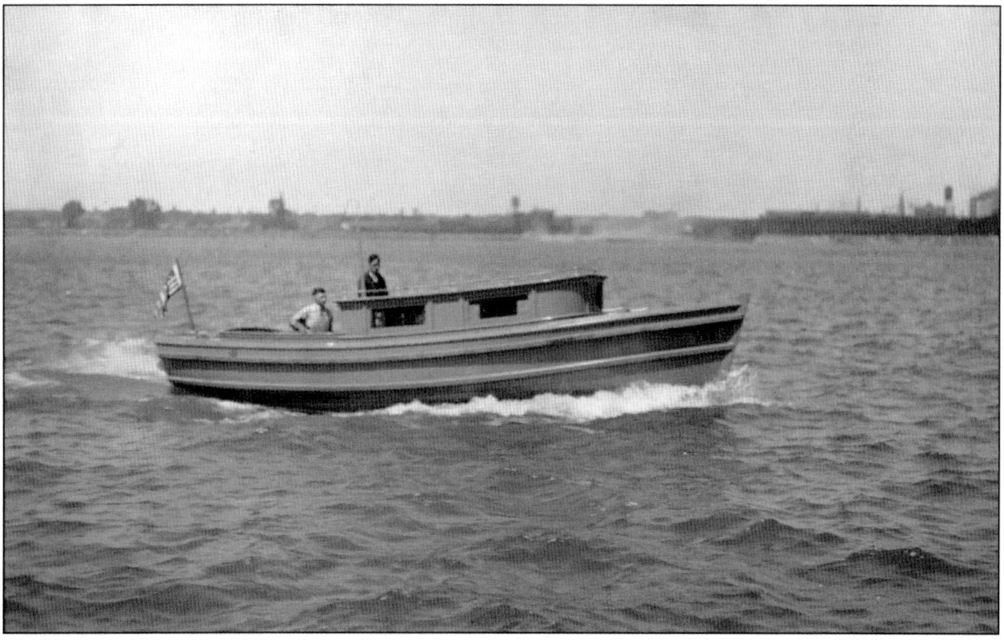

Photographed elsewhere on the Great Lakes, this boat was transferred to the new Galloo Island Coast Guard station for duty on eastern Lake Ontario. It was a single cabin, 36-foot picket boat. (USCG.)

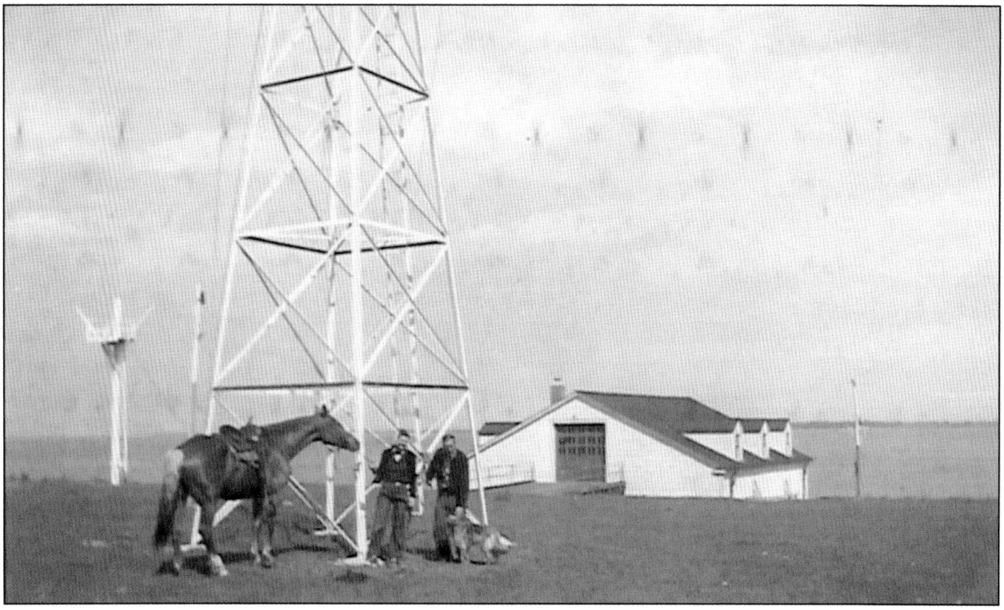

Although more than 50 feet tall and able to protect guardsmen from the weather, the original Galloo Island lookout tower was soon outdated by telephone communications to Sackets Harbor Oswego and by ship to shore radio transmitting from this communications tower near the boathouse. Judy Hovey and Floyd Stevens are with one of the Hovey family horses; they later married. (NCNYCGA.)

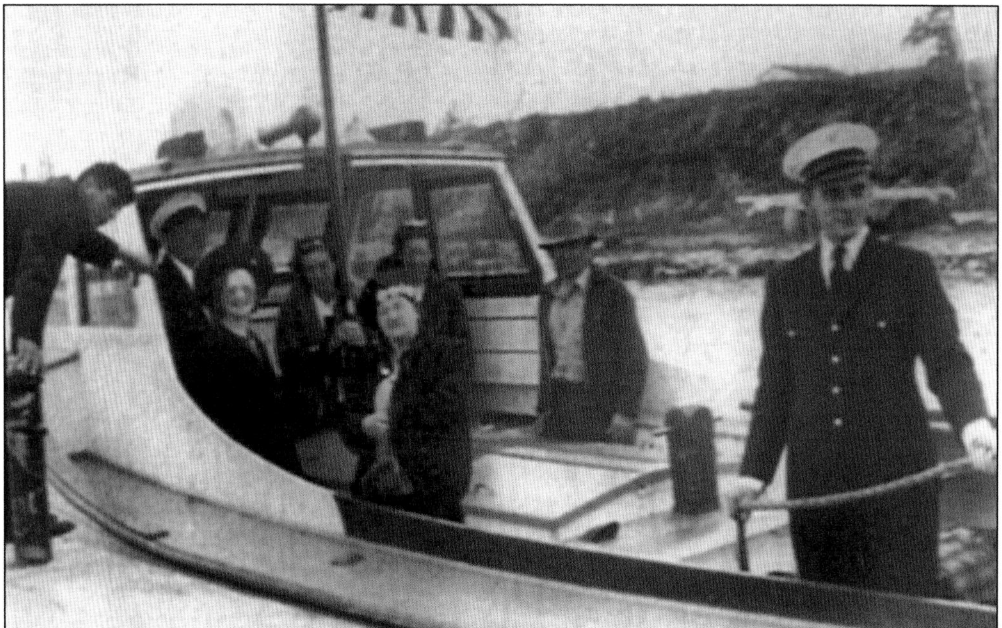

A posting at remote Galloo Island was lonely for guardsmen who stayed on the island for weeks at a time. Visiting day for guardsman Harold Joslyn, right, of Ellisburg was a special occasion in the 1940s. Boats would carry visitors from Sackets Harbor or Henderson Harbor to spend a day on the island. (NCNYCGA.)

The Galloo Island Coast Guard crew normally spent winters in Sackets Harbor. However, they occasionally stayed at Galloo for maintenance operations. During northern New York's long cold winters, family members could visit guardsmen by airplane. Note the skis in place of wheels on the plane. (NCNYCGA.)

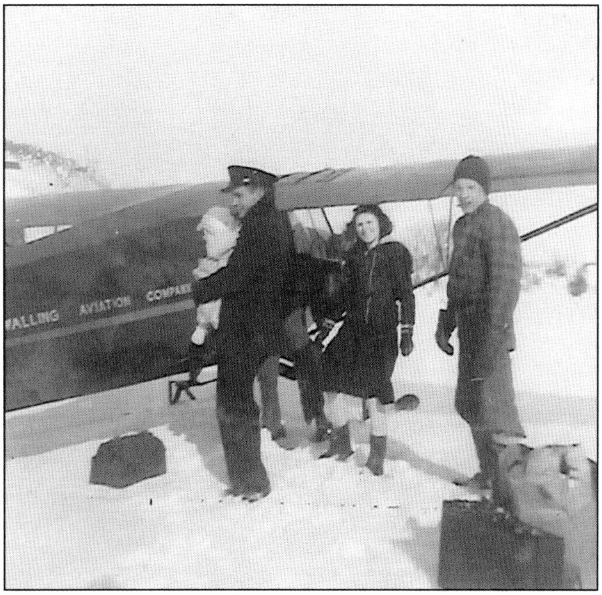

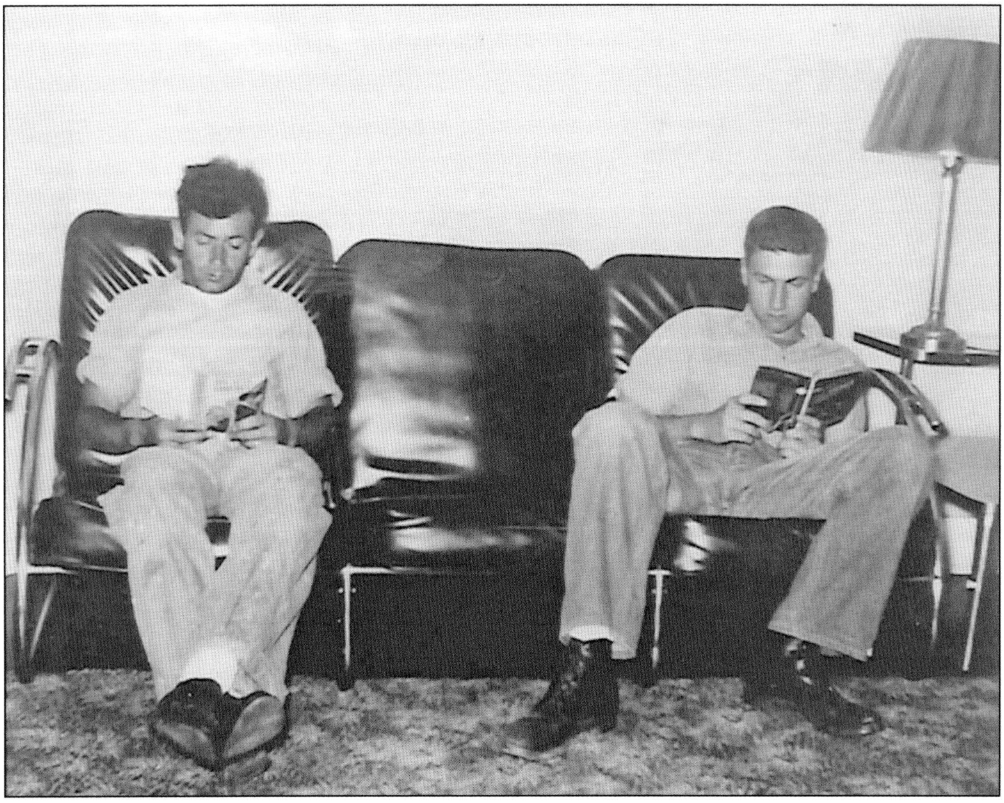

Galloo Island coastguardsmen spent many long and lonely hours at the secluded base, which had no stores, movie theaters, or restaurants. The only entertainment in their spare time was visiting island farm families or personal activities in the station house. Guardsmen Fred Charbanneau (left) and Gordon Koscher are pictured in 1955 spending time reading at the Galloo station. (NCNYCGA.)

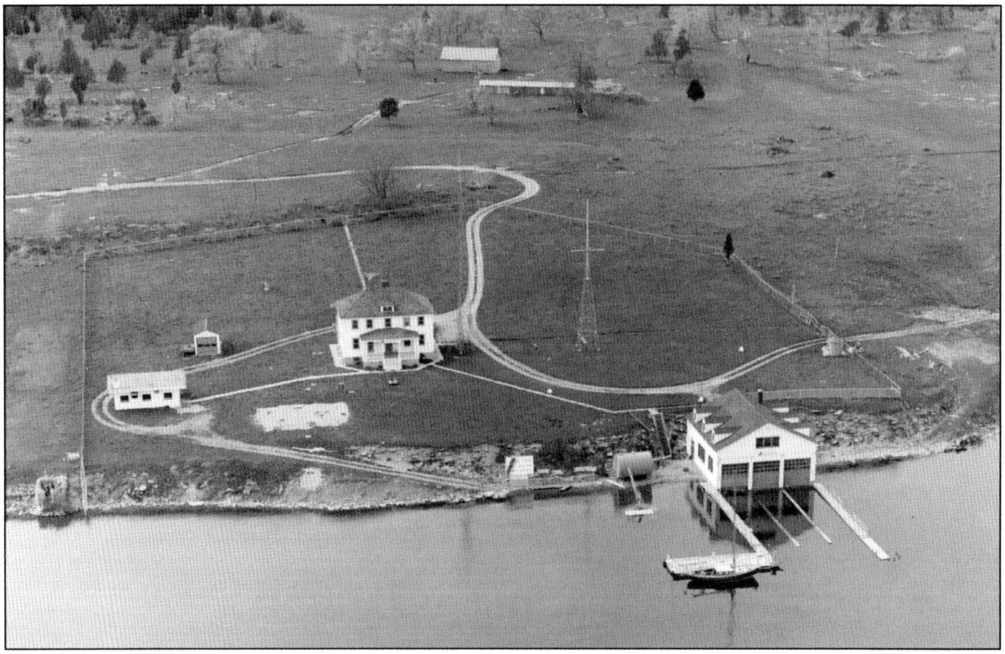

This aerial photograph shows the Galloo Island Coast Guard station in its final year of service. Note that the extremely high water is up to the boathouse doors. Except for the sleek sailing yacht moored at the landing dock, by 1973 the base was deserted when the Coast Guard consolidated operations across Henderson Bay in Sackets Harbor. (USCG.)

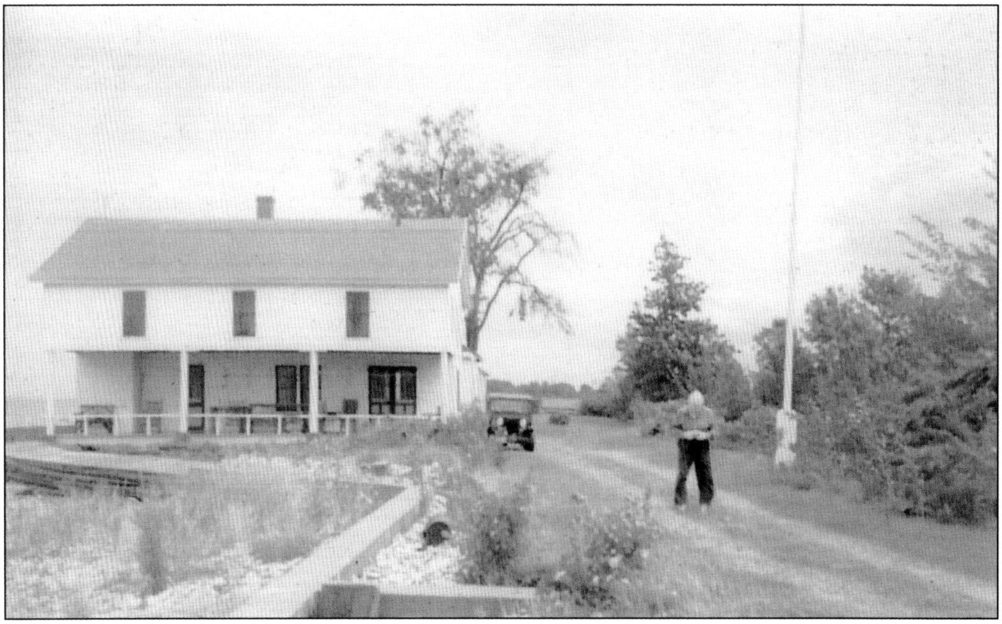

By the 1940s, the original members of the Galloo Island PK Club had died. One of the newer members—former New York State Assembly speaker, banker, farmer, and utility executive Henry Edmund Machold of Ellisburg—purchased the clubhouse in 1944 for his twin children, Earl J. Machold and Doris Machold Davis. This photograph from the early 1950s shows the updated clubhouse with Howard C. Coonley, father of Alice Coonley Machold. (Jack Machold.)

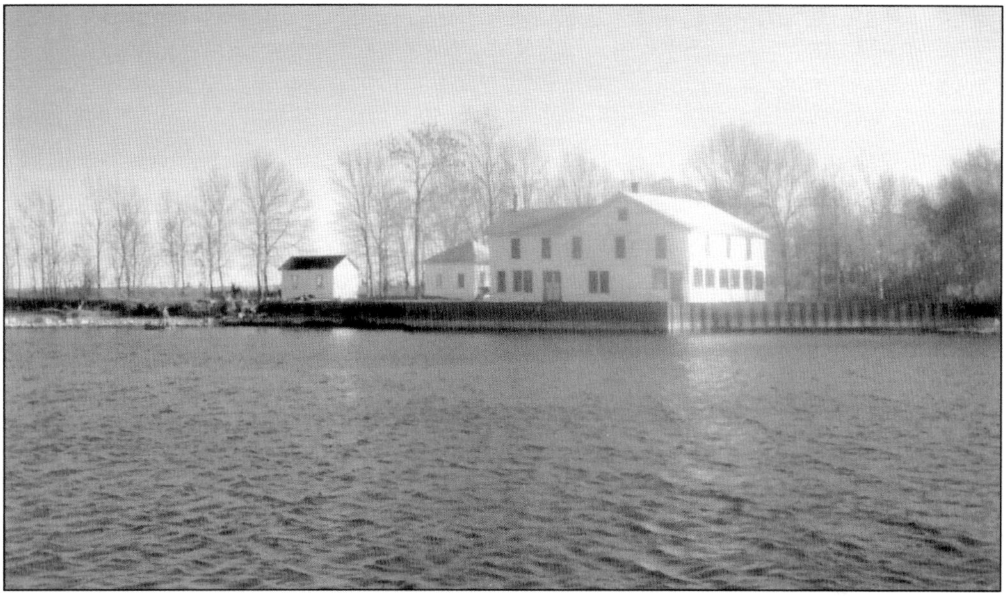

Severe lake storms in the 1950s required a large seawall to be built to save the PK Clubhouse. The porch was enclosed and a generator shack (left) was added. Earl J. Machold was the Niagara Mohawk Power Corporation leader who ushered in nuclear power for the company, but his island retreat had to generate its own electricity. His son and nephews, John Ward Machold, Edmund Machold Davis, and the late Philip Frank Davis Jr., spent many summer days in the 1950s boating and fishing around Galloo Island and riding the Hovey family ponies. (Jack Machold.)

In 1966, the PK Clubhouse was sold to Watertown businessman Larry Smith. A Henderson Harbor summer resident, Smith built a large, multi-slip boathouse on the site of the former Tyler property in Henderson Harbor and spent many summer weekends at the PK Clubhouse. This early 1970s view shows the dock leading from North Pond to the clubhouse. The dock was an ideal sunning spot for snakes. (Greg Smith, GallooIsland.net.)

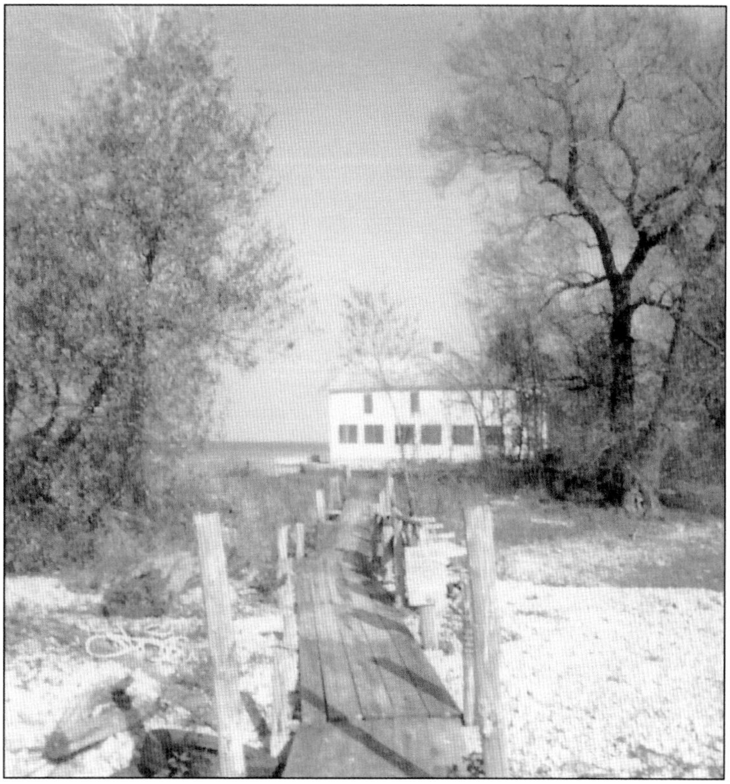

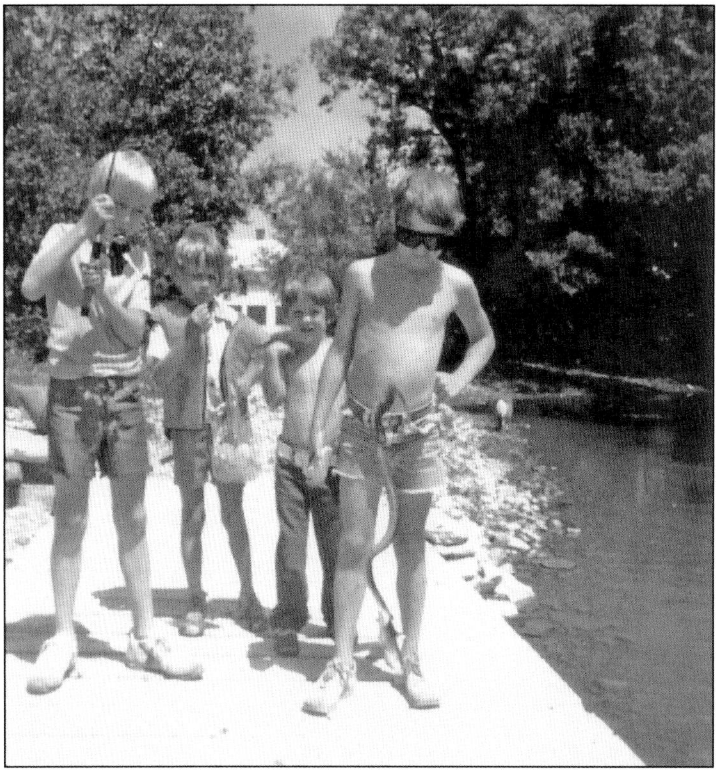

Larry Smith's children, pictured around 1970 on the main dock at the PK Clubhouse on Galloo Island, are enthralled by a snake caught in North Pond. Galloo Island was covered with snakes that often startled island visitors. (Greg Smith, GallooIsland.net.)

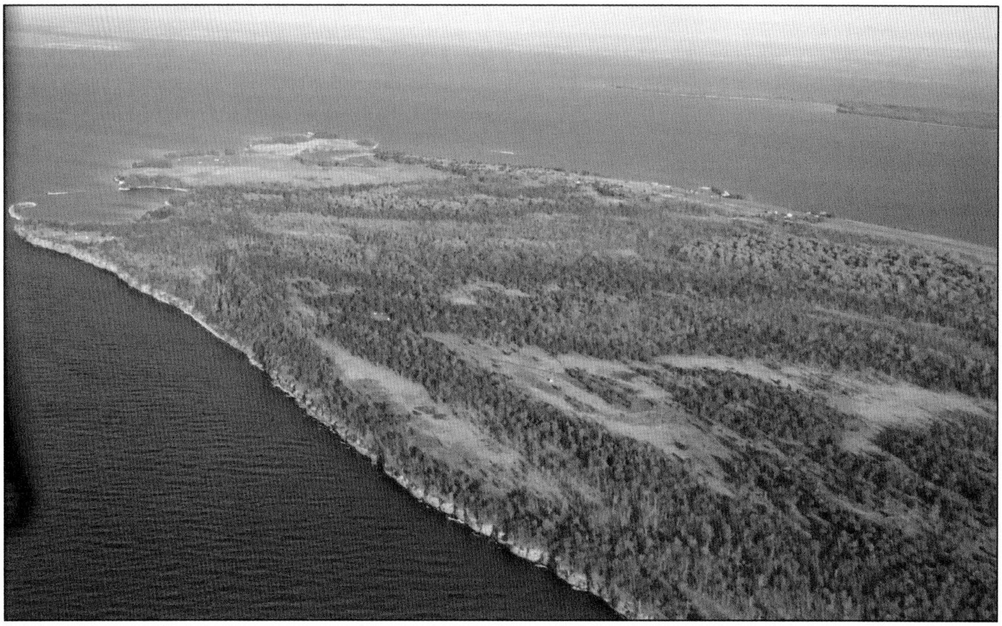

In 2009, a wind farm was proposed for Galloo Island. North Pond is pictured at the left, and the Coast Guard station is at the center on the right. A power transmission line was proposed for underwater or across land from Stony Point to central New York. In 2011, the plan was shelved when power distribution agencies declined a contract to purchase future Galloo Island wind electricity.

Six

GE and Association Island

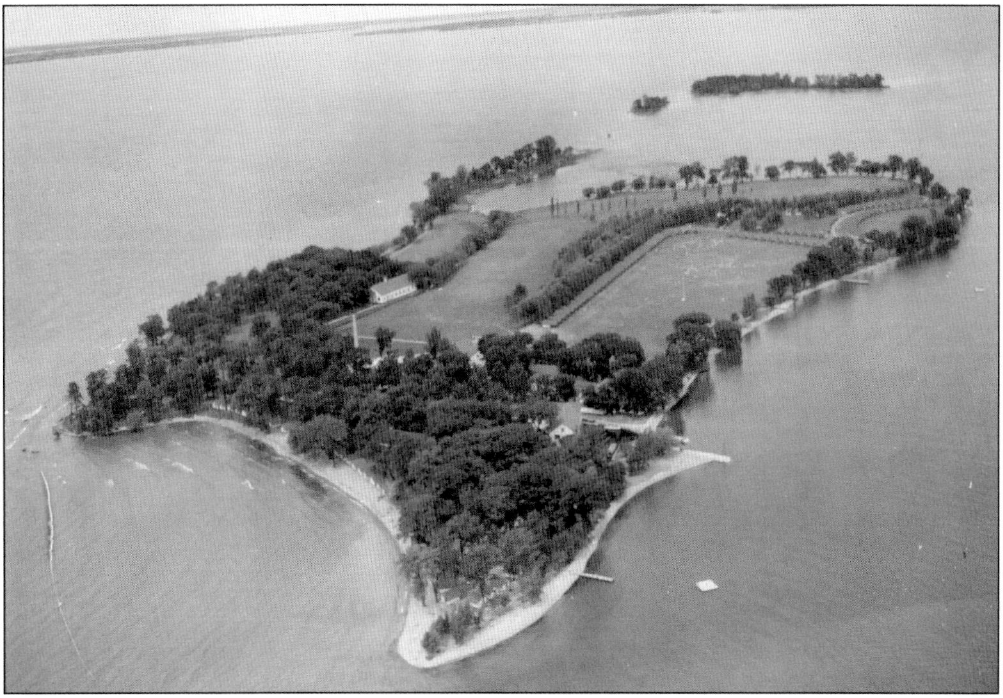

Association Island, originally called Warner's Island, is the largest of the islands surrounding Henderson Harbor at Sixtown Point. The site of a French observation post in 1756, it was also the scene of a gruesome murder of a Native American woman in 1897. It was used for pasturing cattle, camping, and shore dinners until 10 businessmen from an association of electrical lamp companies purchased the island in 1905–1906 for $2,500. (GE.)

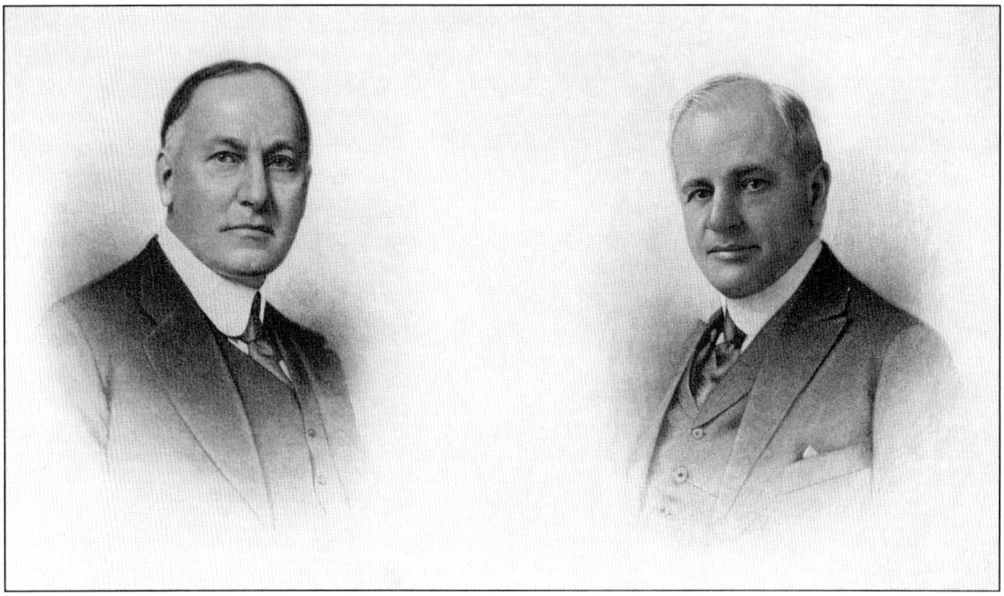

Association Island Corporation was founded by Franklin S. Terry (left) and Burton G. Tremaine, pioneers in the incandescent lamp business. In 1901, Terry and Tremaine helped consolidate small lamp companies into the National Electric Lamp Company (NELC) with financial support from General Electric, or GE. Their goal was to share research but remain competitive. In 1903, Terry arranged a fishing trip to Henderson Harbor, where he and Tremaine determined that Warner's Island would be an ideal location for the NELC's annual encampments. (GE.)

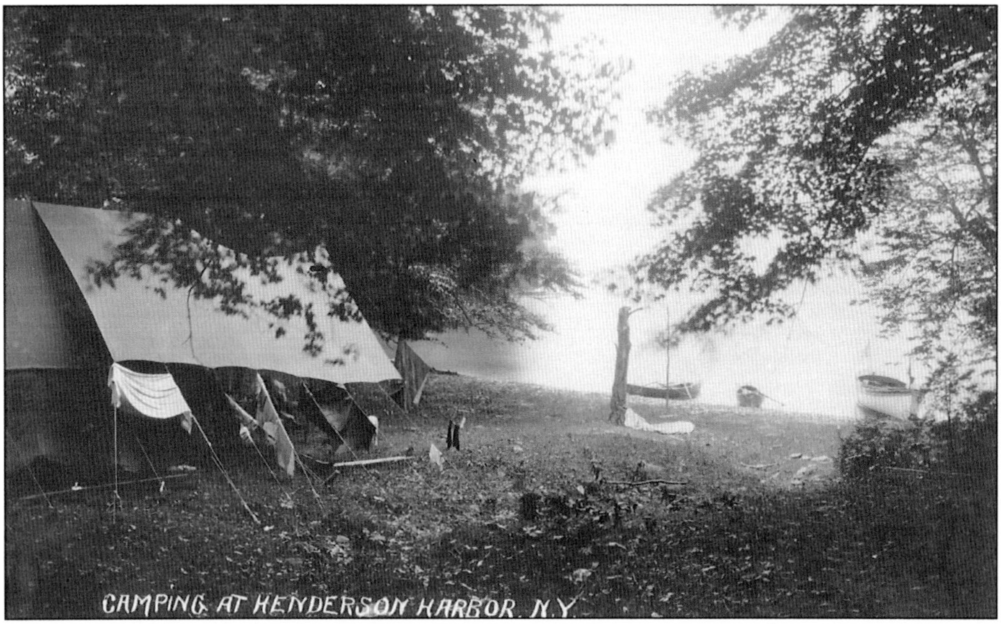

Because of rain during their 1903 trip to Henderson Harbor, NELC members met at a different location the following year. On August 14, 1905, they returned to Henderson Harbor, camping at Colewood (above) on the western shore of Henderson Harbor. During the 1905 and 1906 encampments at Colewood, NELC members agreed to purchase Warner's Island for a permanent summer retreat and changed their name to National Electric Lamp Association (NELA).

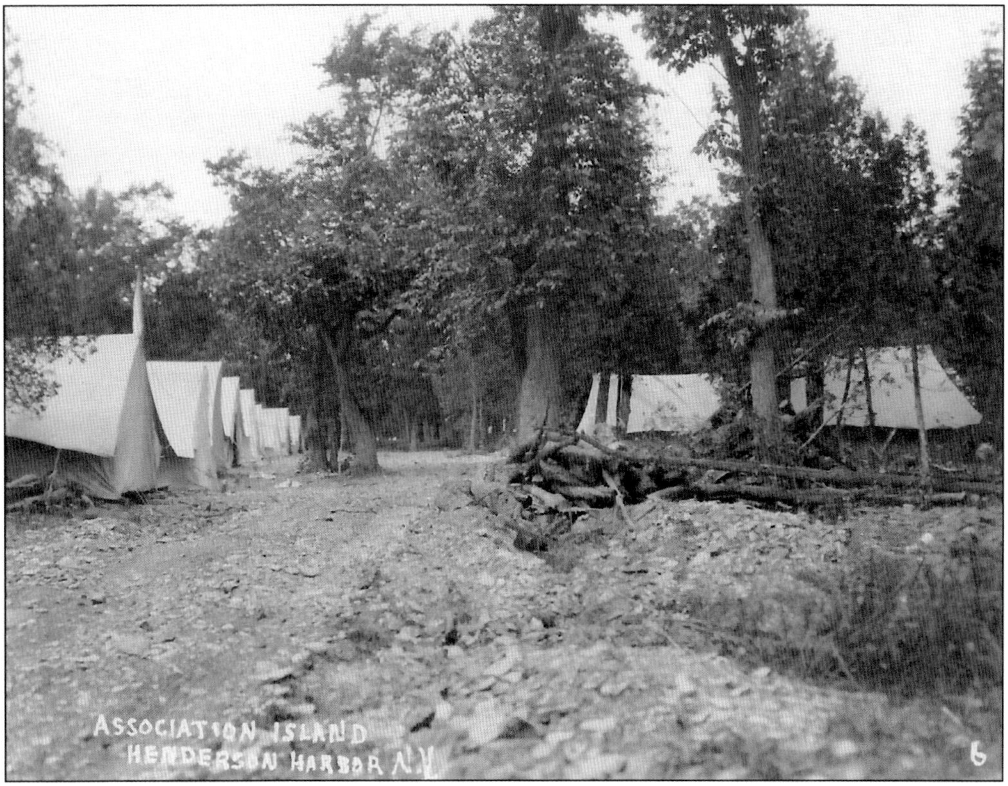

By 1907, the 40 member companies of the NELA had set up a tent campground at Warner's Island, nicknamed Electrical Island by local residents. In the first few years, members could spend only a few weeks at the island because of crude conditions. There were no bathrooms or showers, and tents were pitched on the ground in the woods.

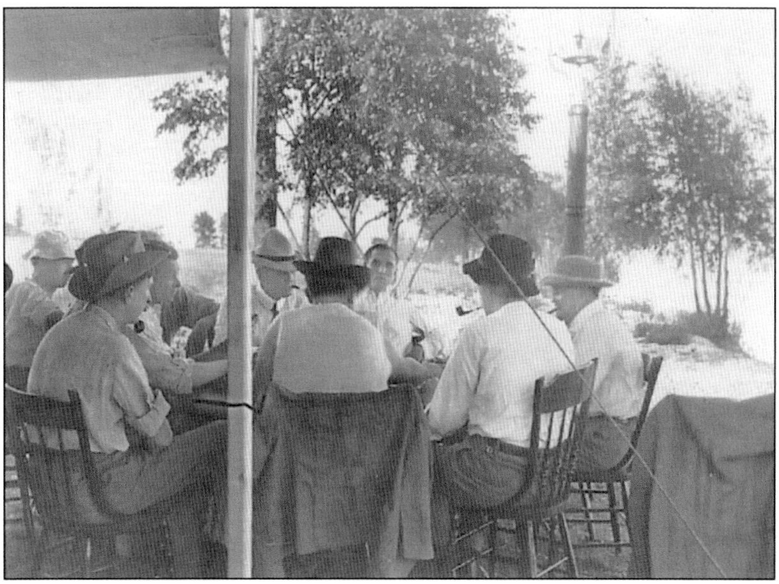

Originally attended by men only, NELA members fished, smoked, ate, drank, played cards, swam in the cool lake waters, and held long discussions about lamp sales. Within a few years, employees were encouraged to bring their families, and soon after, the name Association Island was adopted.

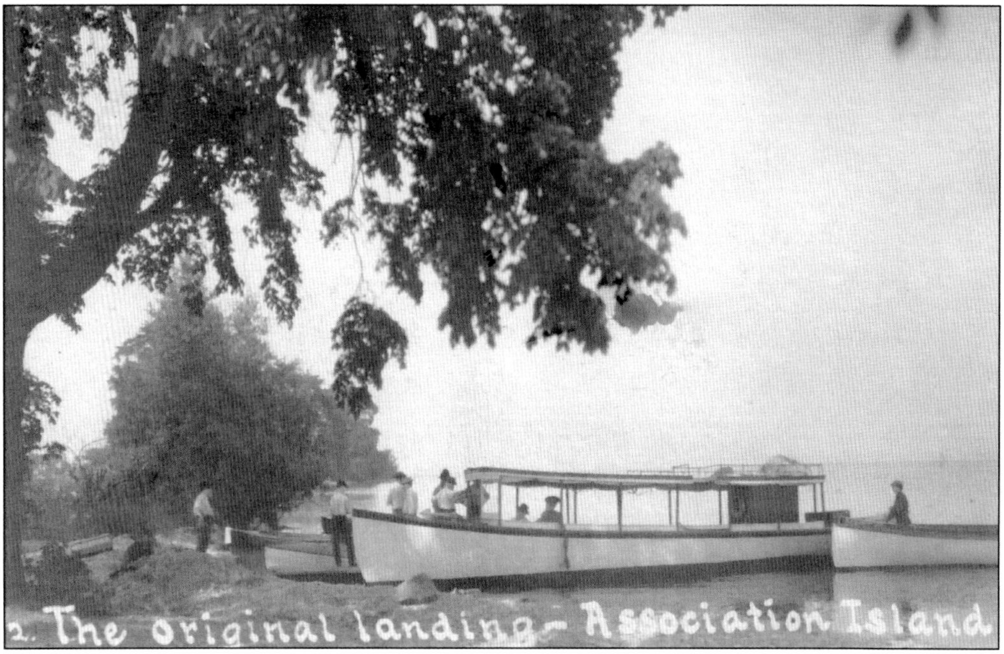

Arriving by a steam-powered launch on the southeast shore of Association Island, the members' first improvement was a dock for the boats arriving from Henderson Harbor. The association of companies proved to be very successful, and sales increased. Only Terry, Tremaine, and a few other key members knew about GE's 75 percent stake in the consolidated lamp companies.

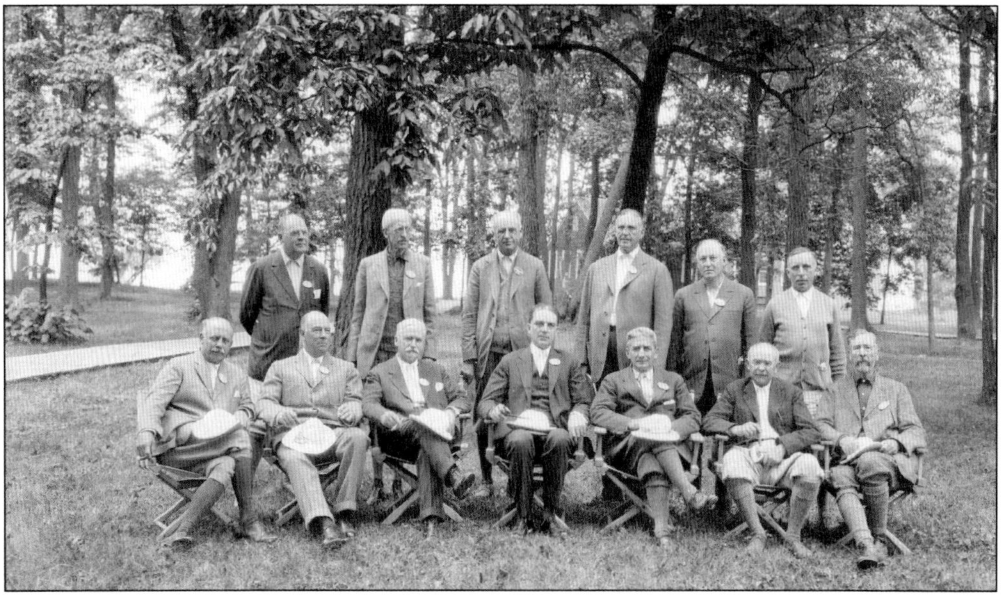

In 1911, the federal government sued GE and the consolidated lamp companies for violation of the Sherman Anti-Trust Act. Through a consent decree in 1912, GE acquired Association Island and installed its own leadership in the Association Island Corporation. Seated fourth, fifth, and sixth from left in this c. 1925 photograph are GE chairman Owen D. Young, president Gerard Swope, and former president Edwin W. Rice; standing third and fifth from left are Burton G. Tremaine and Franklin S. Terry. (GE.)

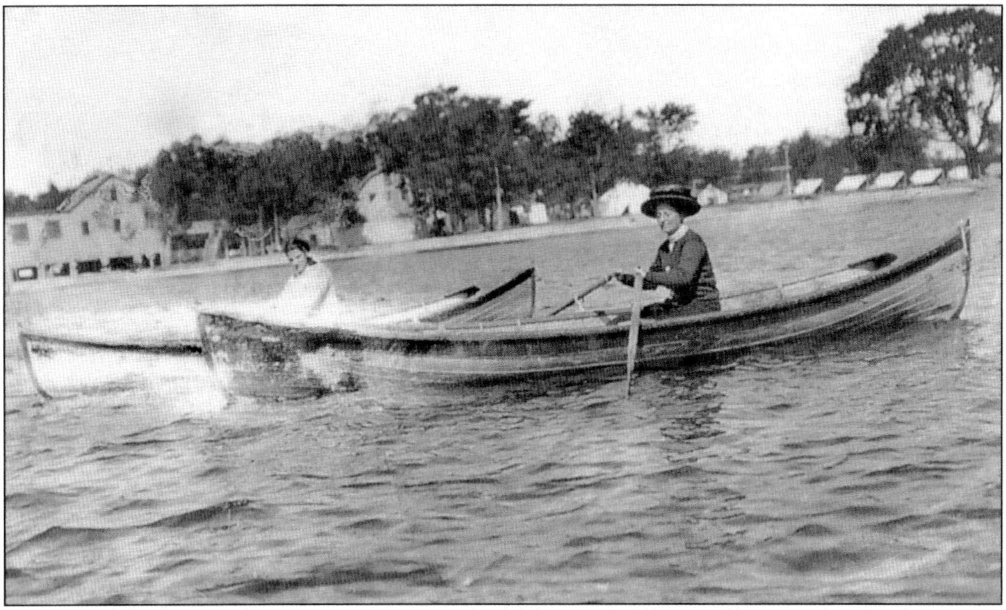

This photograph provides evidence that women were included in all activities in the very early days of Association Island. The boats and fashion date this to be around 1910. In the background are, from left to right, the boathouse, dining hall, and original sleeping tents.

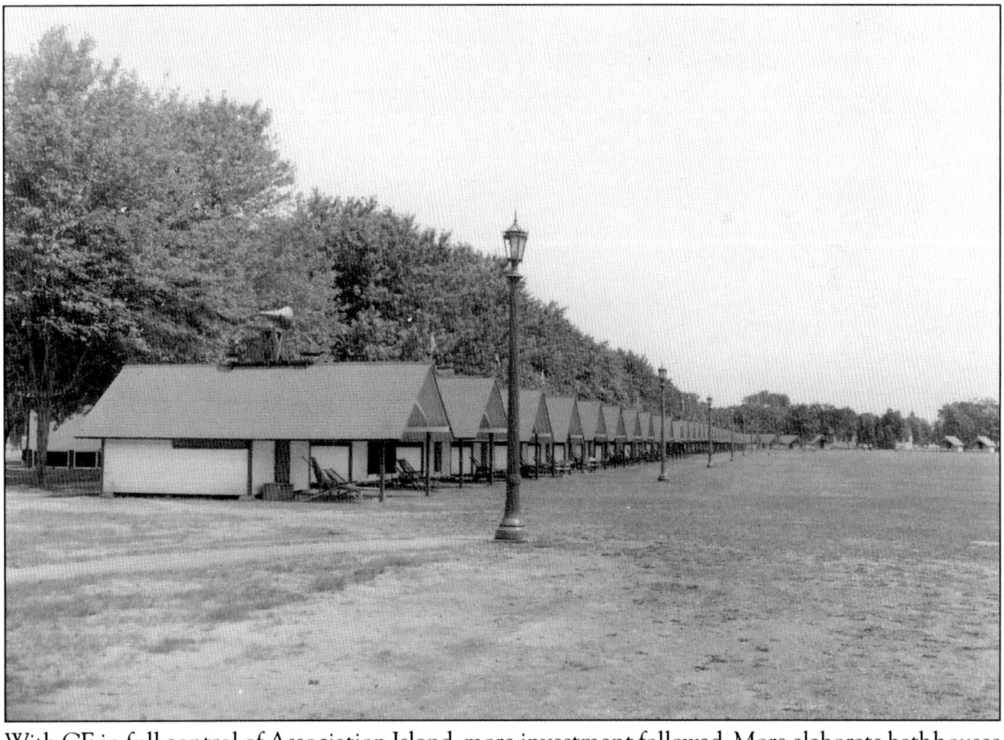

With GE in full control of Association Island, more investment followed. More elaborate bathhouses were installed along with the first of the architecturally significant Association Island cabins. Built by local carpenters, the cabins backed up to tree-lined paths for access by vehicles that carried luggage from the boats. (GE.)

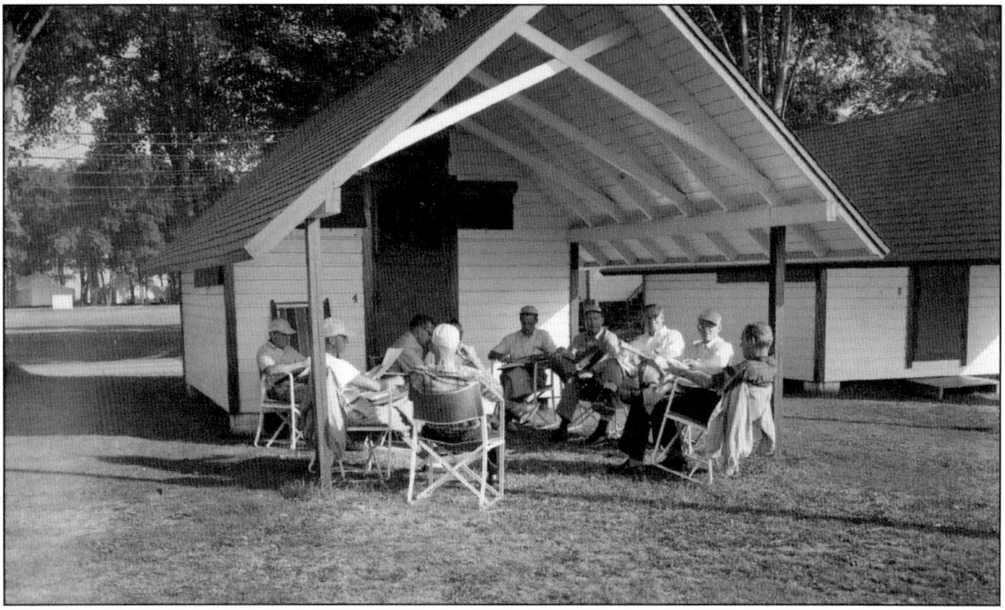

The long overhanging roofs of the Association Island cabins resembled the island's original tents. Facing the parade ground and ball fields, the extended roof provided a quiet sitting area or meeting location. More than 160 of these unique cabins were built. (GE.)

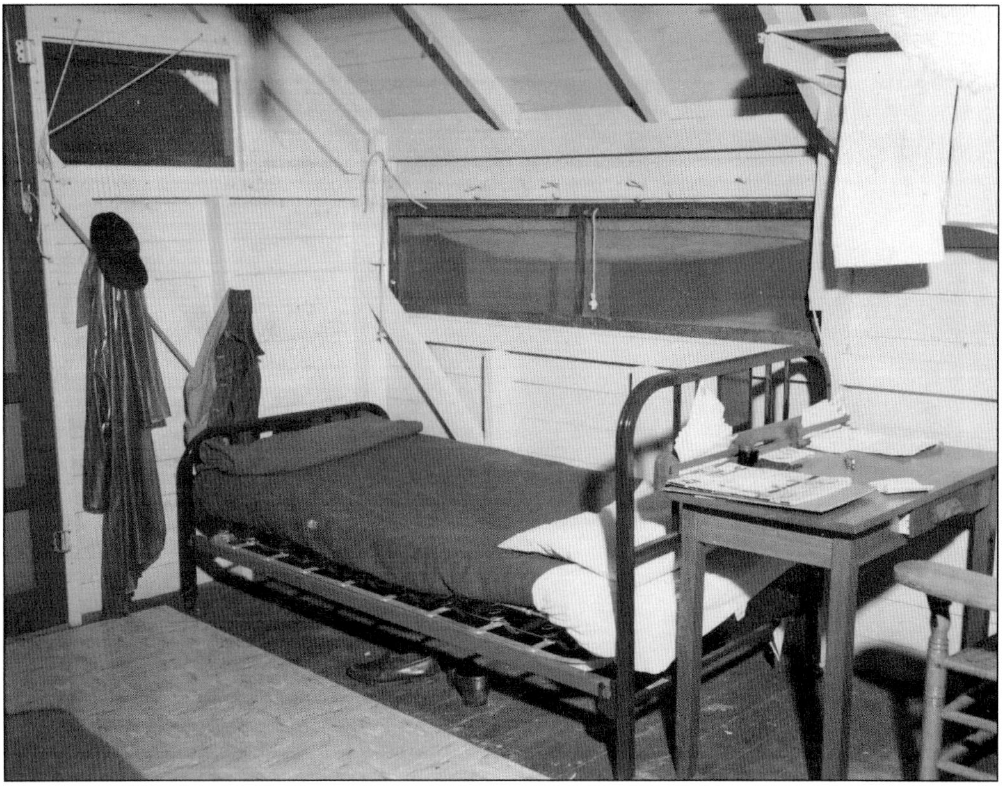

The cabins helped quiet complaints by many campers concerning the crudeness of the tents and lack of activities. The cabins included comfortable beds, screened windows, and electricity. (GE.)

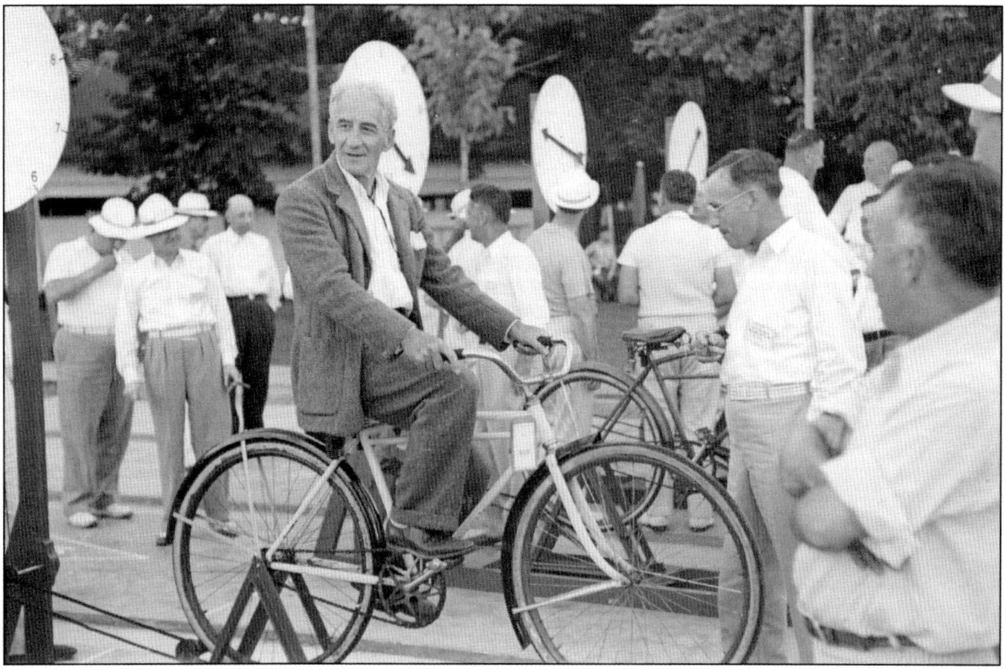

The men responsible for providing comfort for the campers were Gerard Swope, installed as GE president in 1921, and NELA founder Franklin S. Terry. Swope, in this 1937 photograph, pushed the island improvements through the GE board of directors. In court testimony, company vice president Terry discounted challenges that the annual island budget had grown to $250,000 in the 1920s. (GE.)

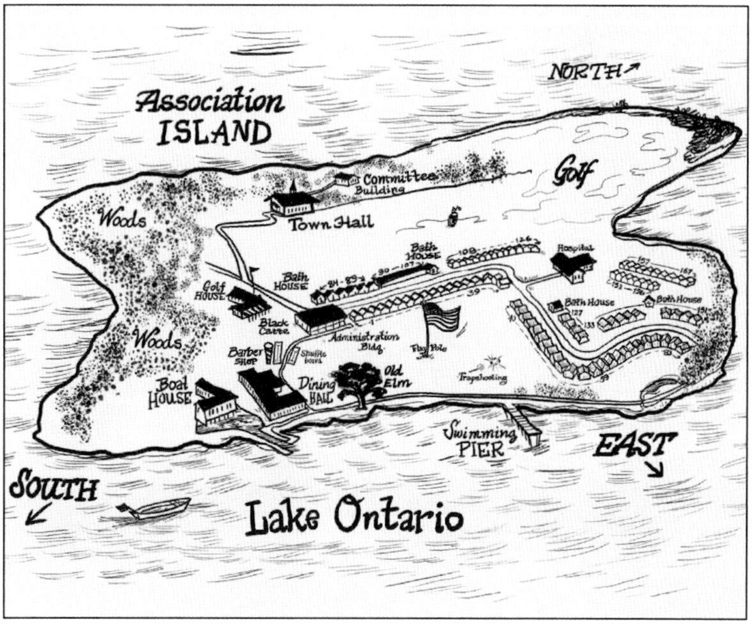

Association Island was fully developed by the late 1920s with its large boathouse, dance hall, dining hall, barbershop, administration building, Black Catte café, town hall, church, committee building, hospital, bathhouses, swimming pier, golf course, ball fields, trap shooting, parade grounds, and sleeping cabins. This diagram was redrawn by artist Emily Anthony from an original island brochure.

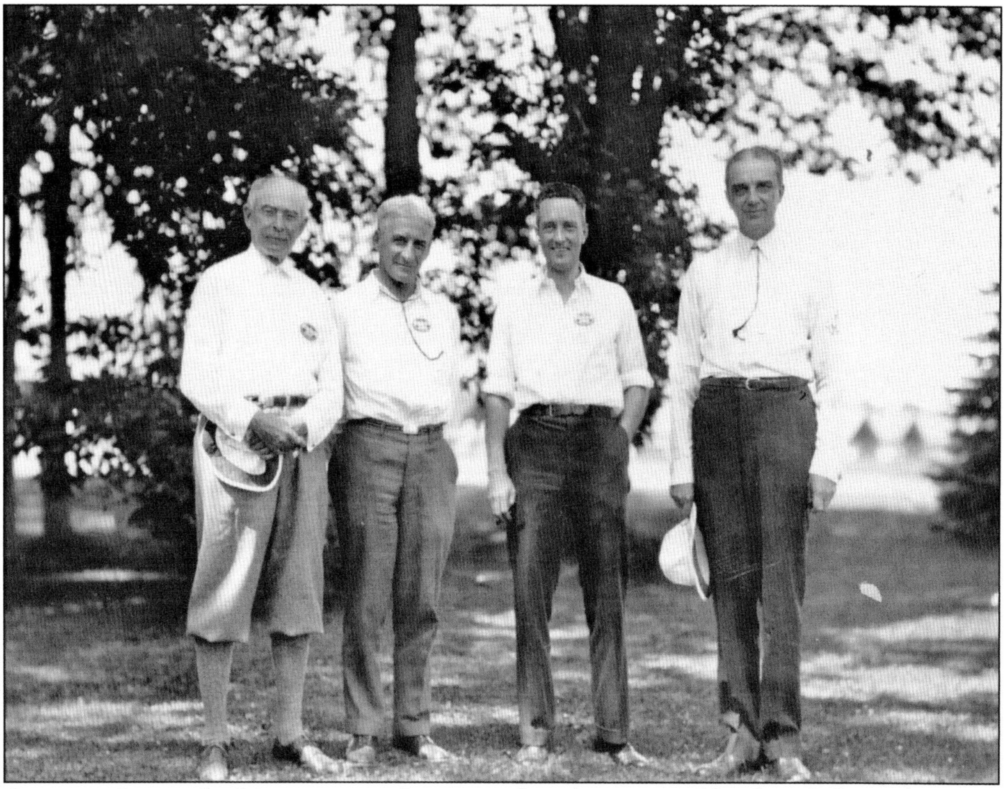

Guest speakers and celebrities were often invited to Association Island, including adventurer Richard E. Byrd, who visited the island in July 1930. Pictured from left to right are former GE president Edwin W. Rice Jr., GE president Gerard Swope, Admiral Byrd, and GE chairman Owen D. Young. The year 1930 was also when GE signed a purchase option for 1,200 acres of land on Carleton Island in the St. Lawrence River. Final plans to move from Association Island, however, never materialized. (GE.)

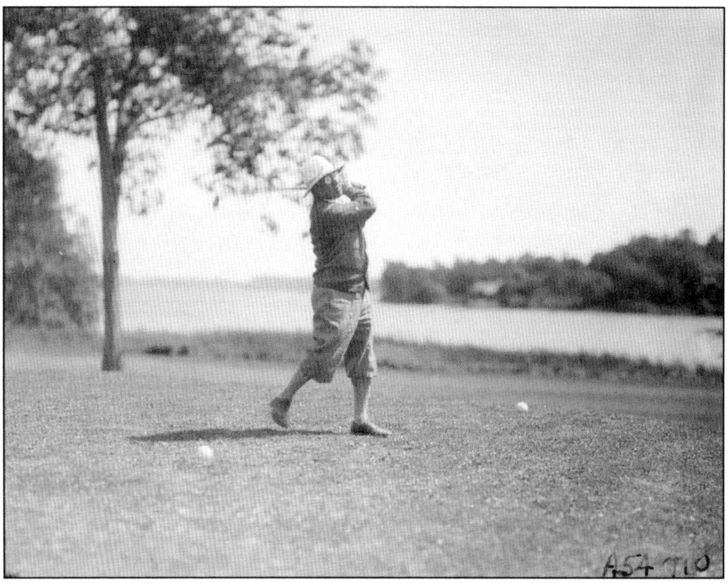

Association Island also included a golf course, and to enlarge it in 1926, GE purchased nearby Hovey's Island and some land on Snowshoe Point from George S. Hovey for $22,500. Golfers had to take a boat to the back nine, but they could tee up their golf balls with magnificent views of Snowshoe Bay (background) and Lake Ontario. (GE.)

Another proponent of Association Island was Owen D. Young, chairman of GE from 1922 to 1939. Pictured here as the ceremonial island police chief, Young was a graduate and trustee of St. Lawrence University in Canton. He founded the Radio Corporation of America (RCA) and helped organize the National Broadcasting Company (NBC). Young also laid the foundation for what became the State University of New York (SUNY). (GE.)

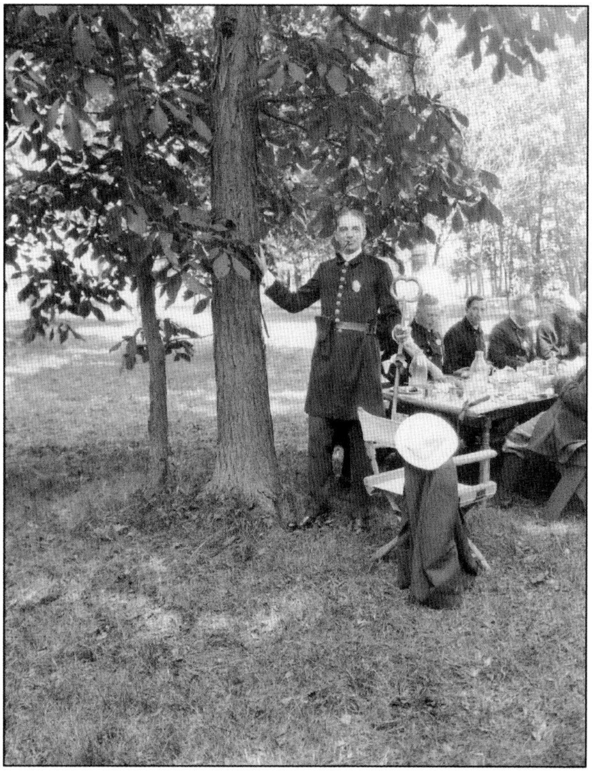

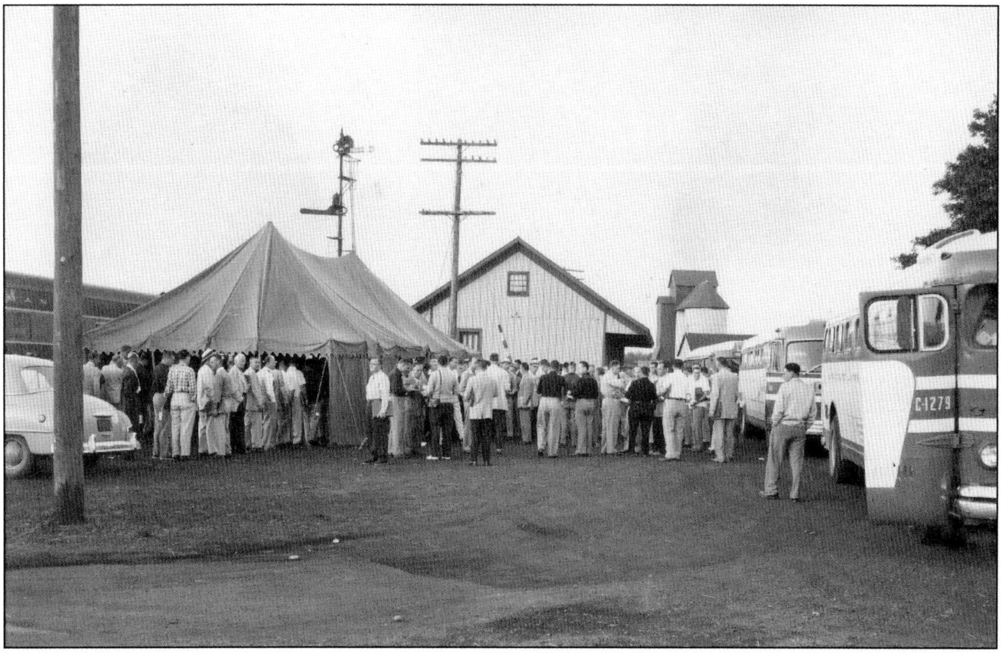

Association Island campers rode the New York Central train to Pierrepont Manor, Adams, or Adams Center, where busses picked them up for the trip to Henderson Harbor. This photograph shows campers disembarking the train in Adams Center. Local residents provided coffee and doughnuts when campers arrived on the overnight train. (GE.)

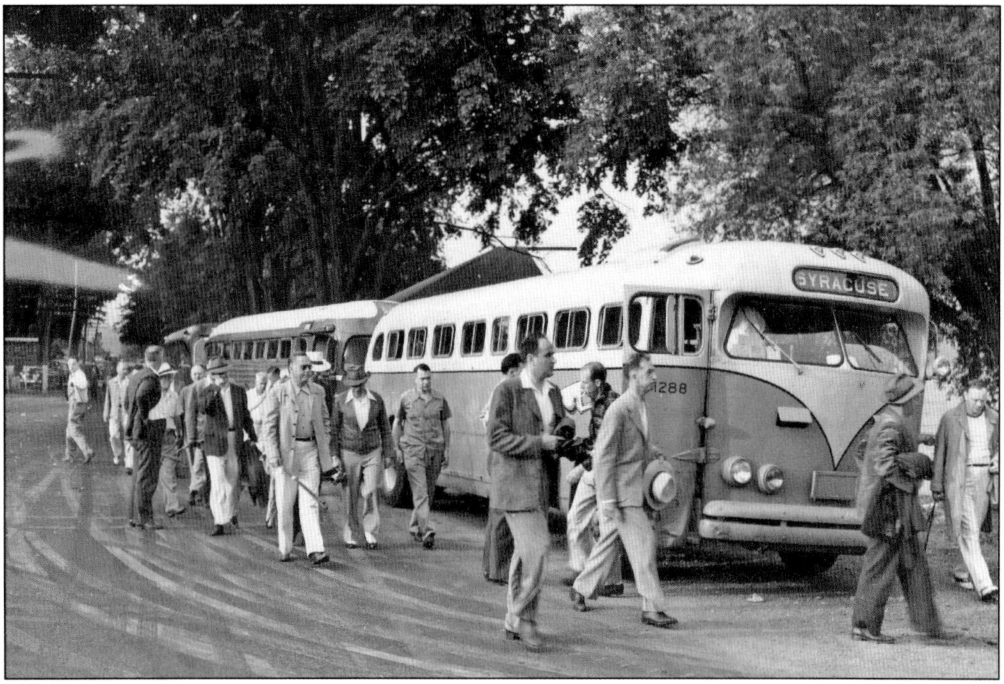

Upon arrival in Henderson Harbor, campers gathered on the GE dock at the former Harbor Inn for a boat ride to Association Island. The influx of hundreds of people at once overwhelmed the small fishing village, but the hotel, restaurant, marina, and store owners loved it. (GE.)

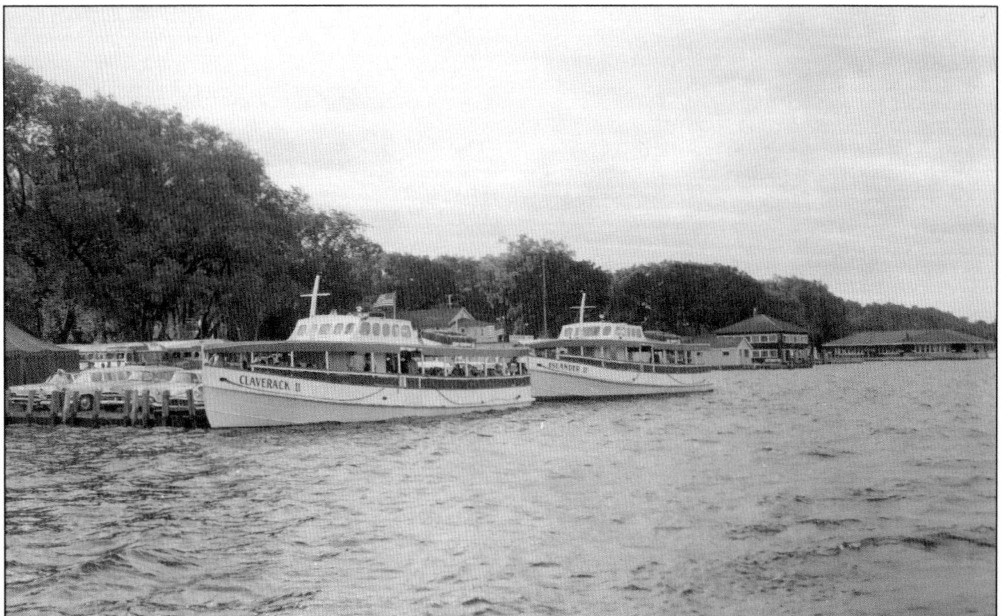

Association Island had many boats during its 50 years. Originally ferried by naphtha launches and local guide boats, by the 1940s campers were carried to the island by larger ferries, such as the *Claverack II* and the *Islander II*. In this photograph, passengers are loading at the GE dock in Henderson Harbor. (GE.)

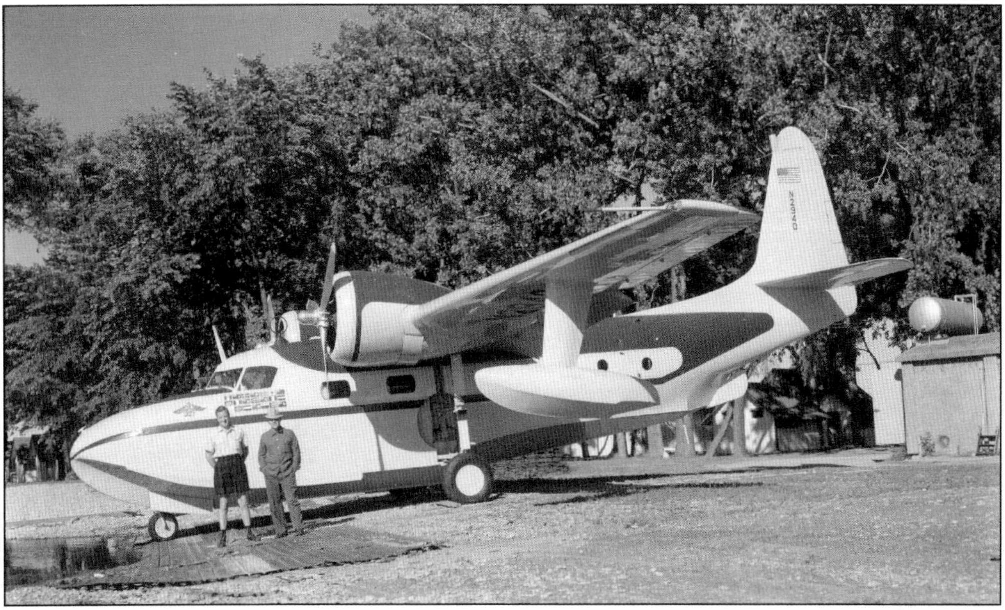

Executive and VIP transportation to Association Island was in a 10-passenger Grumman G-73 Mallard amphibious airplane. This plane was later used by the Virgin Island Seaplane Shuttle in St. Thomas, US Virgin Islands. It suffered a fatal crash in 1986 and was scrapped. (GE.)

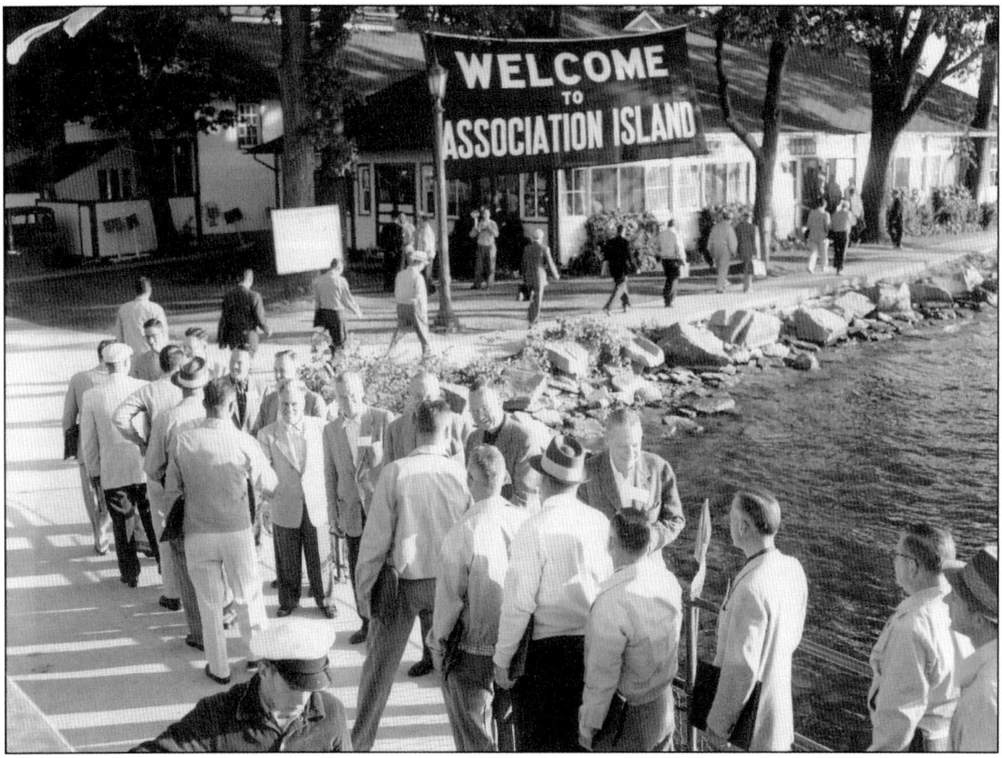

The larger camp meetings at Association Island included hundreds of GE employees and their families. Passengers streamed off the dock to a large greeting sign, the island band, and refreshments. A visit to Association Island was the highlight of their summer. (GE.)

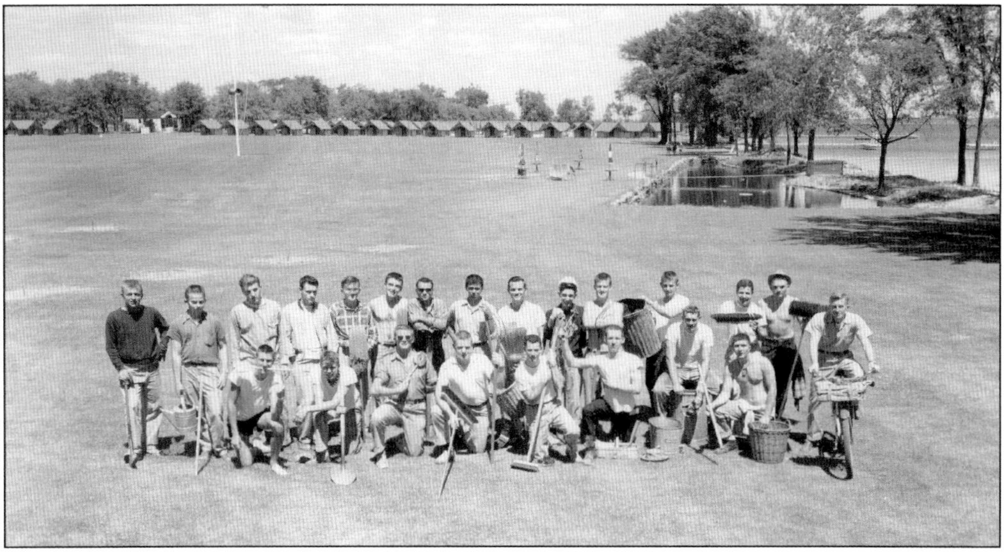

Many hours of work were involved in preparing the island for the summer campers. Island managers were often from Henderson Harbor and local work crews, such as this one posing for a photograph on the parade ground, came from throughout northern New York. (GE.)

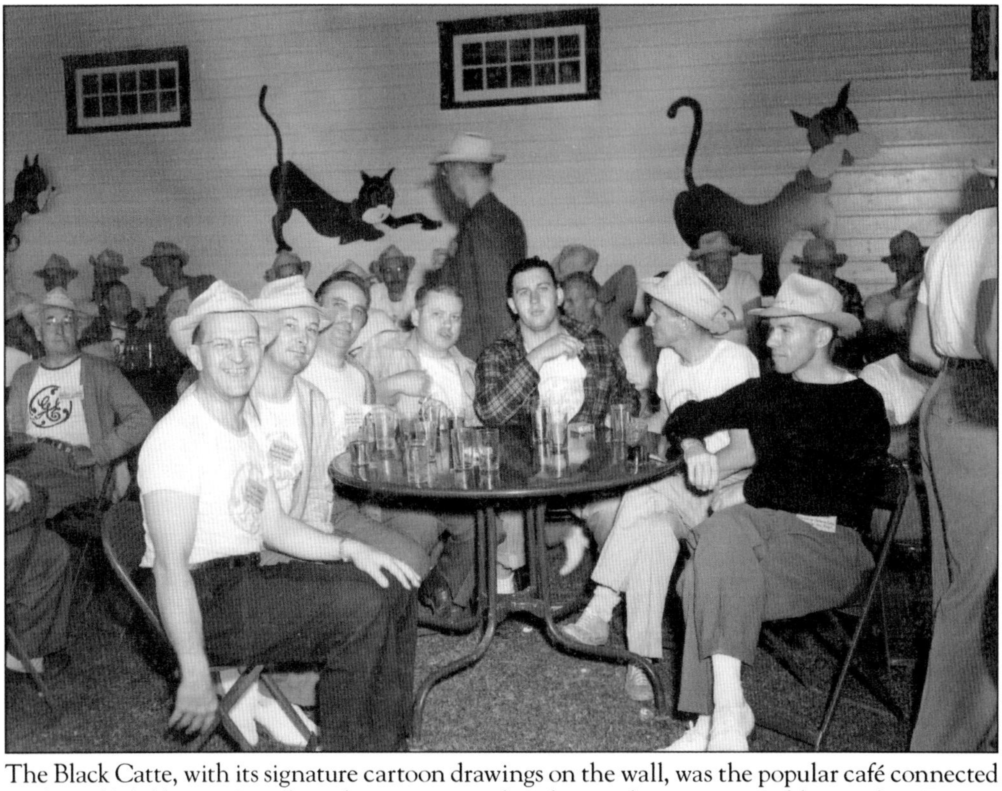

The Black Catte, with its signature cartoon drawings on the wall, was the popular café connected to the golf clubhouse. Local residents were employed as cooks, waiters, and bartenders. During Prohibition, booze smugglers captured near Henderson Harbor in their boat claimed they were hauling their load to Association Island; however, the US Coast Guard could not confirm their story. (GE.)

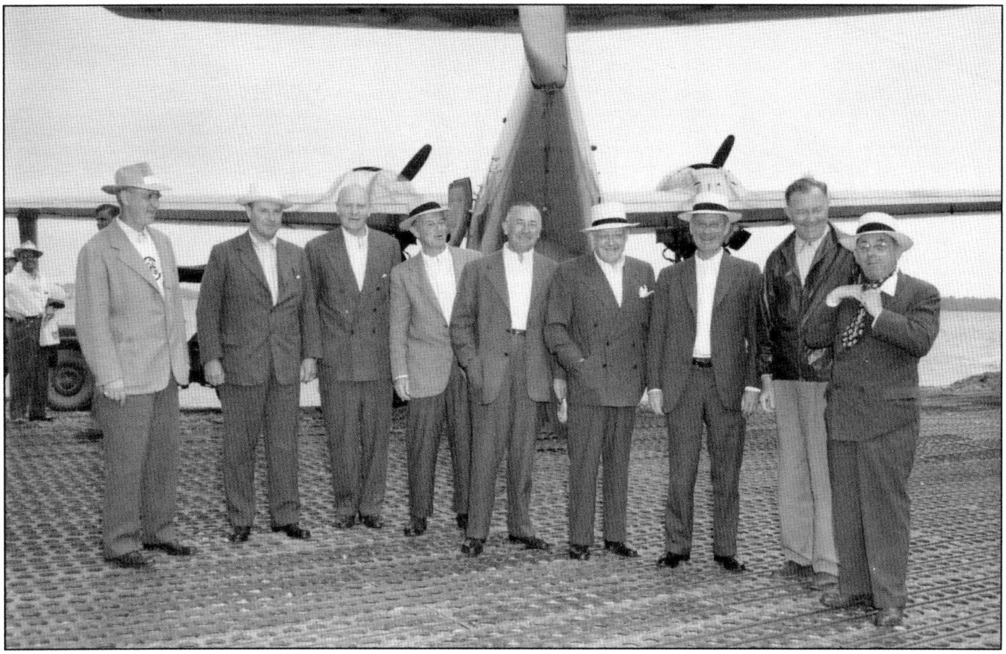

Campers who arrived at Association Island still wearing their ties suffered the traditional, but humiliating, dunk in the lagoon. In this c. 1950 photograph, an executive has arrived on the Grumman Mallard. Upon being informed of the island tradition, he removed his tie, but it was too late. (GE.)

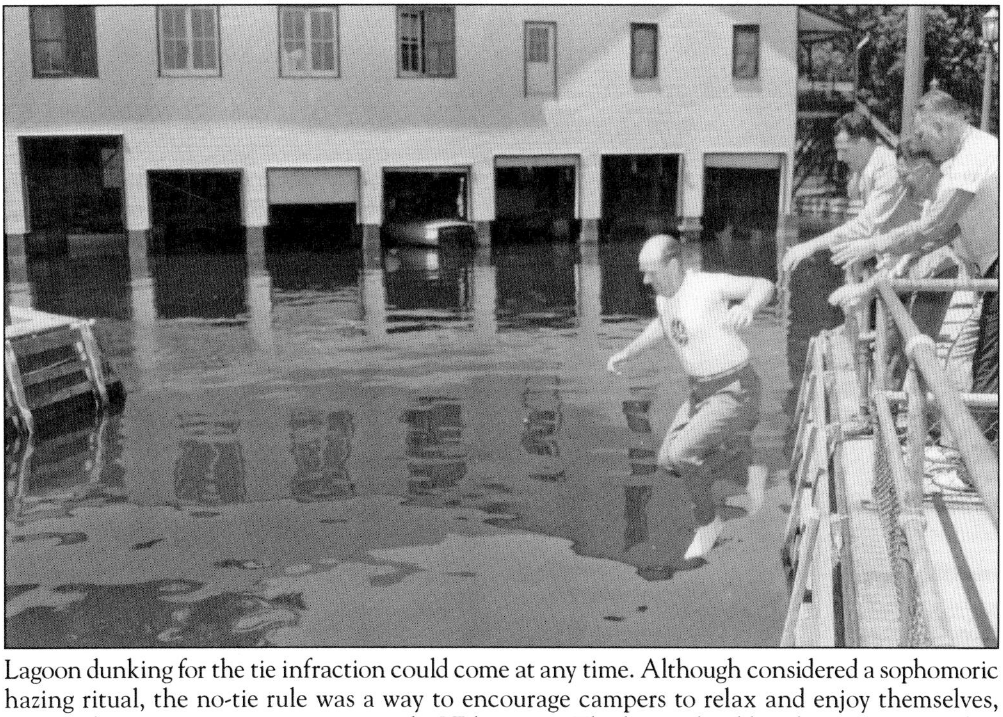

Lagoon dunking for the tie infraction could come at any time. Although considered a sophomoric hazing ritual, the no-tie rule was a way to encourage campers to relax and enjoy themselves, despite the expectation to carry on with GE business. The large island boathouse is pictured in the background. (GE.)

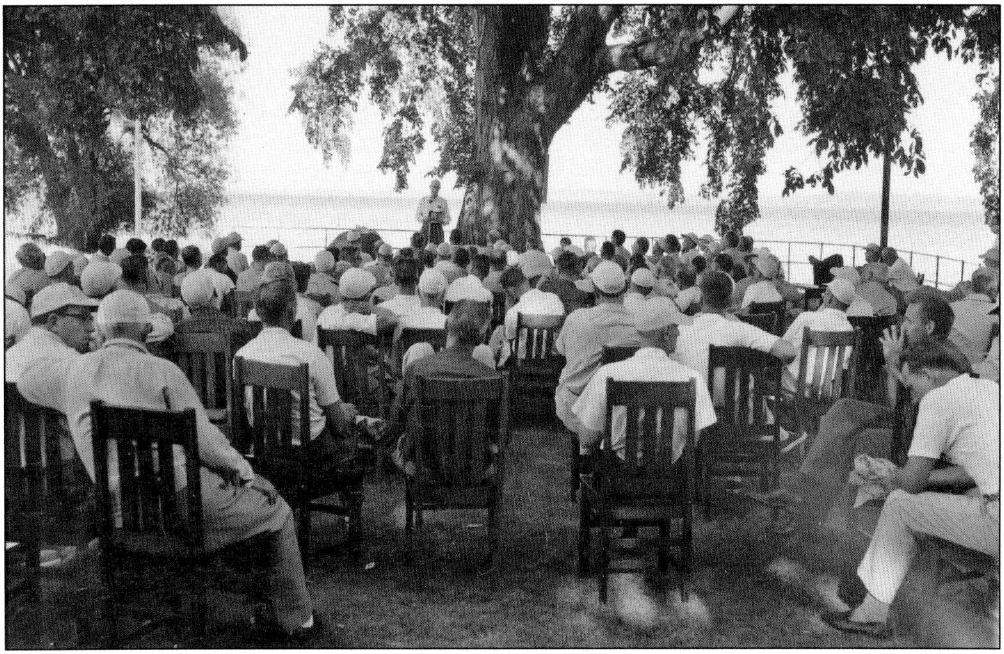

The GE Elfun Society was organized at Association Island in 1928 on a proposal by company president Gerard Swope. A think tank and investment club, the Elfun Society has also grown to become one of the most generous volunteer organizations in the world. The image of Elfun meetings under the famous Association Island elm tree became its signature symbol. (GE.)

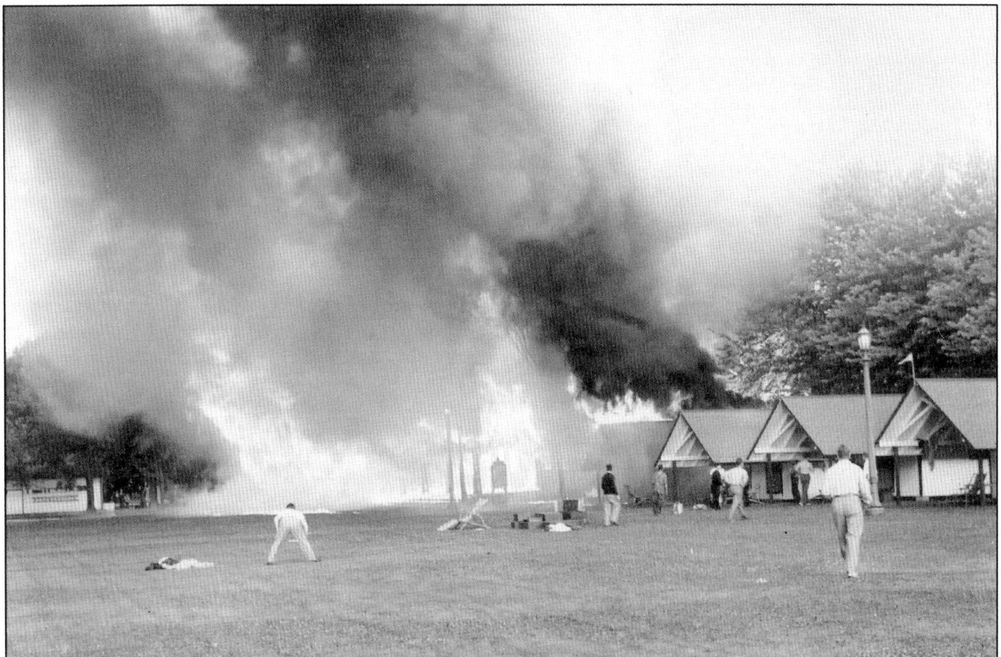

On the morning of July 2, 1946, the one-story administration building caught fire and burned to the ground, destroying one cabin in the process. Of the 275 people on the island at the time, including GE president Charles Wilson, no one was injured. (GE.)

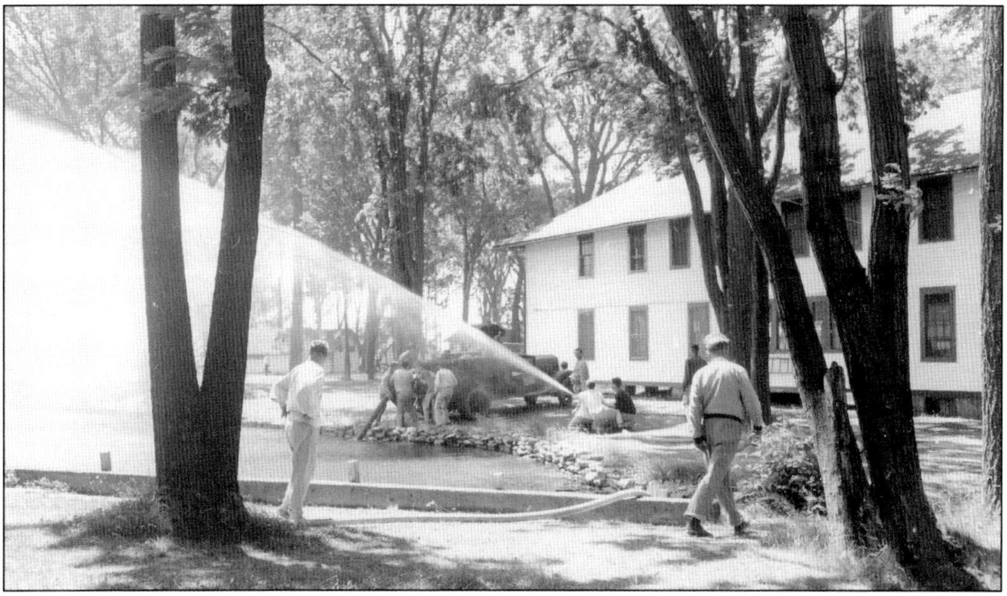

The fire at the administration building prompted more attention to firefighter training. Employees practiced spraying water from the island's only fire truck. Until the construction of a causeway from Snowshoe Point to Association Island after GE pulled out, local fire departments could not get to the island. (GE.)

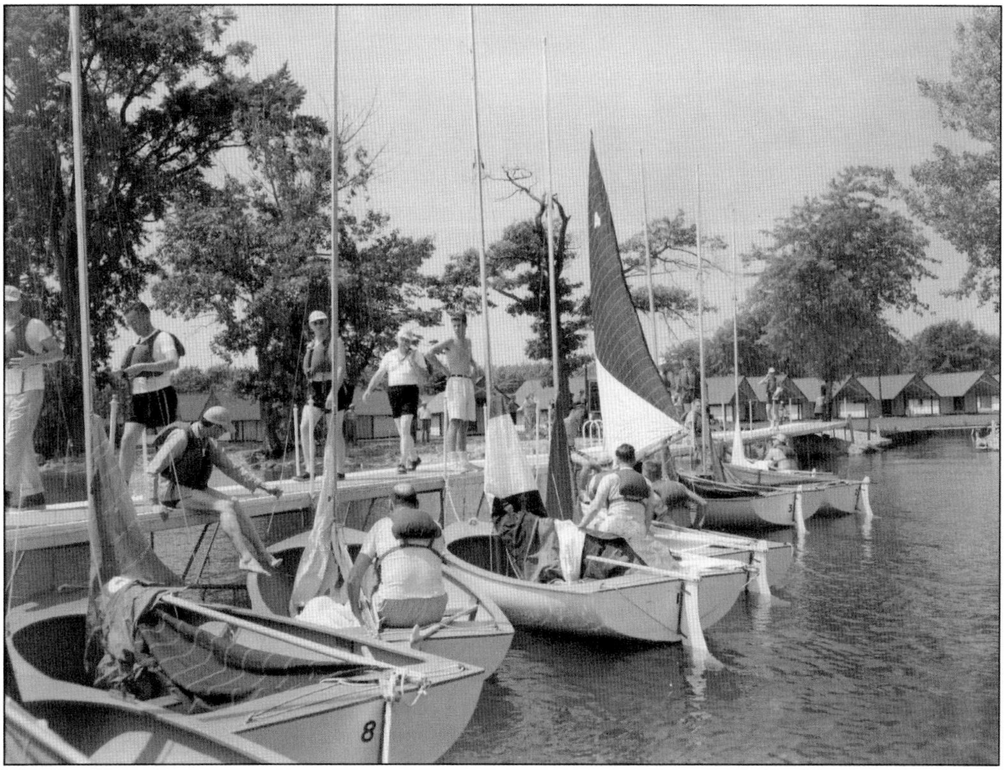

Sailing consumed many summer days at Association Island. Sailing lessons were provided on dozens of small sailboats. The Association Island cabins are visible in the background. (GE.)

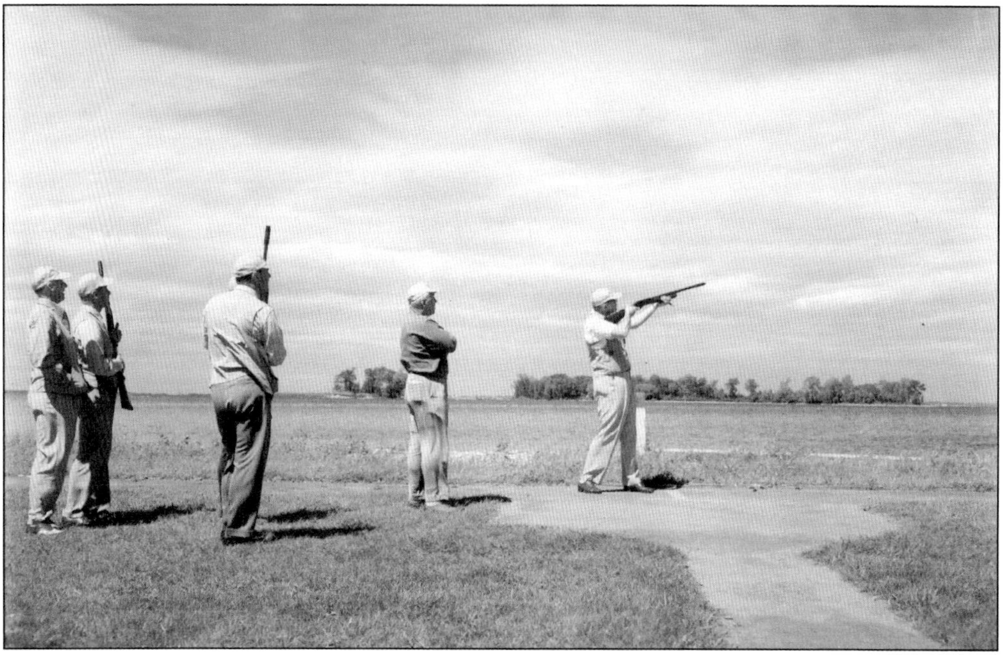

Aside from fishing, trap and skeet shooting was popular. The shooting range was on the north side of the island where the shot was projected over the water. In the background of this photograph, Davis Island (center) and Sixtown Island are visible. (GE.)

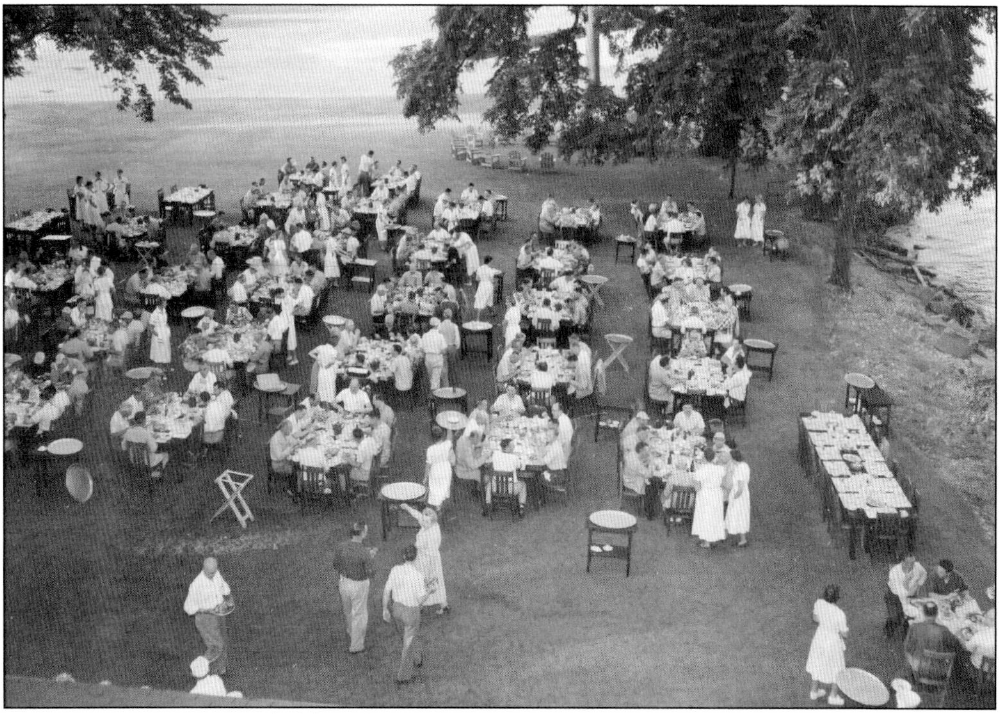

Large banquets were often held on the expansive lawn overlooking the lake. Near the dining hall, these banquets could easily be moved inside in the event of stormy weather, which was common on Lake Ontario, even in the summer. (GE.)

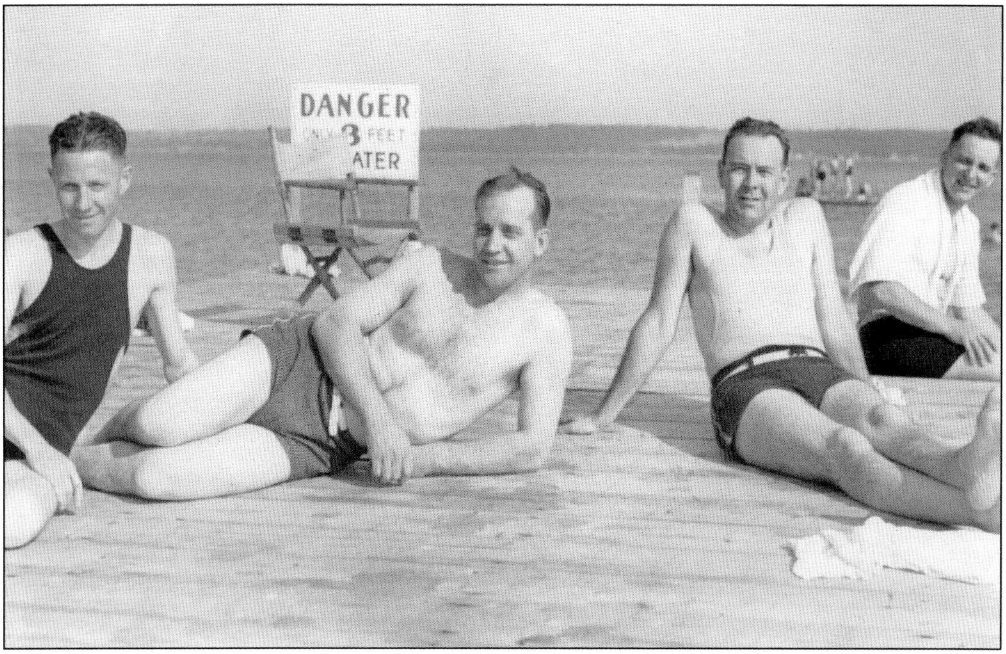

Swimming has always been a primary activity at Henderson Harbor. On the main Association Island dock, these campers pose for a GE photographer during the summer of 1936. The rock cut for the recently built New York State Route 3 can be seen at the far background to the left of a swimmer's head. Also notice the other swimmers on a raft. (GE.)

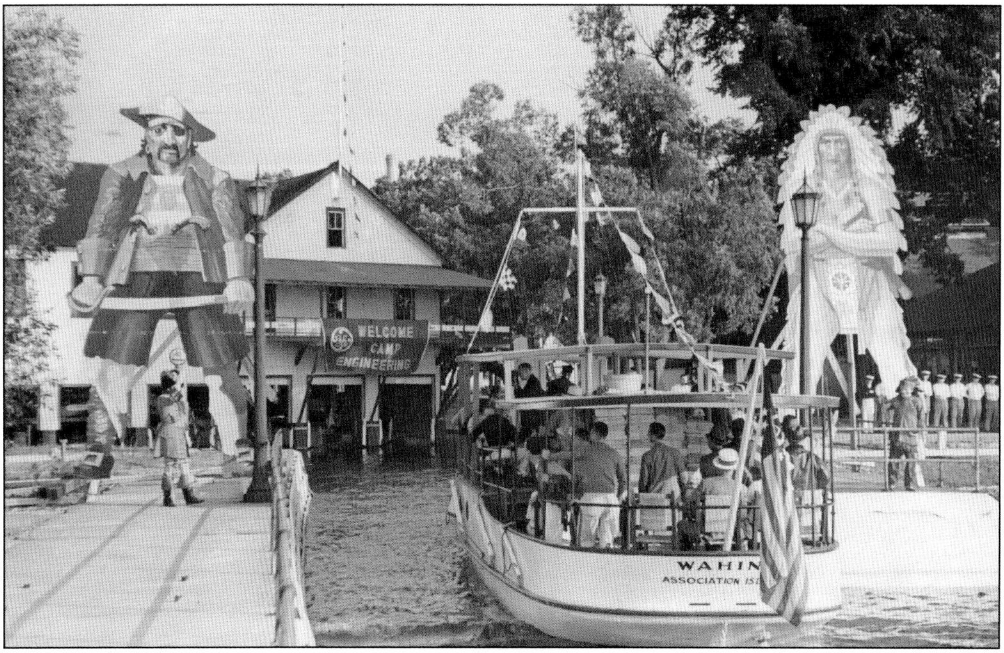

Author Kurt Vonnegut Jr. spent time on Association Island in the 1940s. His first novel, *Player Piano*, satirized corporate activities in the 1950s. In 1957, citing inadequacies for training managers and the need for better internal communications, GE pulled out of Association Island. Two years later, the company donated the entire property to the New York YMCA for one dollar. (GE.)

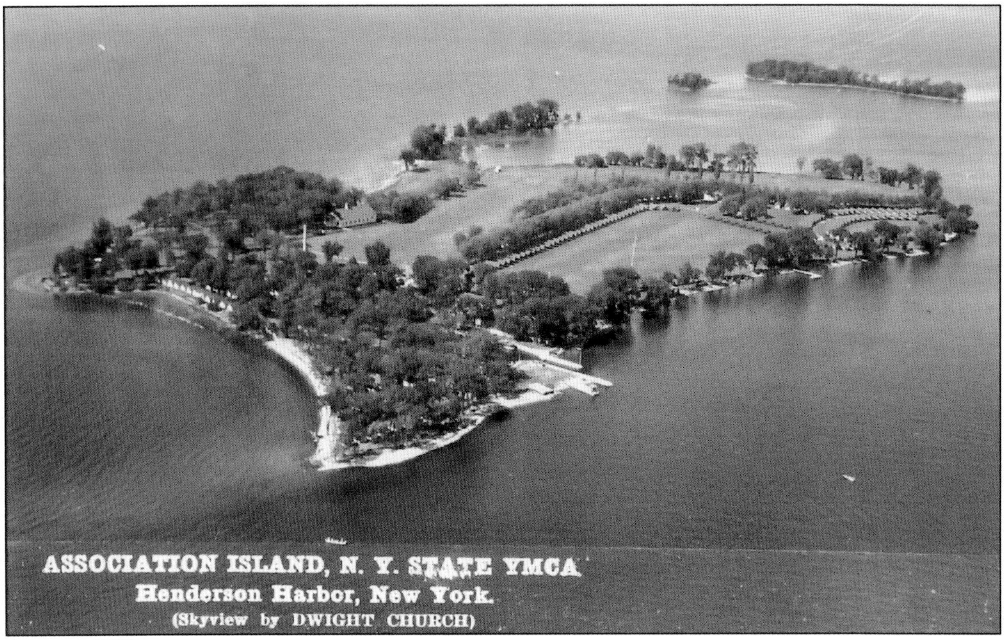

The YMCA operated Association Island as a family and youth center for nearly a decade until their money ran out. After failed attempts to sell the island in 1969 for $400,000 and private development, a nonprofit organization used it as a training facility for US Olympic sailors. When the 1976 Olympics ended, the island was deserted once again and fell into virtual ruins. (Church.)

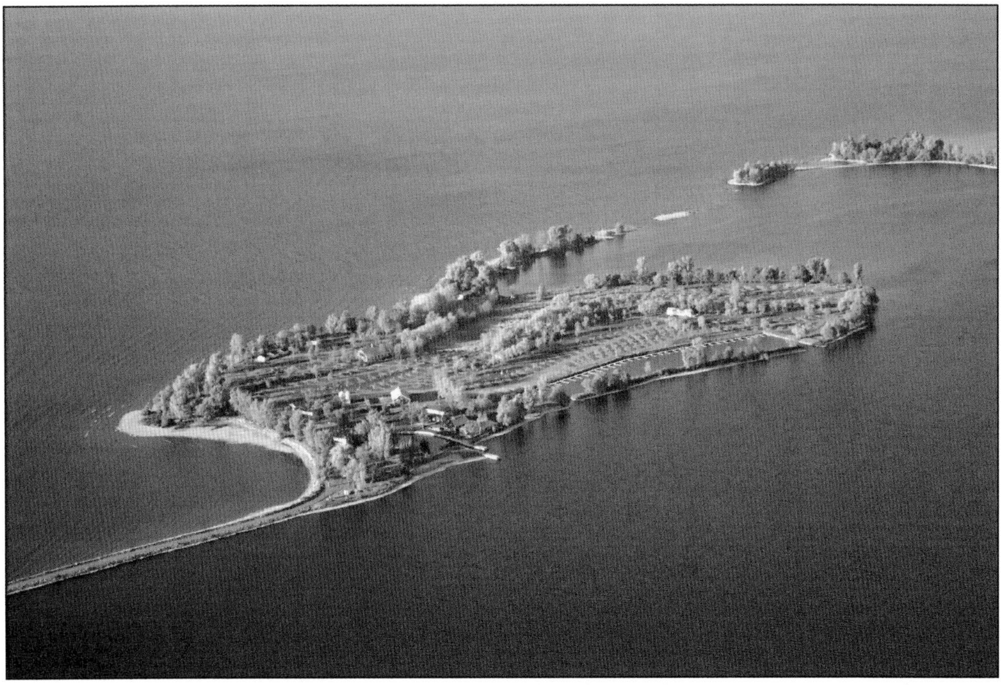

Since 2002, Association Island has been renovated and turned into an RV resort and marina, accessible by a causeway (left). It has regained its status as the jewel of the islands around Henderson Harbor.

Seven

Big Sandy

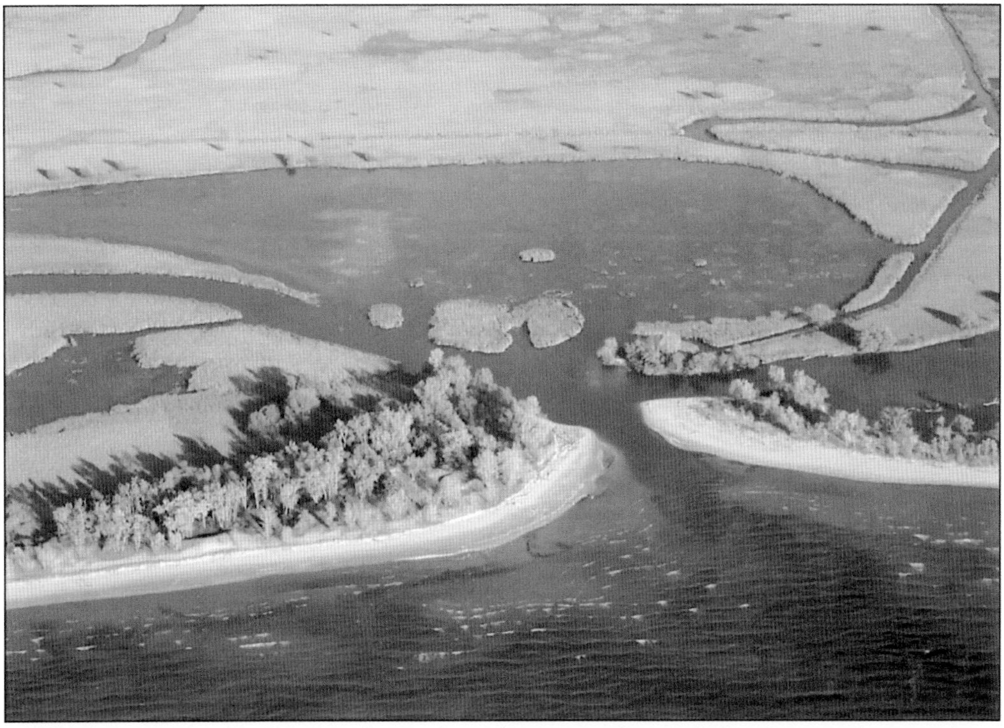

Big Sandy is the mouth of Big Sandy Creek on the eastern shore of Lake Ontario along northern Mexico Bay. Sand dunes protect the north branch (left) and south branch (right), providing shelter for mariners. This was the location of the 1814 Battle of Big Sandy, when the US Navy defended its Sackets Harbor–bound munitions and armaments from the British.

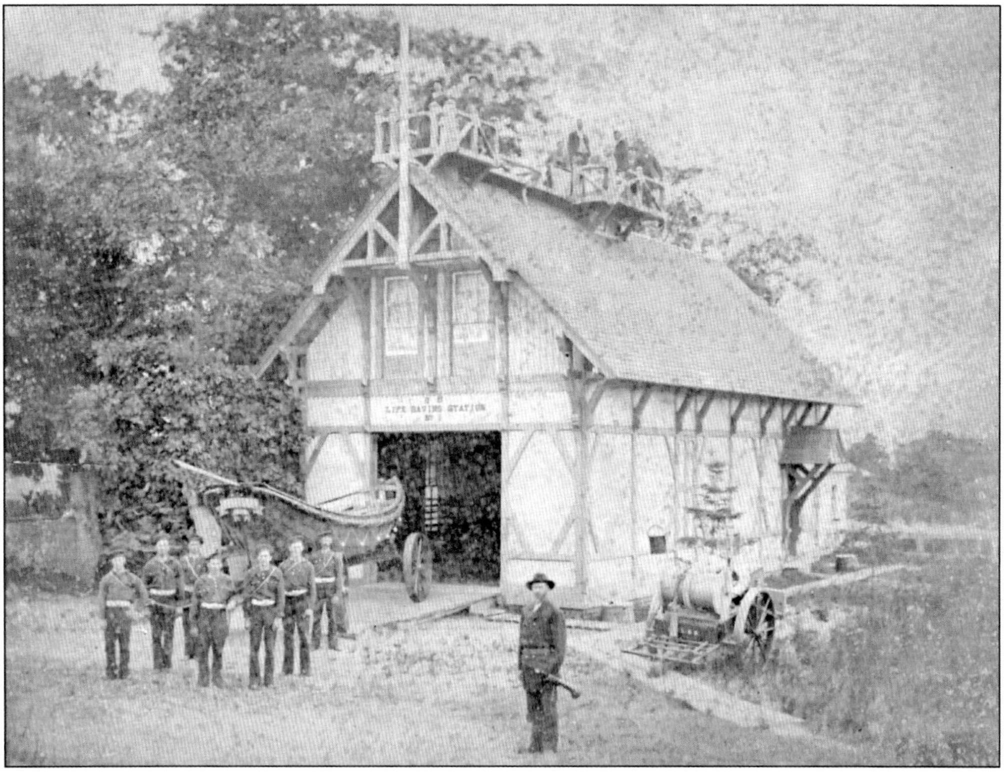

In 1874, Big Sandy Life Saving and Coast Guard Station was established on the north side of Big Sandy Creek at a time when lake schooners were often blown into Mexico Bay, known as the "graveyard of Lake Ontario." An 1876-style station, the preassembled building was shipped from Michigan in September 1876 and opened in 1877. In this rare early photograph of the new station, it is labeled No. 1, before the name Big Sandy was installed above the door.

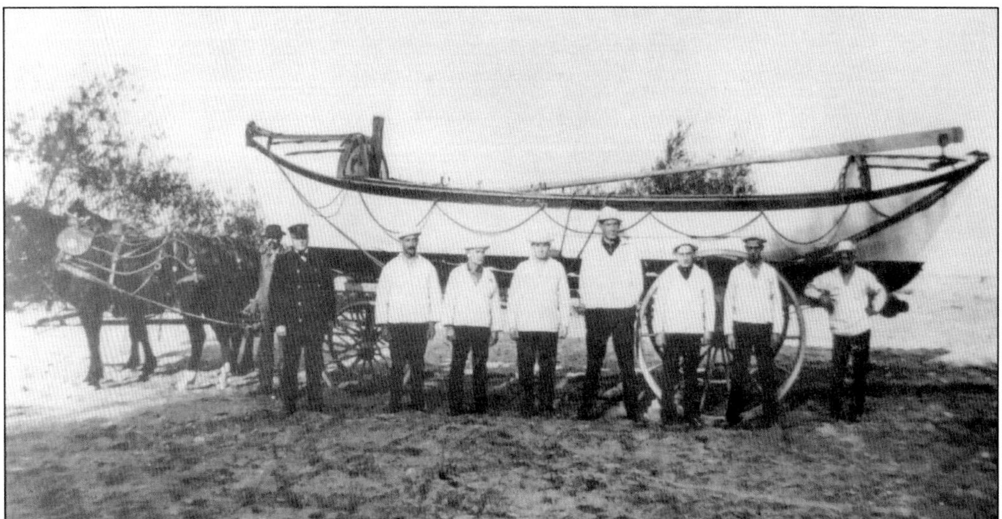

Another rare and early photograph shows the Big Sandy crew and lifeboat on the beach. The long oar in the lifeboat was used for a rudder. Since most shipwrecked schooners were driven to the beach, rescues required great skill and strength at rowing through the surf. (USCG.)

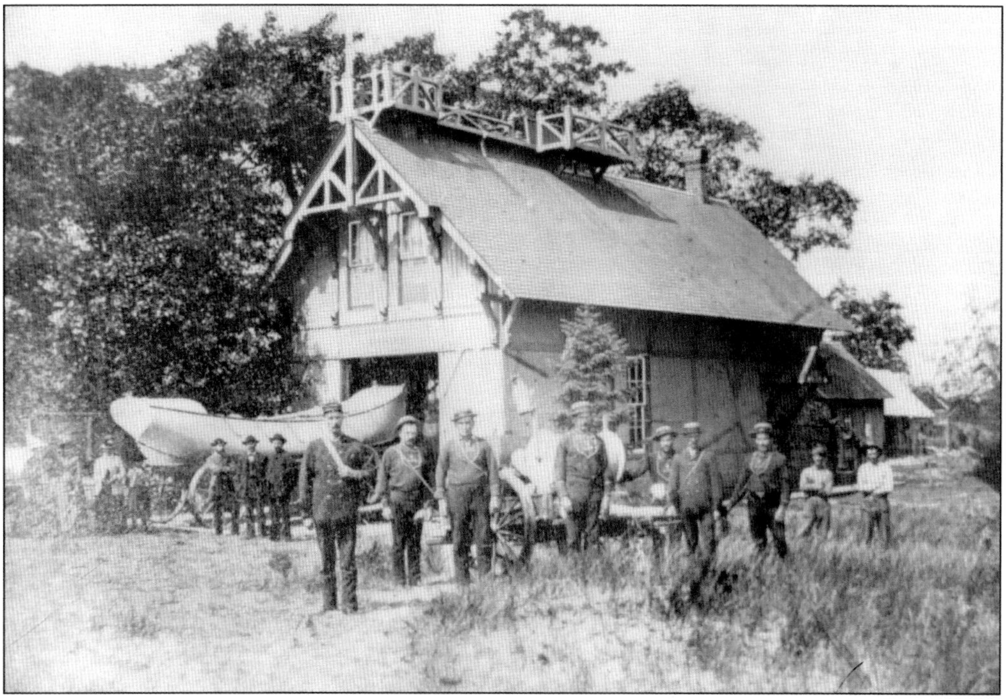

A violent storm in the first week of December 1886 wrecked two schooners in Big Sandy territory, and the surfmen were kept busy for several days. A telephone was installed in the station in 1889. When this photograph was taken, the name "Big Sandy" had replaced No. 1 above the door.

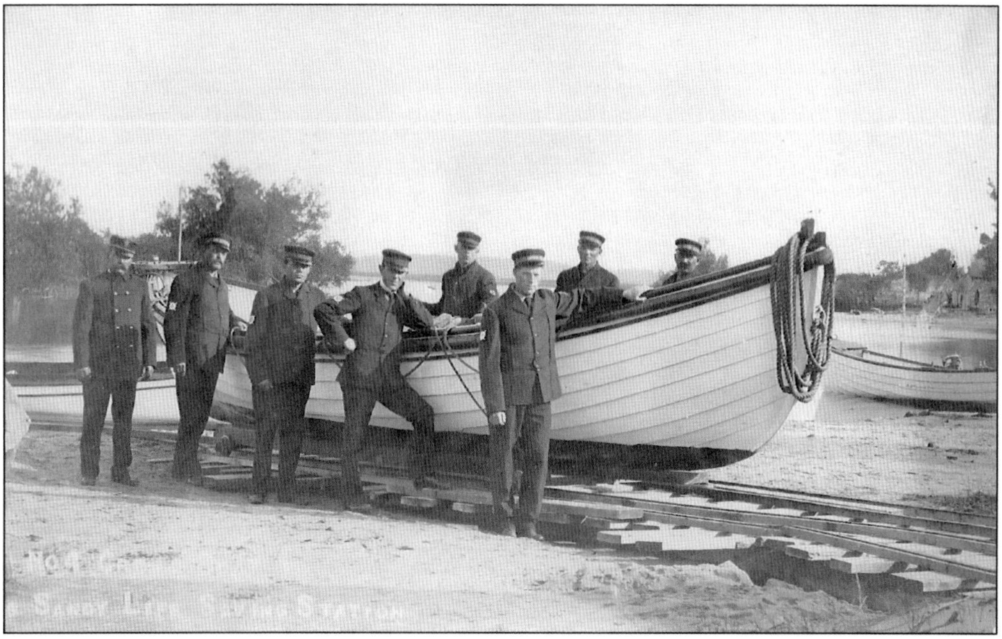

Lifeboats were drawn from the station to the creek on steel tracks. If a rescue was near the station, the boats were launched from the mouth of the creek. If it was several miles away on the beach, the crew would haul the lifeboat on a trailer and launch into the surf.

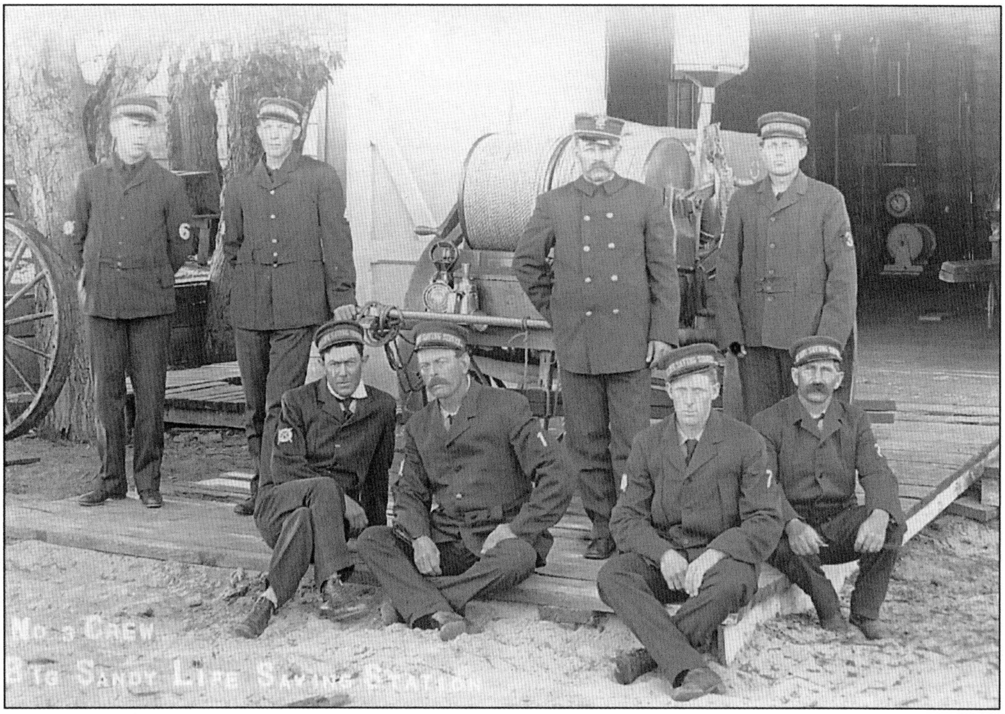

The Big Sandy crew is pictured around 1900 in front of the station house with the coils of rope used during rescues. From left to right are Wade Allen, Leslie Eveleigh, Earl Hungerford, Fayette "Fay" Noble, Capt. William Hagadone, Ed Dre?, Byron Otis, and Frank Williams. (USCG.)

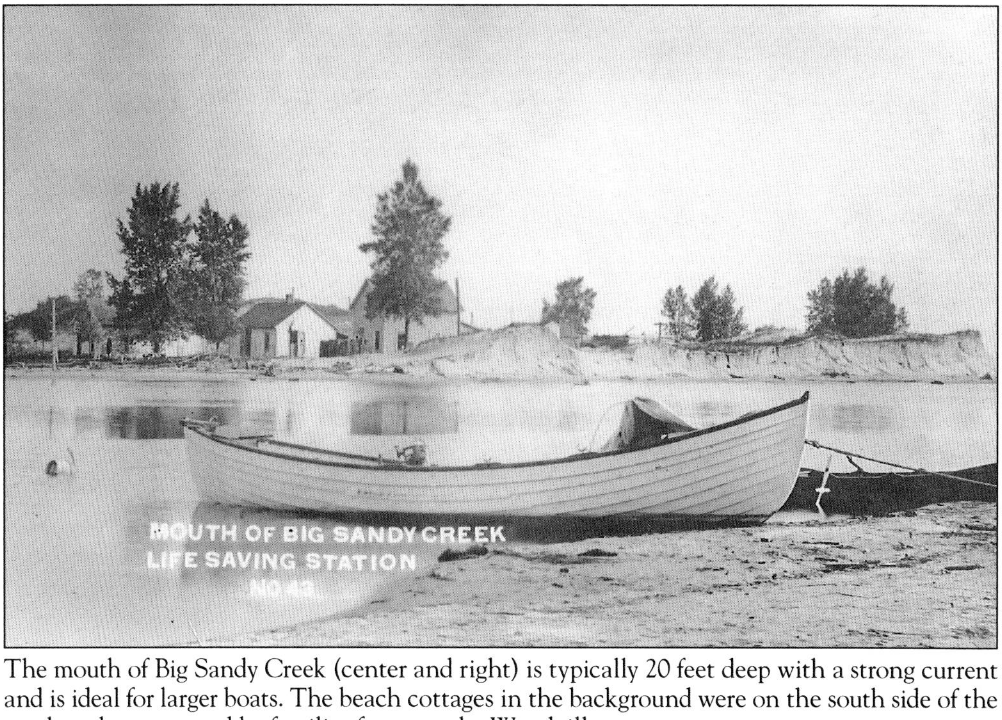

The mouth of Big Sandy Creek (center and right) is typically 20 feet deep with a strong current and is ideal for larger boats. The beach cottages in the background were on the south side of the creek and were owned by families from nearby Woodville.

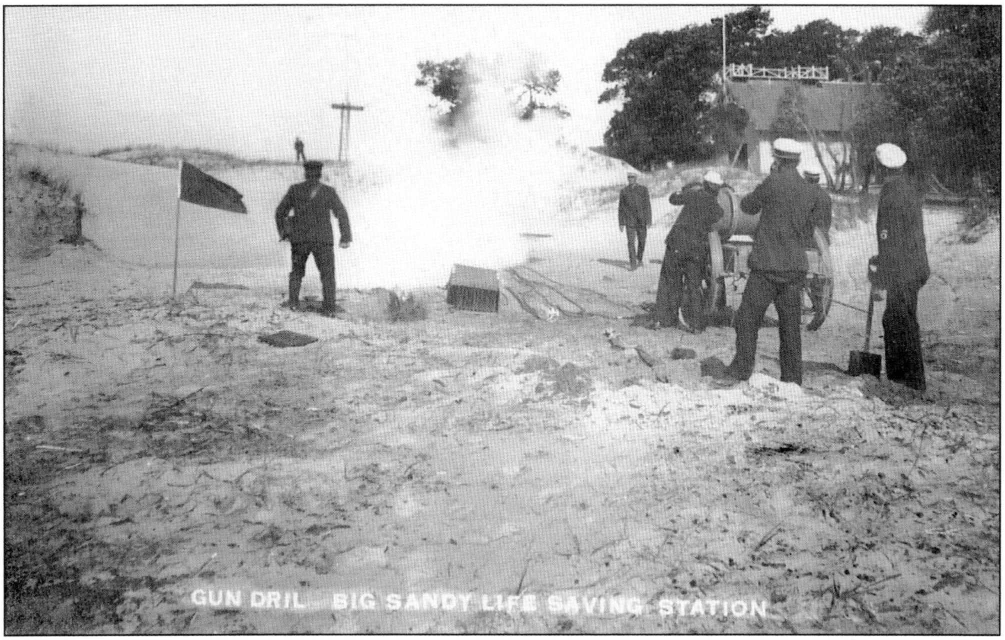

The Big Sandy crew fires a line during a gun drill on the beach. The station is pictured on the right in the background. During a near-shore rescue in rough seas, surfmen would fire a line from their cannon to the wrecked ship and tie it off on the beach. They would run a breeches buoy on the line to the ship and haul in marooned sailors.

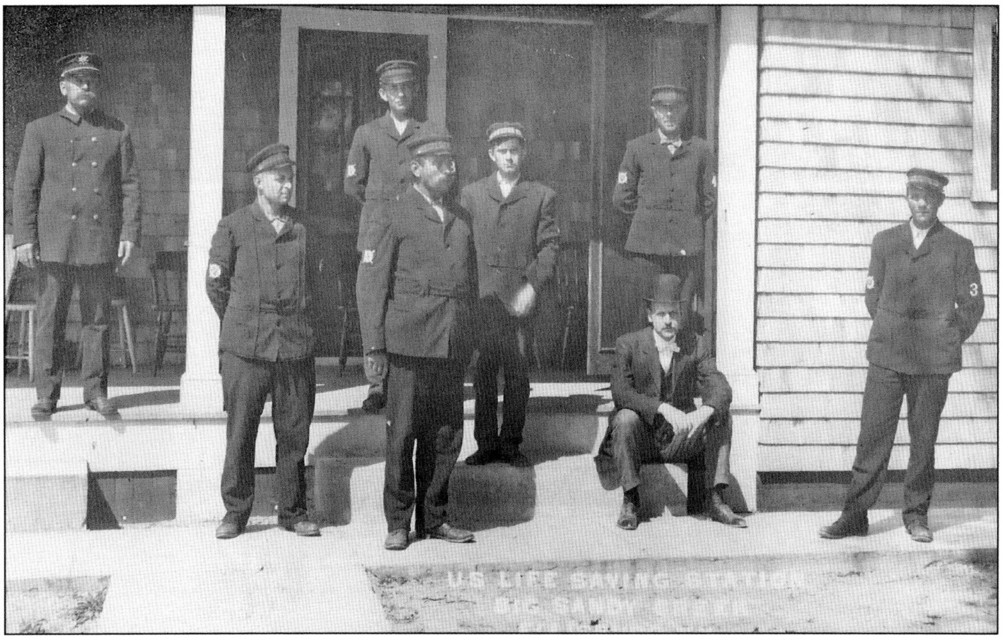

By World War I, motorized vessels had taken over shipping on the lake. Big Sandy was merged into the US Coast Guard in 1915, and many people suggested Big Sandy be moved to Galloo Island because beach rescues were diminishing. In 1916, displaying gallant bravery during the rescue of four people from the sunken steamer *Roberval*, the crew's heroics won them a reprieve, and Big Sandy remained open.

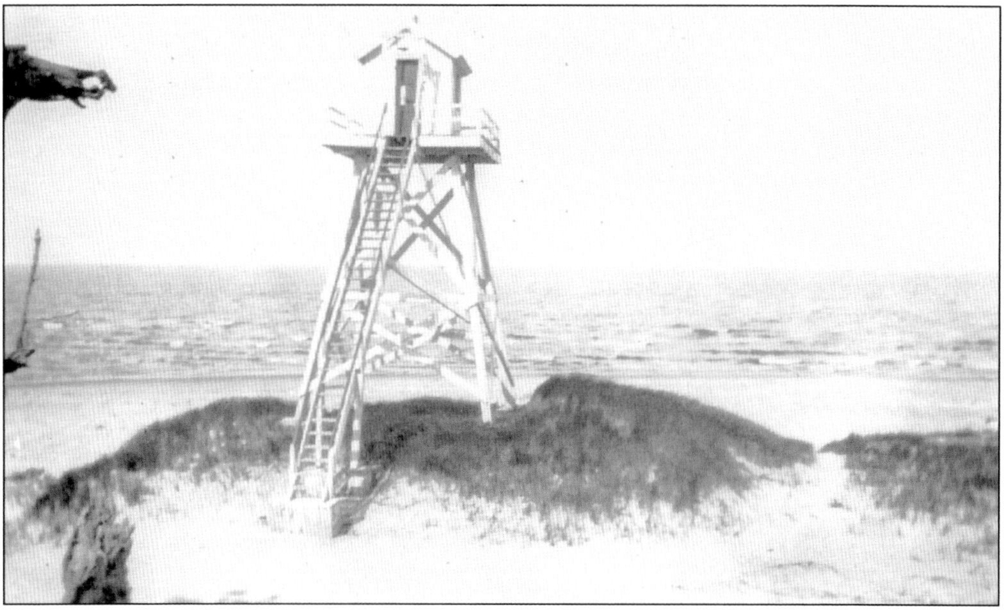

The Big Sandy rooftop lookout may have proved inadequate for a full view of the lake because this large lookout tower was constructed on the beach. The mouth of the creek is at the left. (Torre Parker-Lane.)

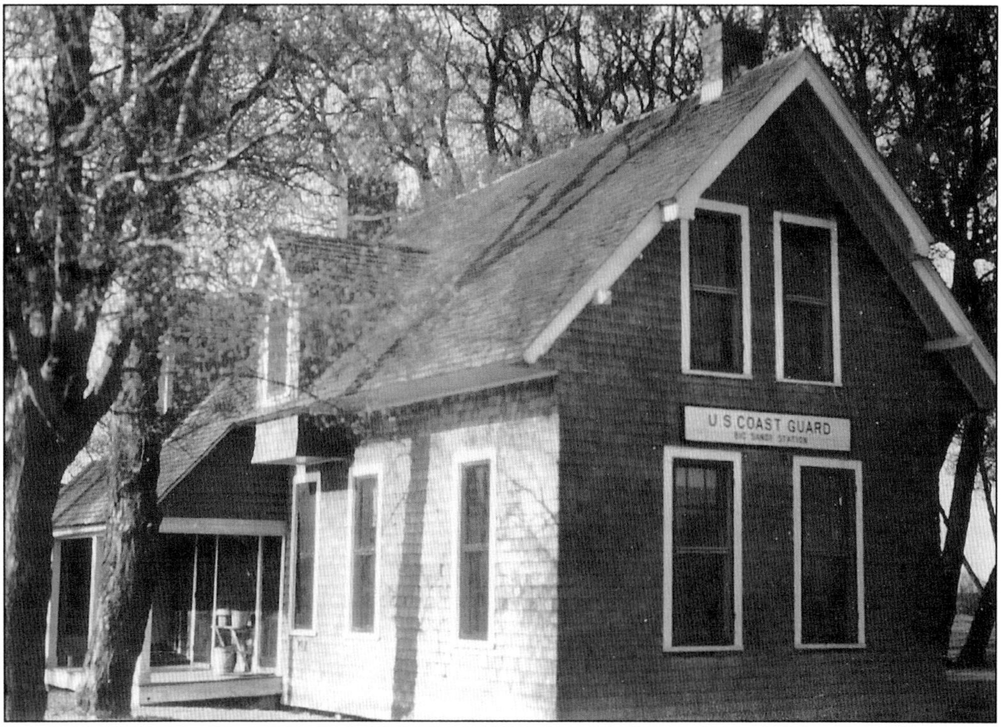

The Big Sandy keeper's house was built a few feet away from the station. It was common for the keeper's family to stay with him during the open season. (Torre Parker-Lane.)

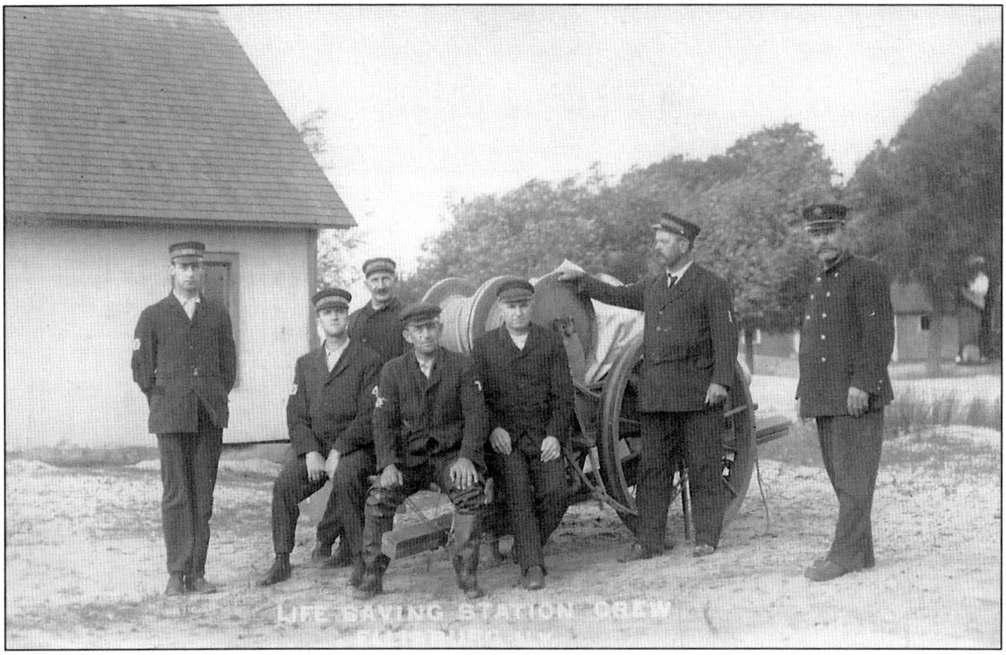

In July 1921, Big Sandy was abandoned by the federal government for financial reasons. The crew was transferred to other stations, and the buildings and equipment were planned for a sale. At its closing, the station was left in charge of Boatswain's Mate Fayette "Fay" Noble of Ellisburg, pictured second from right.

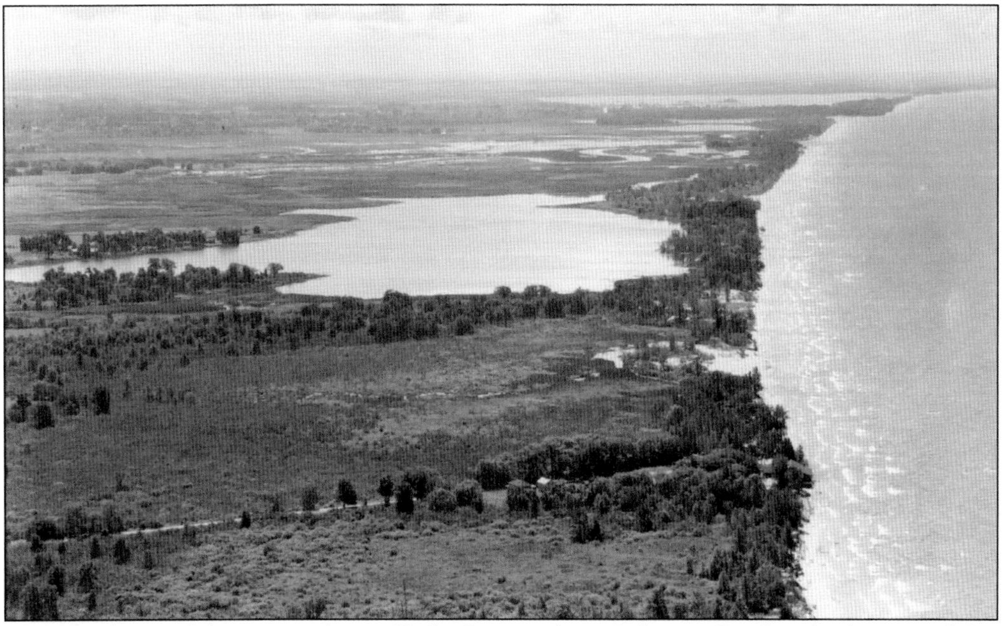

This aerial view of the eastern shore of Lake Ontario shows Lakeview Pond in the foreground, Big Sandy, and Sandy Pond in the background. By early 1924, with Big Sandy still closed and a law enforcement crackdown on the Atlantic Ocean's rum row during Prohibition, booze smugglers turned to the Great Lakes. This remote shoreline saw a dramatic increase in smuggling. The road to Southwick farm and beach is in the foreground. (Church.)

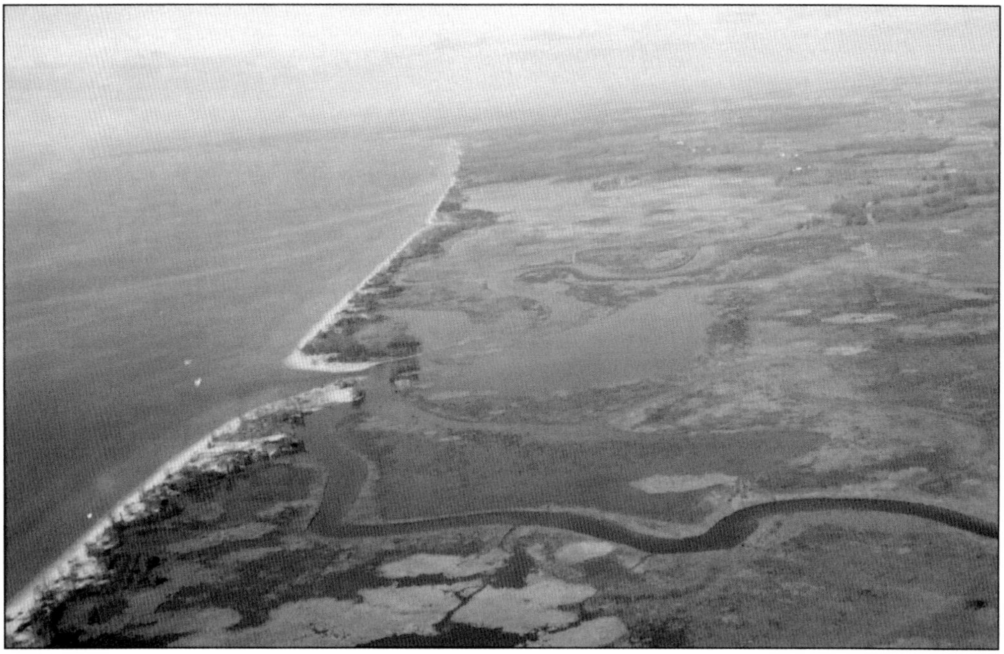

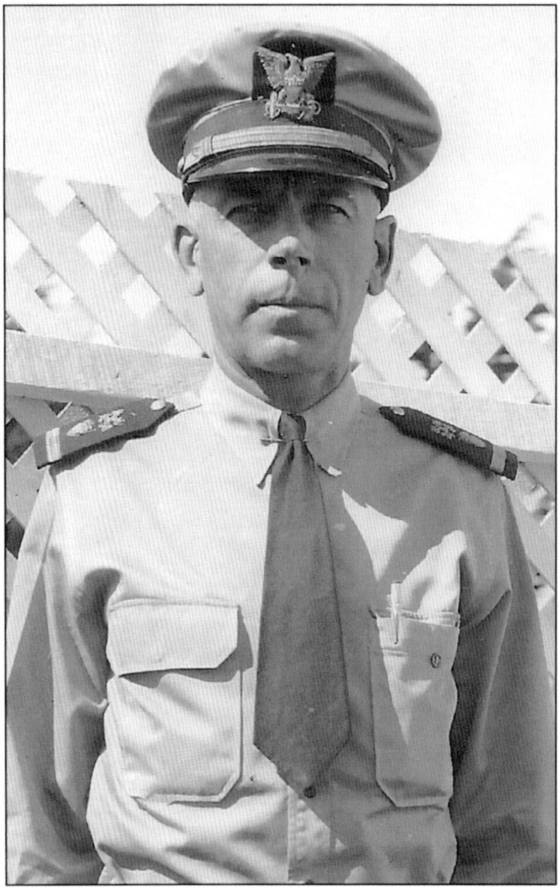

At 2:00 in the morning on August 12, 1924, smugglers boldly steered their 35-foot cabin cruiser past Big Sandy and up the south branch of Big Sandy Creek (bottom). Giving chase at the South Landing Bridge, two maintenance guardsmen fired their guns at two trucks loaded with booze from the boat. The trucks and the boat escaped but left behind were 175 cases of Dow Canadian Ale. Big Sandy was immediately reopened under new orders to stop rumrunning on the lake. (Church.)

Capt. Paul W. Tifft of Sandy Creek was placed in command of the reopened Big Sandy station. Tifft and Oswego station keeper George E. Jackson of Woodville reported to district headquarters that smuggling on the lake had increased dramatically. Their primary complaint, however, was that farmers on the lakeshore could "make more money selling unloading privileges than working the soil. It seems that nearly everyone will aid the bootleggers," Jackson wrote. (Arlene Tifft Dana.)

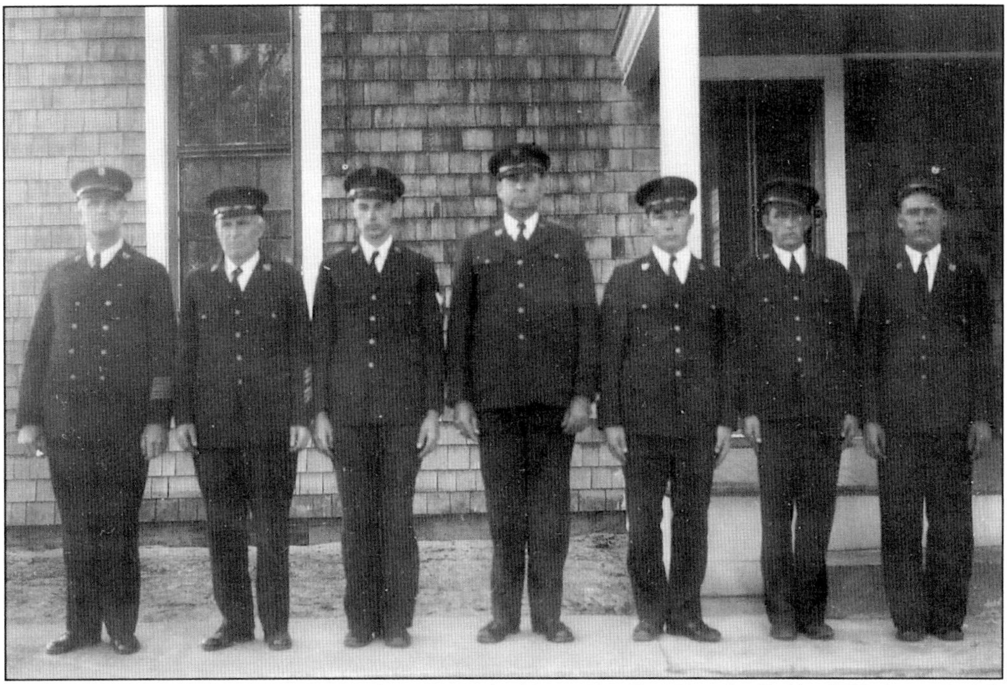

Captain Tifft's first crew at Big Sandy consisted of Isaac H. "Ike" Wright (left) of Ellisburg, Ralph M. Matteson (center) of Belleville, and Harvey E. Richardson (third from right) of Ellisburg. These three men would participate in some of the most significant arrests of bootleggers on eastern Lake Ontario. (Torre Parker-Lane.)

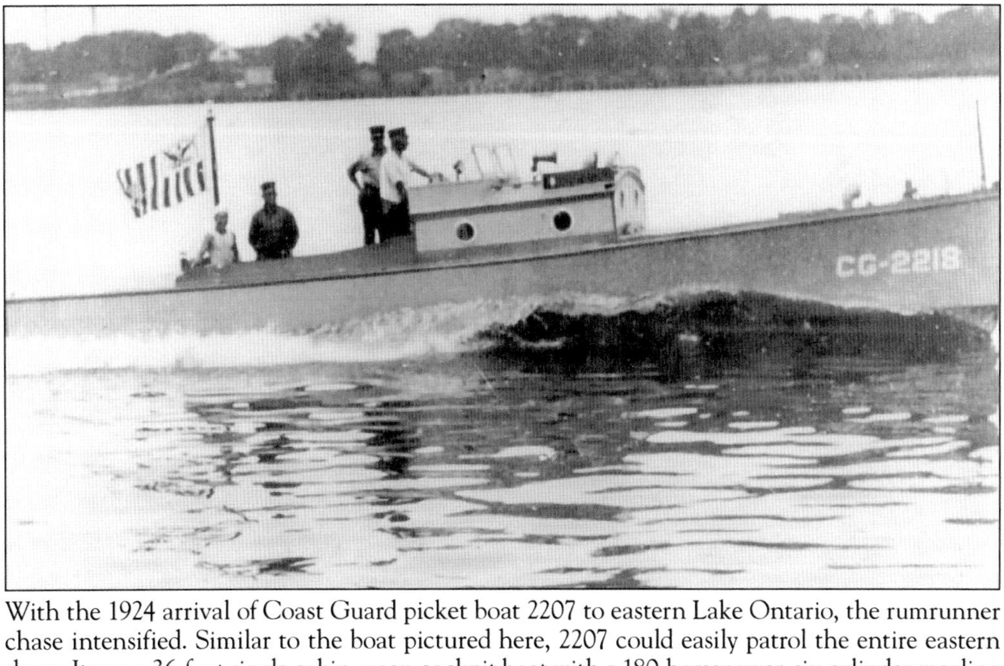

With the 1924 arrival of Coast Guard picket boat 2207 to eastern Lake Ontario, the rumrunner chase intensified. Similar to the boat pictured here, 2207 could easily patrol the entire eastern shore. It was a 36-foot single cabin, open cockpit boat with a 180-horsepower, six-cylinder gasoline engine. Top speed was 24 knots, but that was not fast enough to keep up with the fastest rum boats. (USCG.)

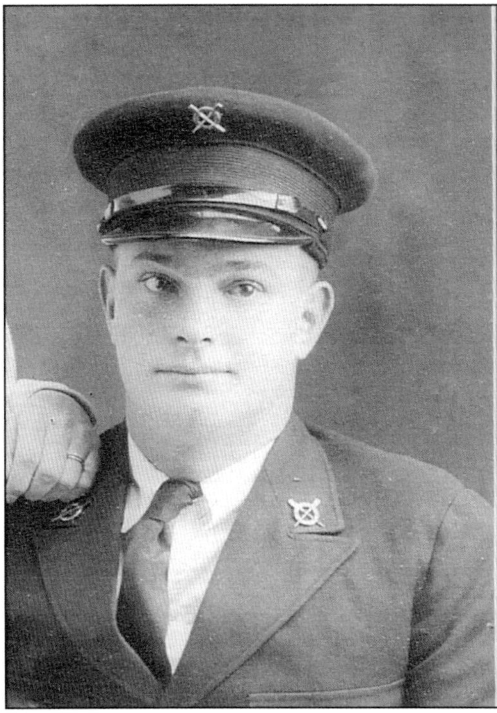

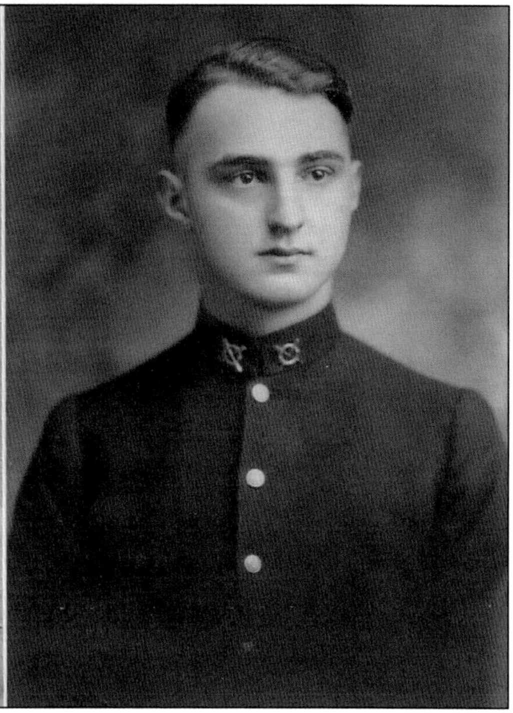

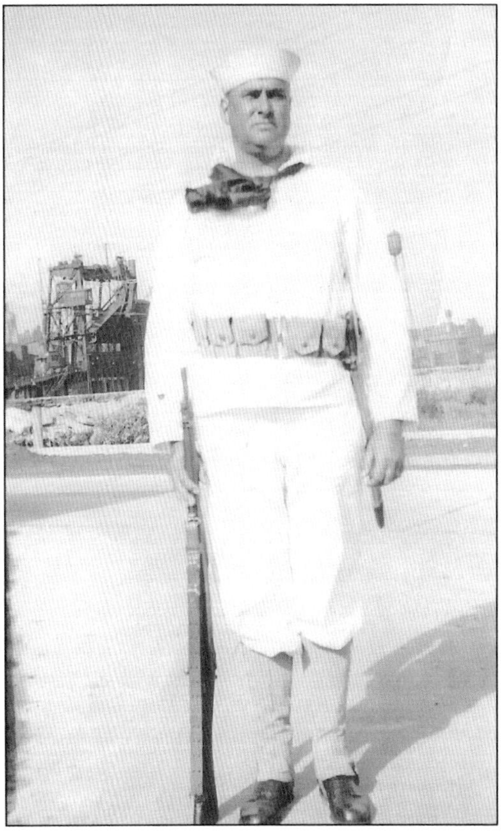

Brothers Maurice Lyndon Matteson (left) and Ralph Minor Matteson of Belleville began their Coast Guard careers at Big Sandy. Lyn Matteson's stint had a traumatic beginning when, in July 1925, a 19-year-old co-recruit from Lorraine drowned in Big Sandy Creek in front of the station while they were swimming. Unable to save his mate, Matteson shied away from recreational swimming for the rest of his life. Ralph Matteson later became the first captain in the Galloo Island Coast Guard station. (The Matteson family.)

Isaac H. "Ike" Wright gained notoriety for rowing a surfboat six miles from Big Sandy to Stony Point on New Year's Eve 1929 to arrest a smuggler, who turned out to be Wright's former schoolmate from Sandy Creek, unloading Canadian whiskey. Wright's widow, Hazel Ethridge Wright, told the author that her husband was aware of local guardsmen, police, and farmers who received booze and cash for helping the bootleggers. (Torre Parker-Lane.)

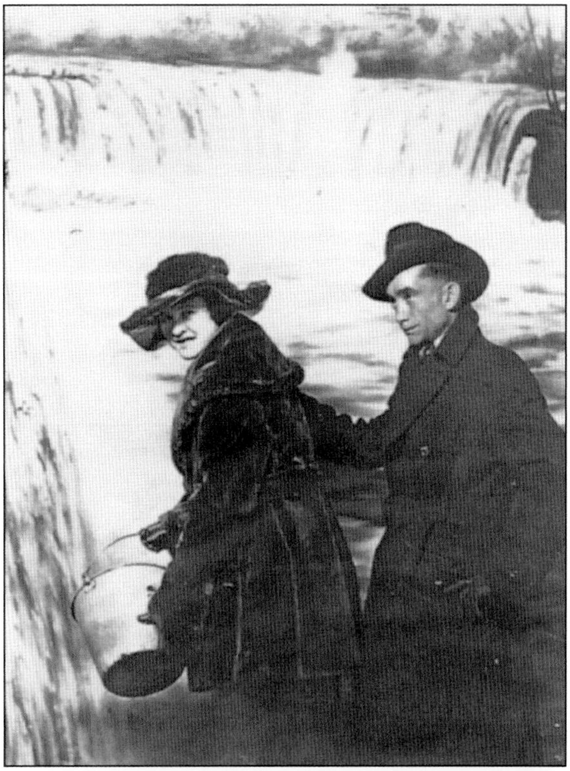

Anthony "Tony" Kane of Solvay was one of the most notorious rumrunners on Lake Ontario. Kane is seen here in a c. 1920 carnival photograph with his wife, Lola Major Kane. Kane owned boats and trucks to haul bootleg booze. Sandy Pond was his favorite drop-off location, but his third and final smuggling arrest was in March 1929 at Henderson Harbor's Snowshoe Point. (Jack Major.)

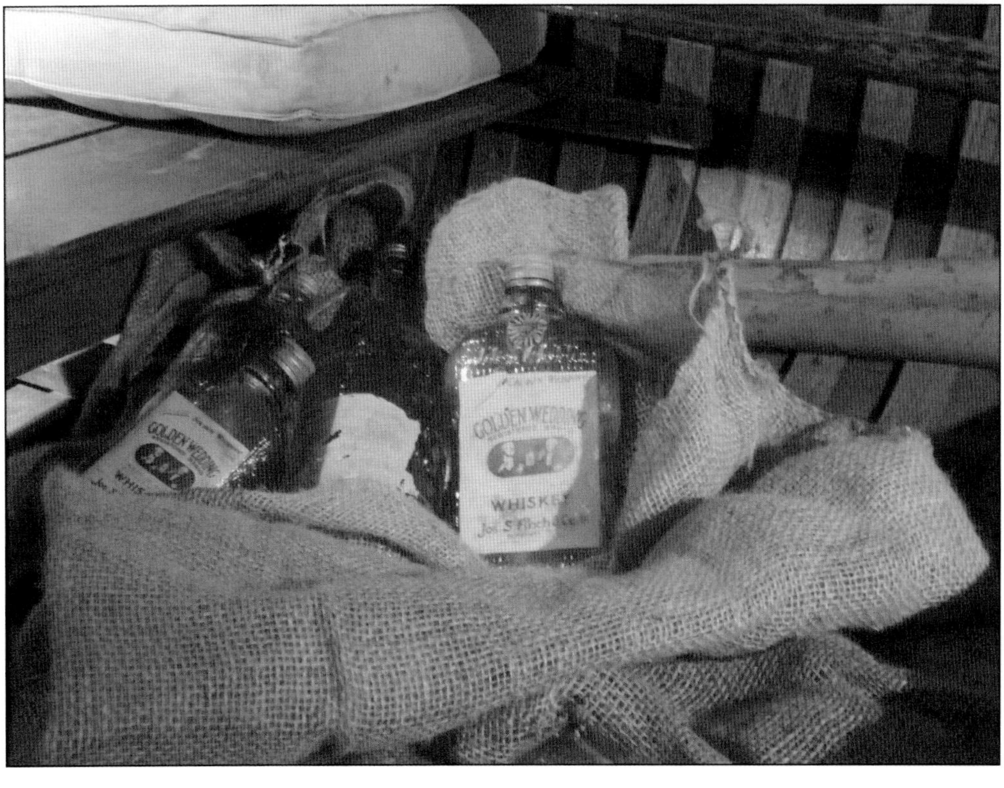

When Tony Kane was arrested at Snowshoe Point by Big Sandy captain Paul W. Tifft and surfman Harvey E. Richardson, he and two other men were hauling 74 bottles of Golden Wedding whiskey, like those pictured, across the ice from Stony Island. Richardson later told Canadian author C.W. Hunt for his book *Booze Boats and Billions* that he and Captain Tifft witnessed an after-hours courtroom scene where they believed Kane paid a bribe to avoid prison.

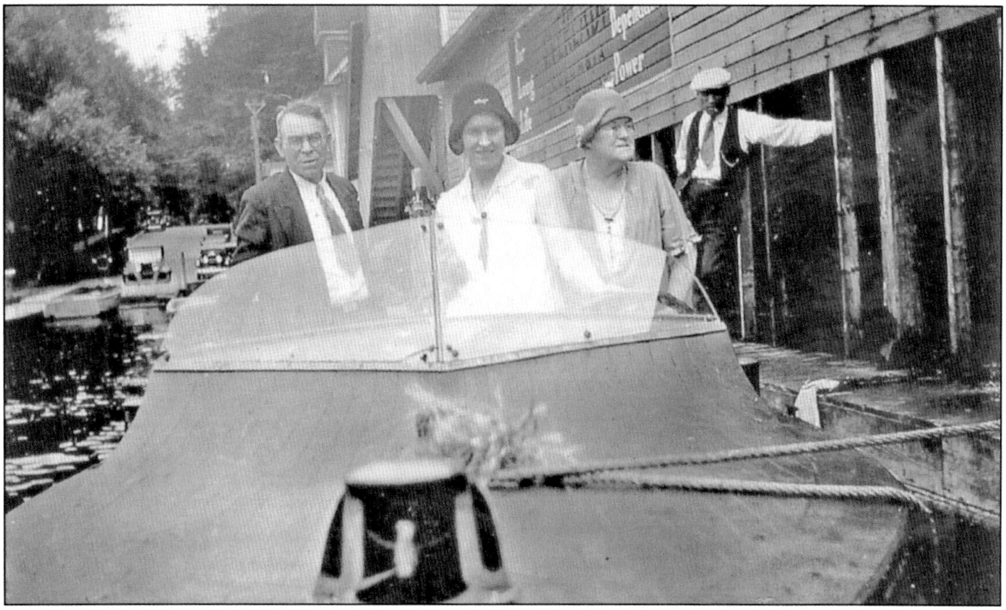

Tony Kane continued smuggling with his 30-foot mahogany boat *Firefly* after his Henderson Harbor arrest. Lola Major Kane is pictured in front with her parents, John and Rosa Major, in Alexandria Bay. In late December 1930, Kane and fellow rumrunners William Assman, also known as Wild Bill Sheldon, of Rochester and Cecil Phillips of Bath, Ontario, capsized in the *Firefly* between Main Duck Island and Kingston, Ontario. Their bodies were found in 1931. The shadowy looking man in the background is unidentified. (Jack Major.)

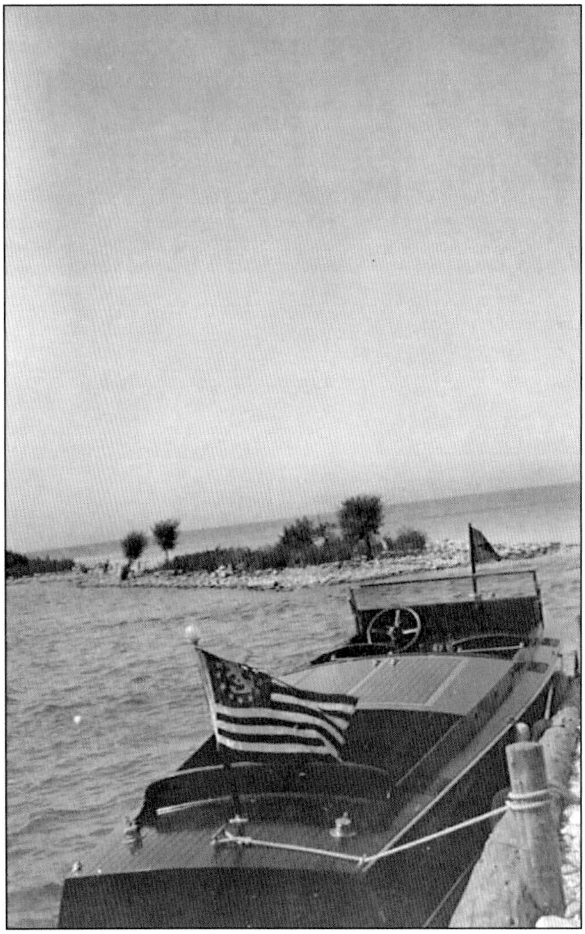

In August 1928, Henderson Harbor summer residents John C. and Beulah Marsellus, their boatman, and family were returning to Henderson Harbor in their 26-foot Chris Craft runabout. While cruising in front of the PK Clubhouse on Galloo Island, they were fired upon by what appeared to be a pleasure boat. It turned out to be the Coast Guard, in a confiscated vessel, demanding the Marsellus boat heave-to for a liquor inspection. (John D. Marsellus.)

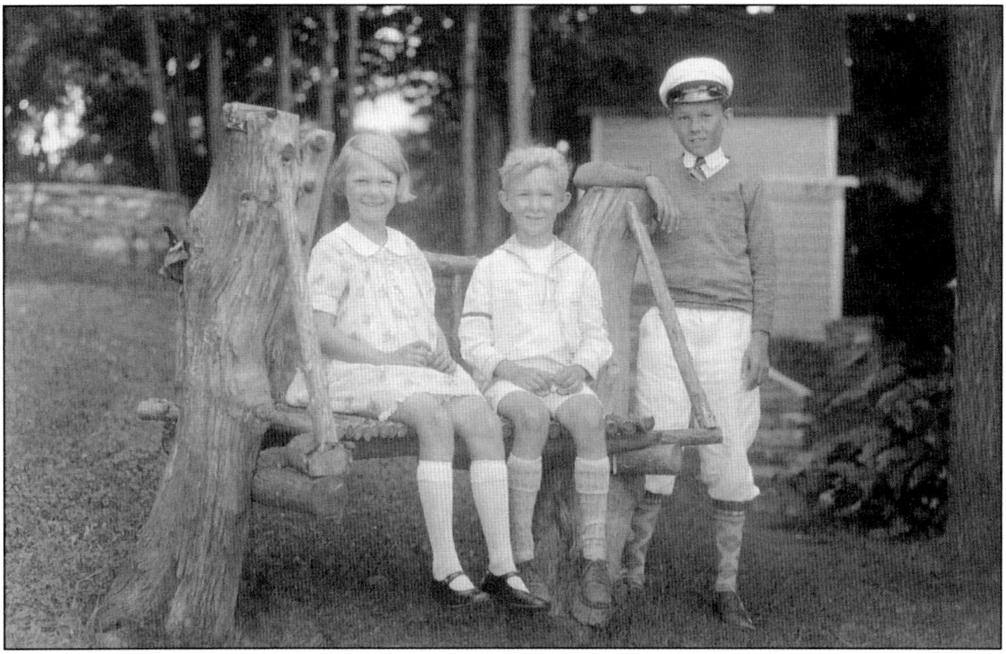

The Marsellus children, Betty, Richard, and John F., were also in the boat when the Coast Guard bullets flew over their heads. Marsellus was cleared and allowed to continue, but he complained about the incident in a letter to the undersecretary of the US Treasury, Ogden Mills. He said his family and the PK Club members on shore were placed in danger. (John D. Marsellus.)

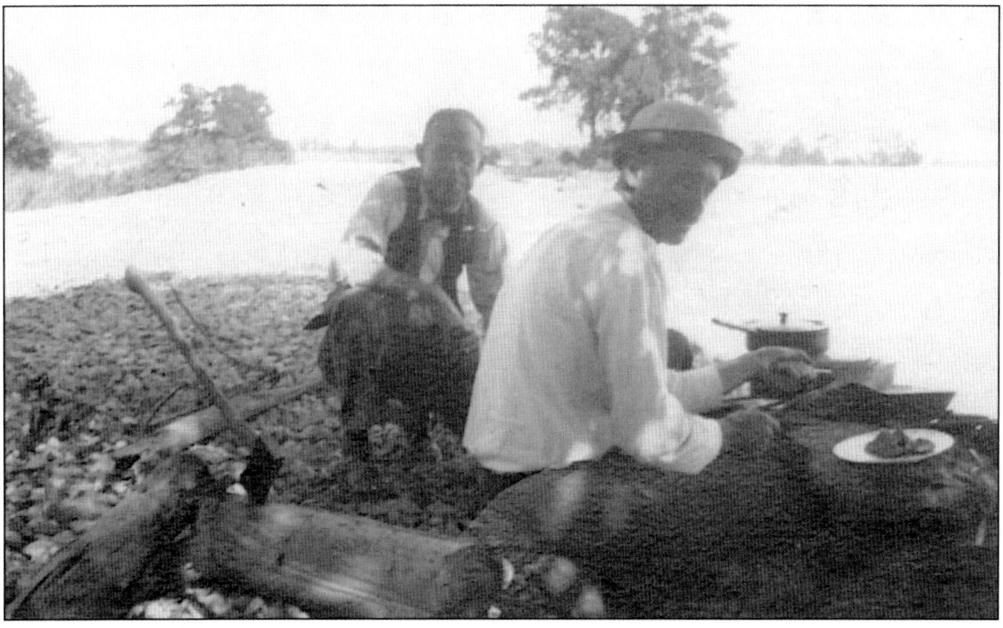

John C. Marsellus (left), pictured at a shore dinner, was the owner of the prestigious Marsellus Casket Company of Syracuse. In reply letters from the Coast Guard, the incident was downplayed and it was suggested that the Coast Guard had a duty to detain all boats and enforce Prohibition. However, publicity of the event contributed to public disdain for the interdiction tactics of the Coast Guard. (John D. Marsellus.)

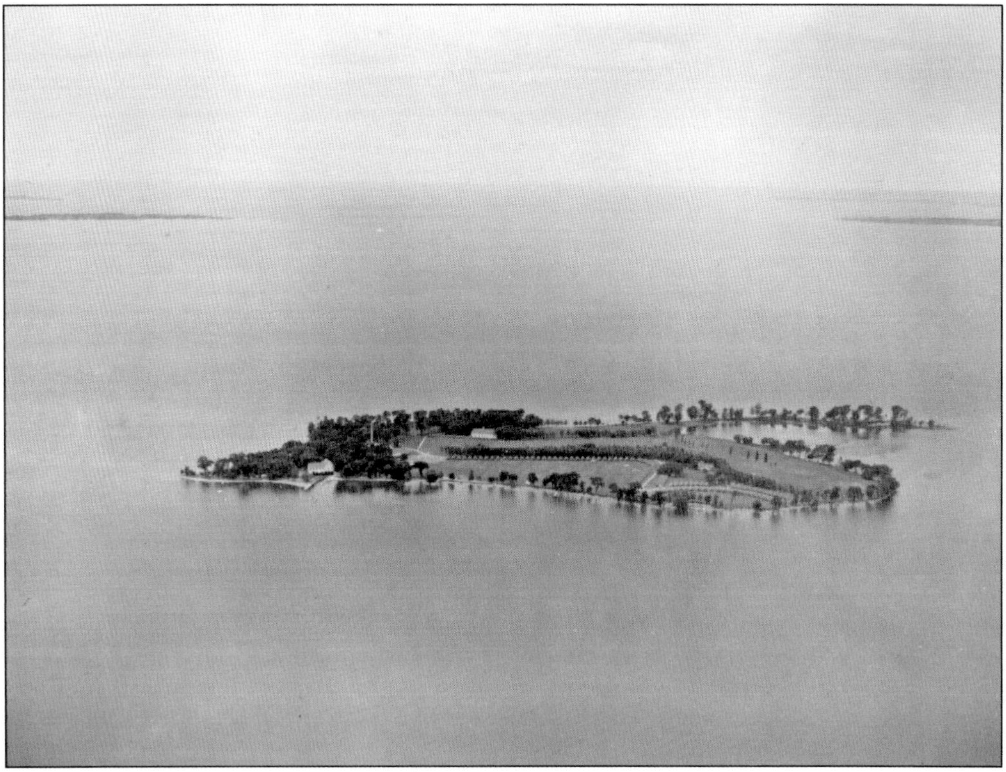

On June 29, 1928, the crew of Coast Guard picket boat 2206 captured three rumrunners in the motorboat *Anna*, offshore from Henderson Harbor, and confiscated 40 bags of Canadian ale. The Coast Guard report indicates the smugglers tried to bribe their captors, payable when they made their delivery to Association Island. Instead, all but one case of the evidence was dumped into the outer portion of Henderson Harbor (foreground). (Church.)

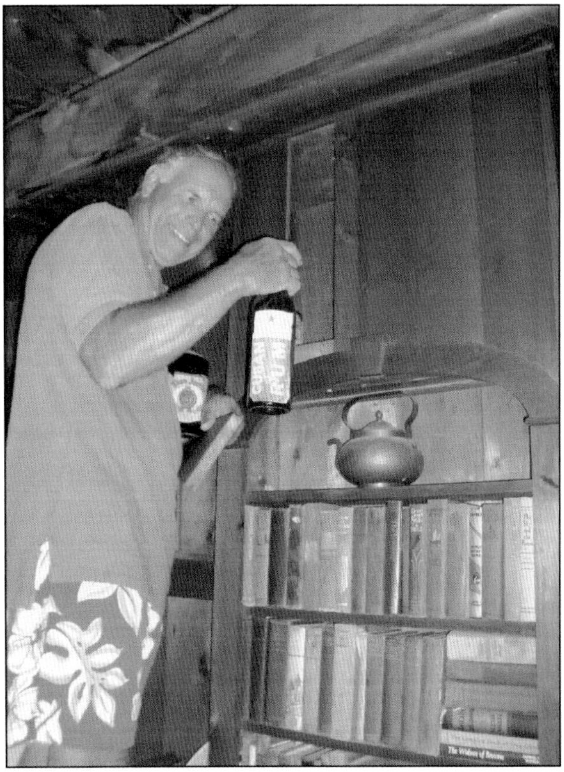

Henderson Harbor summer resident Jeff Averill displays a bottle of Cuban rum removed from a secret compartment in the wall of his family's summer cottage at Highland Park. Discovered only recently, several bottles of Prohibition-era booze had apparently been hidden in the wall to the right of his hand by his parents or grandparents for more than 75 years.

Eight

Boats and Marinas

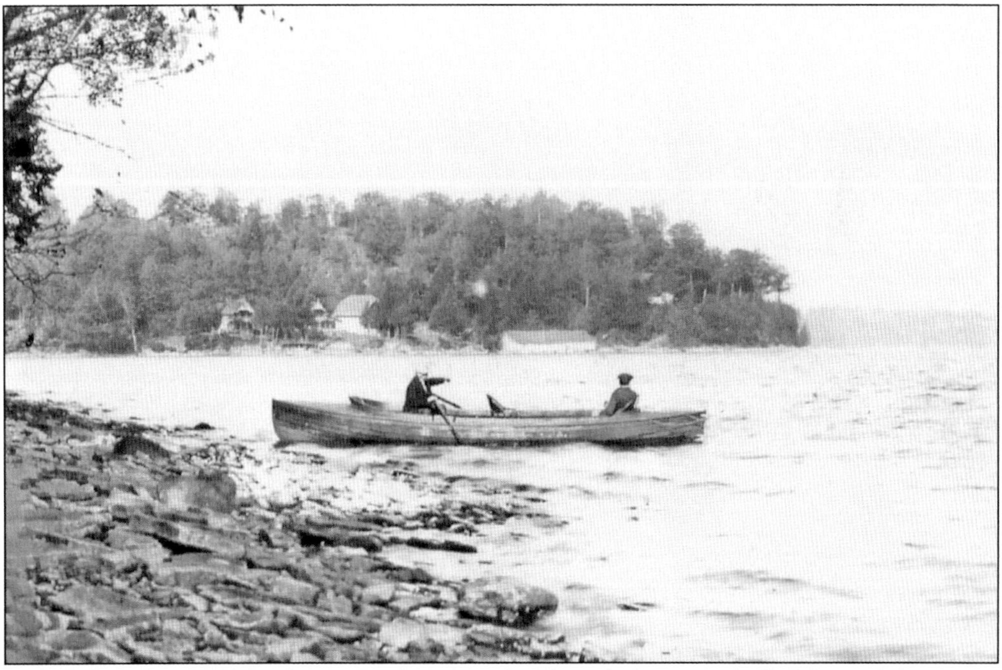

Early fishing boats of Henderson Harbor were double-ended rowing skiffs. Many of them were handmade by James Bassett, who had a boat building shop on the north end of Henderson Bay. This appears to be a Bassett boat on the shore of Cedarwood with Highland Park in the background. Cane-backed chairs with the legs cut off served as boat seats.

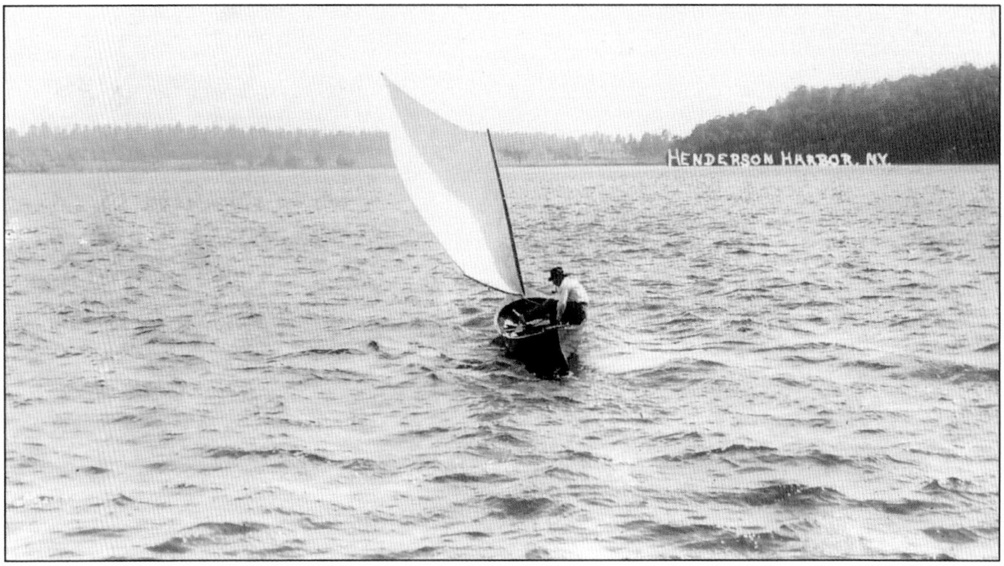

Pleasure sailboats in Henderson Harbor were as simple as this sailing dinghy on the western shore near Highland Park. It is believed that the sailor is Earl Amos Averill of Highland Park.

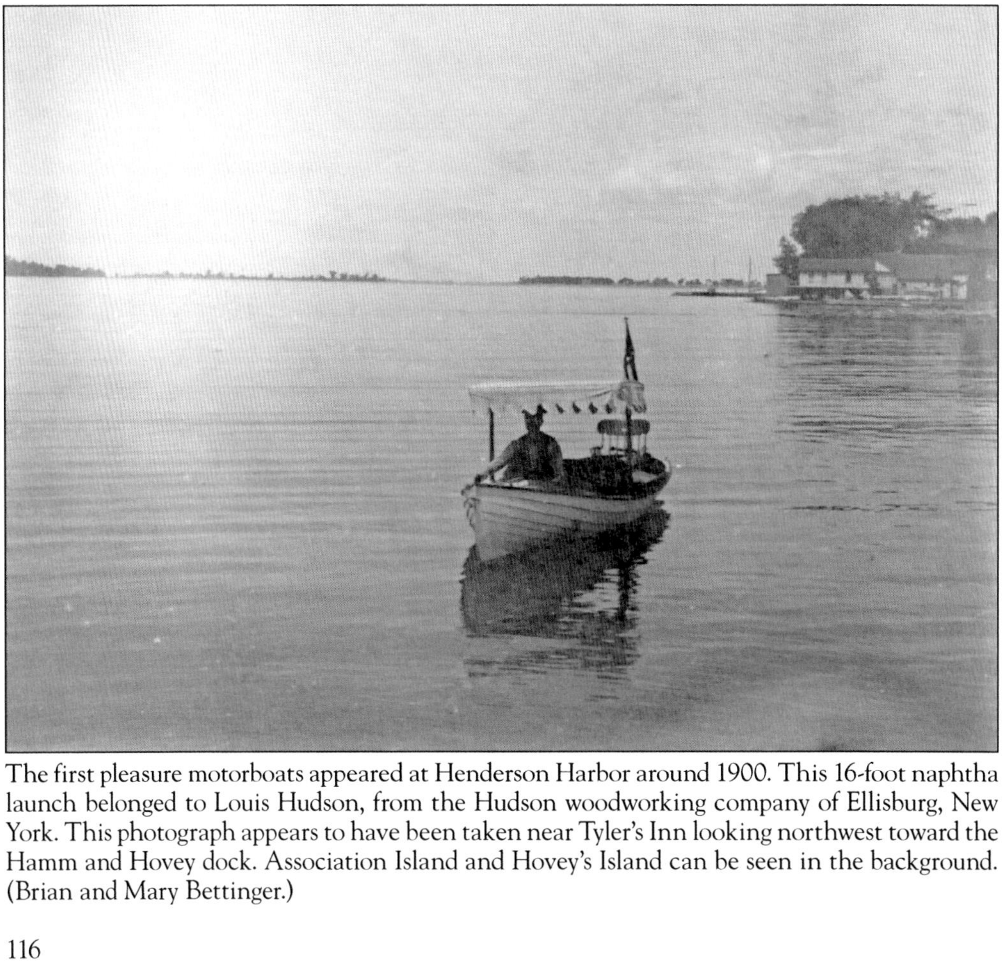

The first pleasure motorboats appeared at Henderson Harbor around 1900. This 16-foot naphtha launch belonged to Louis Hudson, from the Hudson woodworking company of Ellisburg, New York. This photograph appears to have been taken near Tyler's Inn looking northwest toward the Hamm and Hovey dock. Association Island and Hovey's Island can be seen in the background. (Brian and Mary Bettinger.)

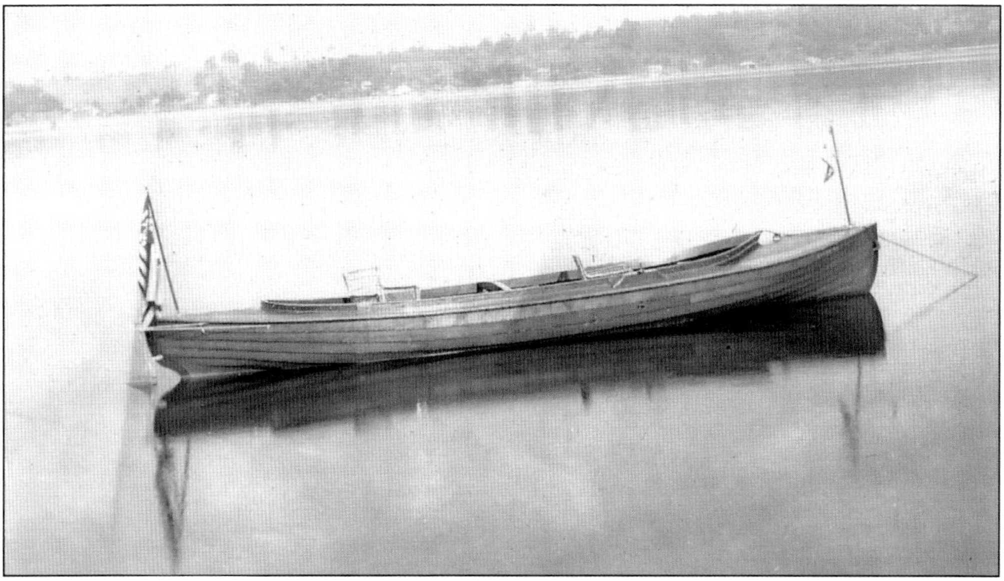

A well-known naphtha, then gasoline, launch in Henderson Harbor was the *Bluebird*, which was owned by Earl and Bertha Waite Averill. Built by the Bassett family of Henderson Harbor, Bertha Averill cruised in the *Bluebird* from Highland Park to Webster's cottage, the Cedars, on Harbor Road (now the Brown Owl), and gave rides to members of the Daughters of the American Revolution, holding their final meeting of 1915. (The Averill family.)

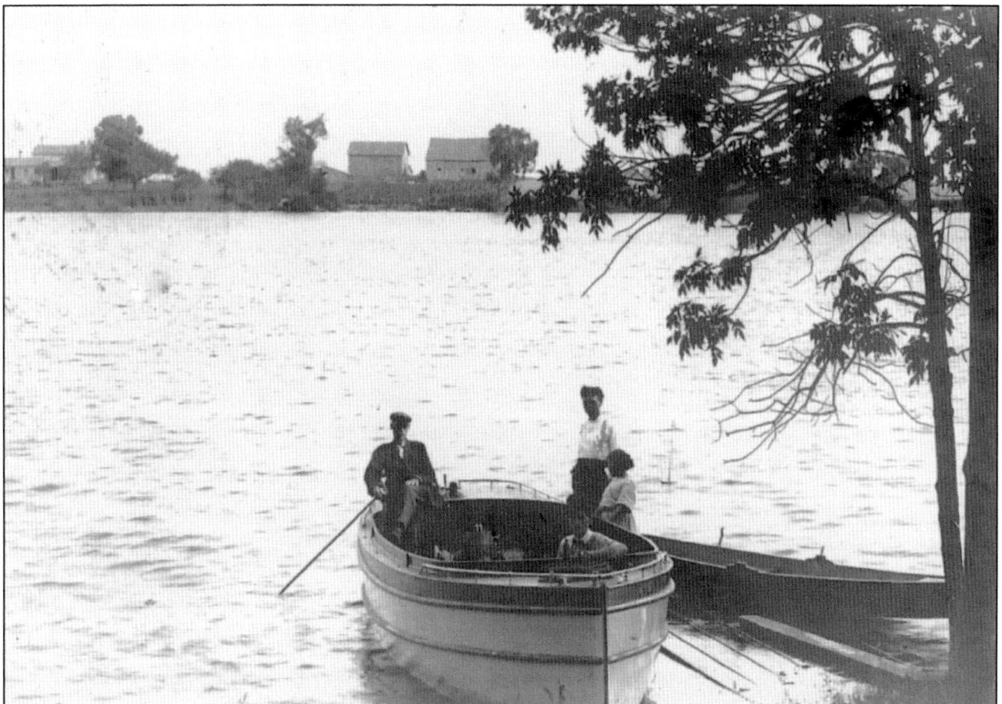

Tied to the Horton family dock in Snowshoe Bay, this fish and work boat has a small inboard gasoline engine. The occupants of the boat are unidentified. The George and Winnie Hovey farm and Snowshoe Inn on Hovey's Island is pictured in the background.

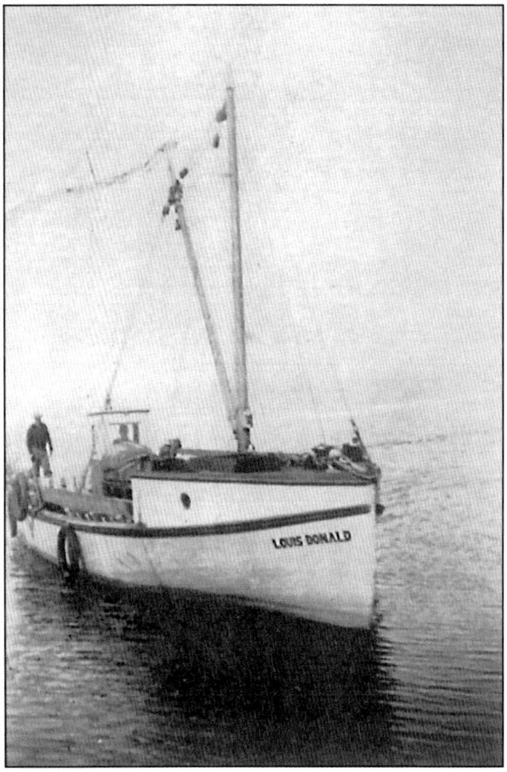

The *Louis Donald* was a 40-foot cattle boat used primarily to haul livestock and supplies from Henderson Harbor and Sackets Harbor to Galloo and Stony Islands. Owned and operated by Rudolph Gowing, the *Louis Donald* was well equipped for cattle and sheep but often carried people too. (NCNYCGA.)

The Barnes family of Paradise Park first sailed into Henderson Harbor in their large yawl, *Themis*. From left to right are Anna Barnes Taylor, Mary Barnes Barrett, Eva Snaith Barnes, unidentified, Helen Barnes Jewell, and John Barnes (lower left). Family patriarch E. Austin Barnes is walking on the dock. Austin and Eva Snaith Barnes purchased the Paradise House hotel at Paradise Park. Their sons George and John Barnes developed the Lightning sailboat. (The Averill family.)

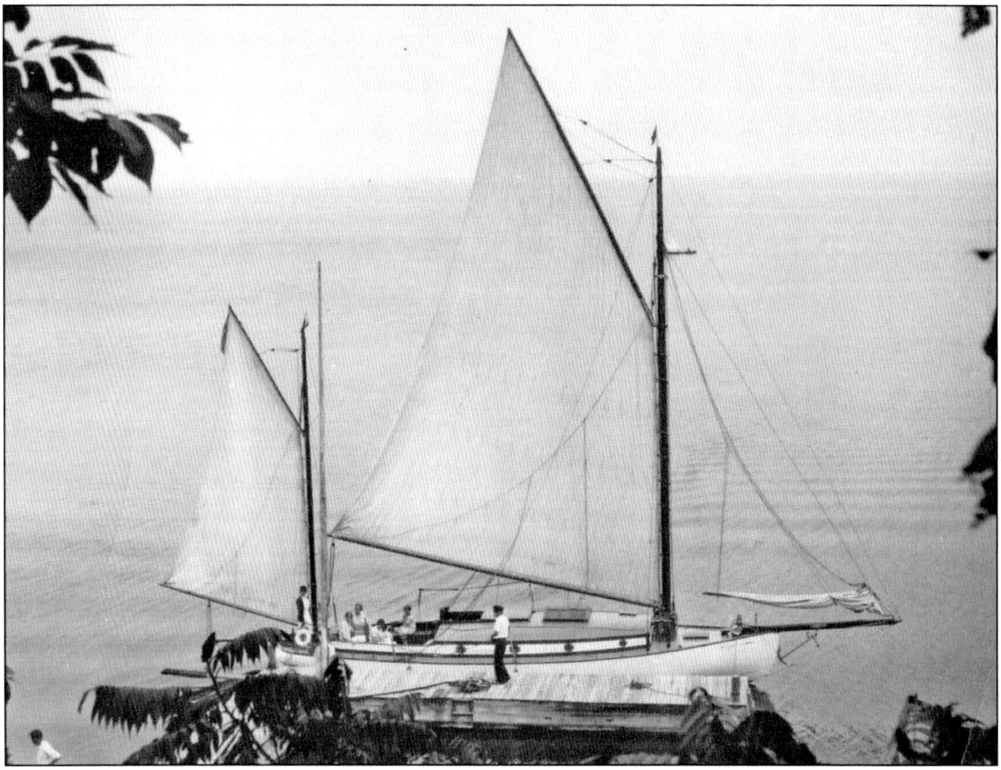

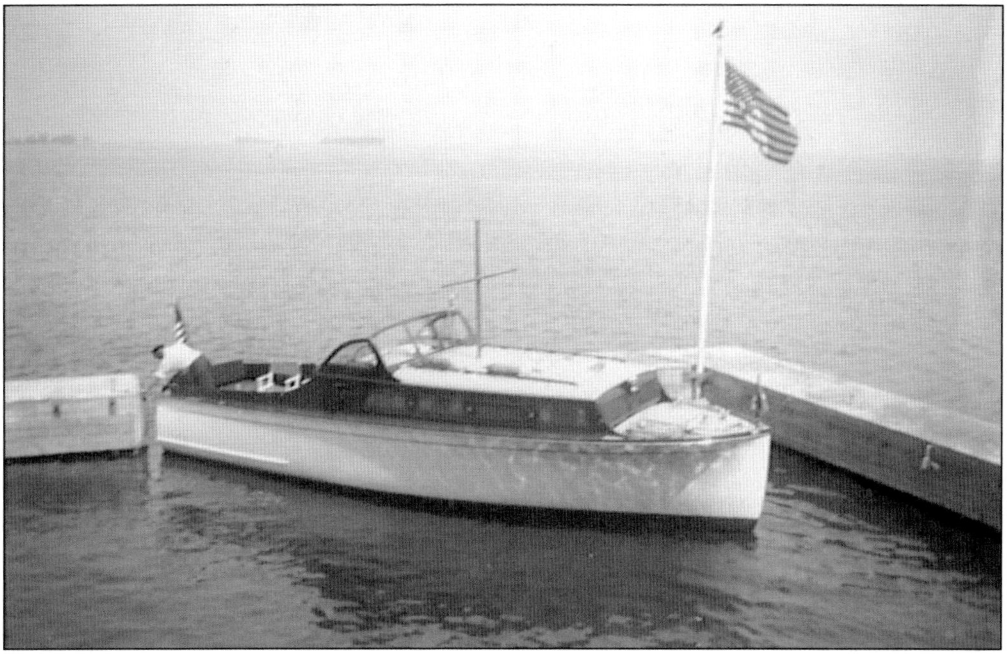

One Marsellus family boat was the *MARS*, a short version of the family name. The *MARS* was a Richardson cruiser. It was owned by John C. Marsellus in the 1930s and 1940s. (John D. Marsellus.)

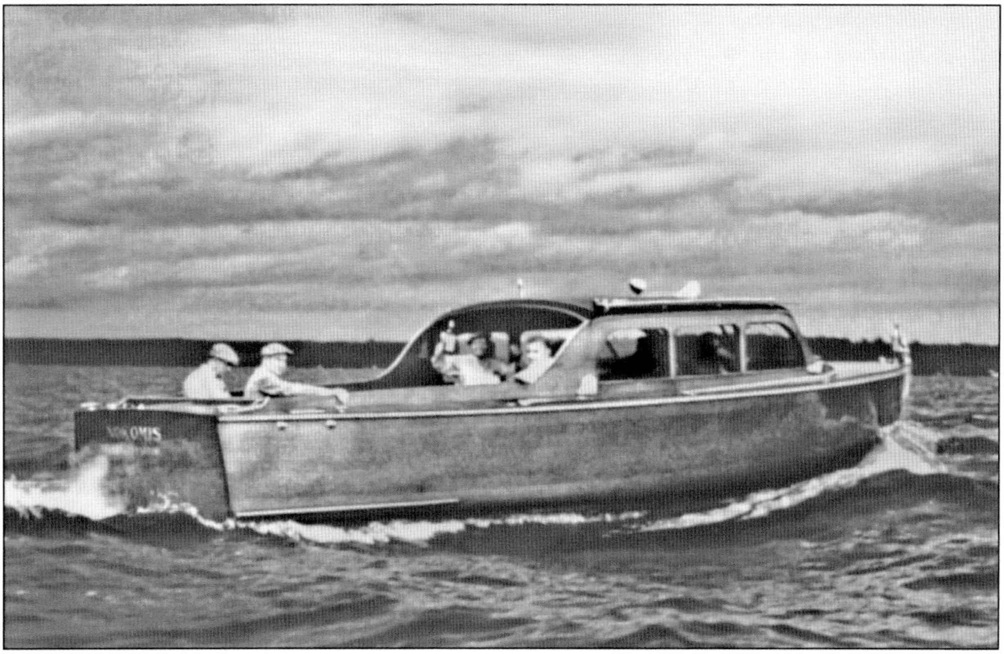

Nokomis was the name given to two boats owned by Earl J. Machold of Ellisburg. President of the Niagara Mohawk Power Corporation, Machold's first boat was this 1935 thirty-foot cruiser built by Hutchinson Boat Works of Alexandria Bay. Machold, seen here in the cabin holding an object for the camera, owned the PK Clubhouse on Galloo Island from 1944 to 1966 with his twin sister, Doris Machold Davis. Machold's boatman was Rudolph Gowing. (Jack Machold.)

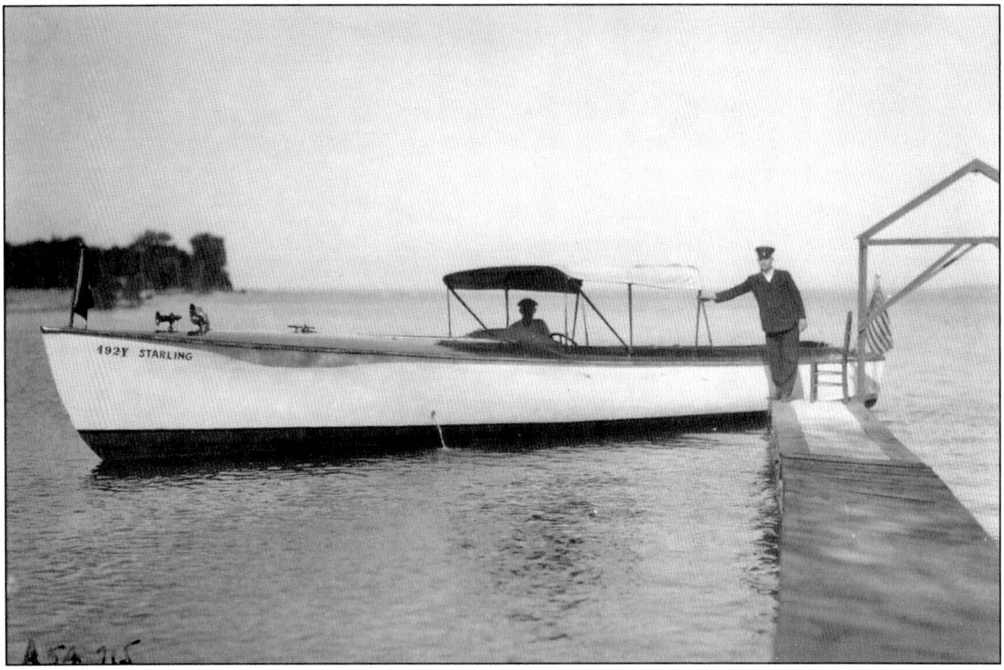

GE installed many boats in Henderson Harbor to ferry passengers to and from Association Island. One of the earliest GE boats was the *Starling*, seen here at the island dock in a c. 1920 photograph. Several of GE's early boats, such as the *Claverack* and *Kommanche*, were destroyed by fires caused by exhaust sparks igniting gasoline fumes in the bilge. (GE.)

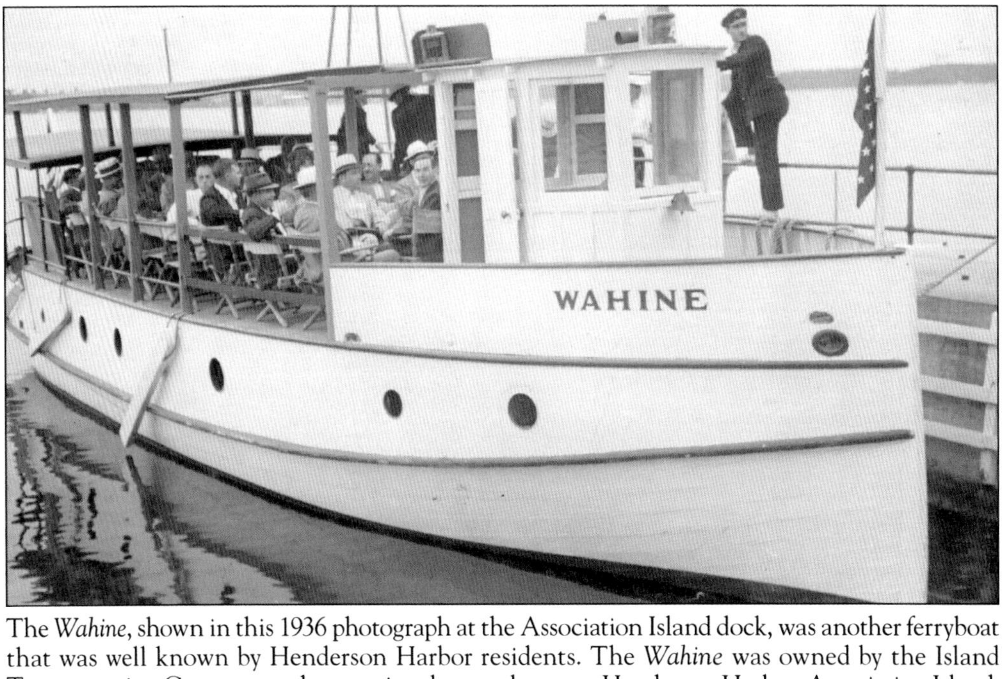

The *Wahine*, shown in this 1936 photograph at the Association Island dock, was another ferryboat that was well known by Henderson Harbor residents. The *Wahine* was owned by the Island Transportation Company and ran a triangle route between Henderson Harbor, Association Island, and Sackets Harbor starting in 1912. (GE.)

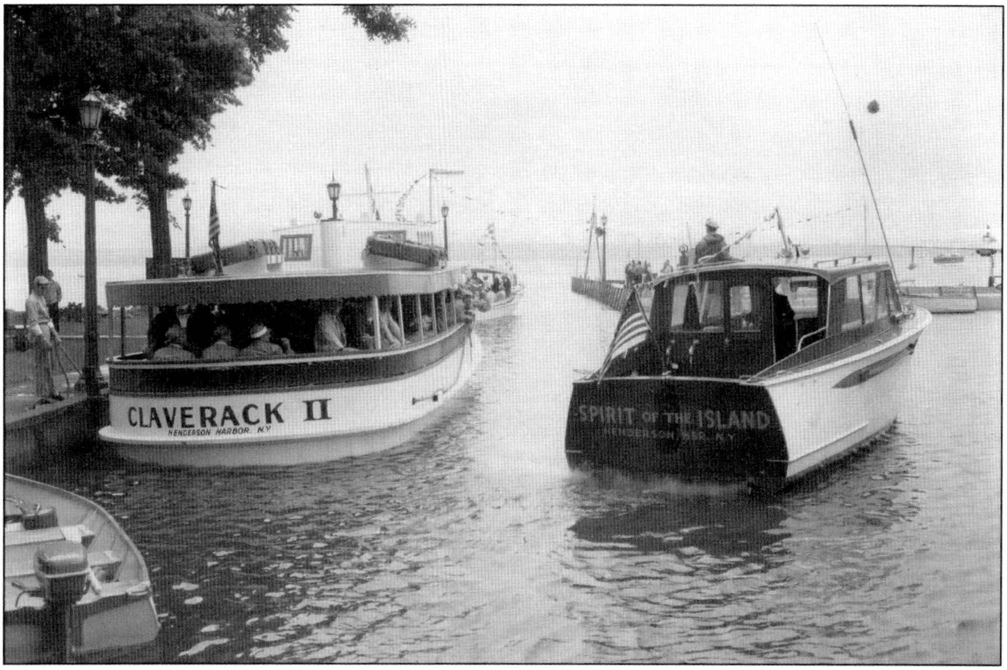

The *Claverack II* and *Islander II* were twin boats. Because several busloads of GE campers arrived in Henderson Harbor at the same time, running two ferry boats maximized the efficiency of trips to and from Association Island. At right is the *Spirit of the Island*, a fishing and pleasure boat for GE that ferried VIPs. (GE.)

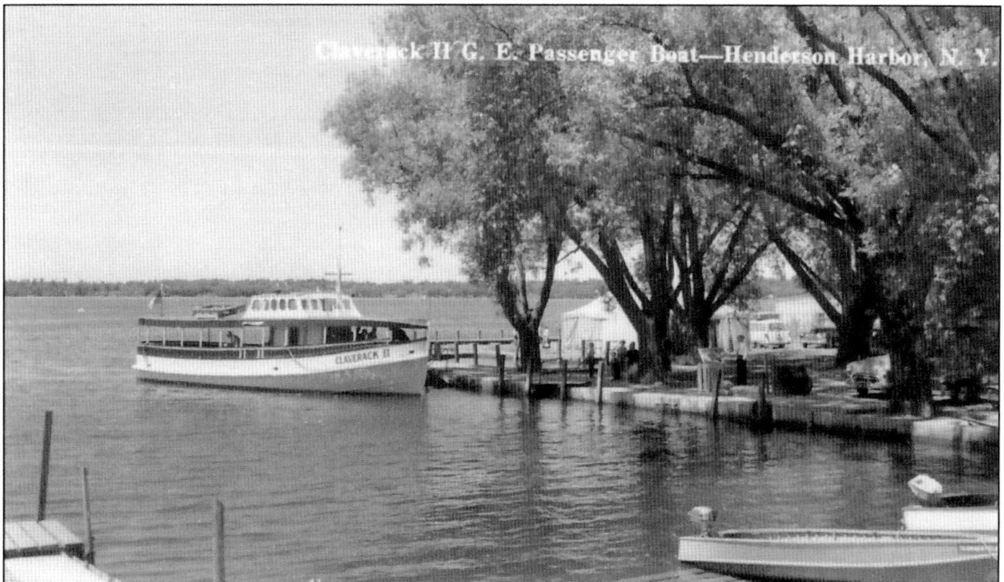

The *Claverack II* arrives at the GE dock at Henderson Harbor to load passengers in the early 1950s. The former Harbor Inn dock, GE acquired this property and razed the massive four-story Harbor Inn in the 1930s. Notice the tent set up to check in passengers as they arrived by bus. Two small outboard launches are pulled bow first onto the busy boat ramp that was once located in the heart of Henderson Harbor.

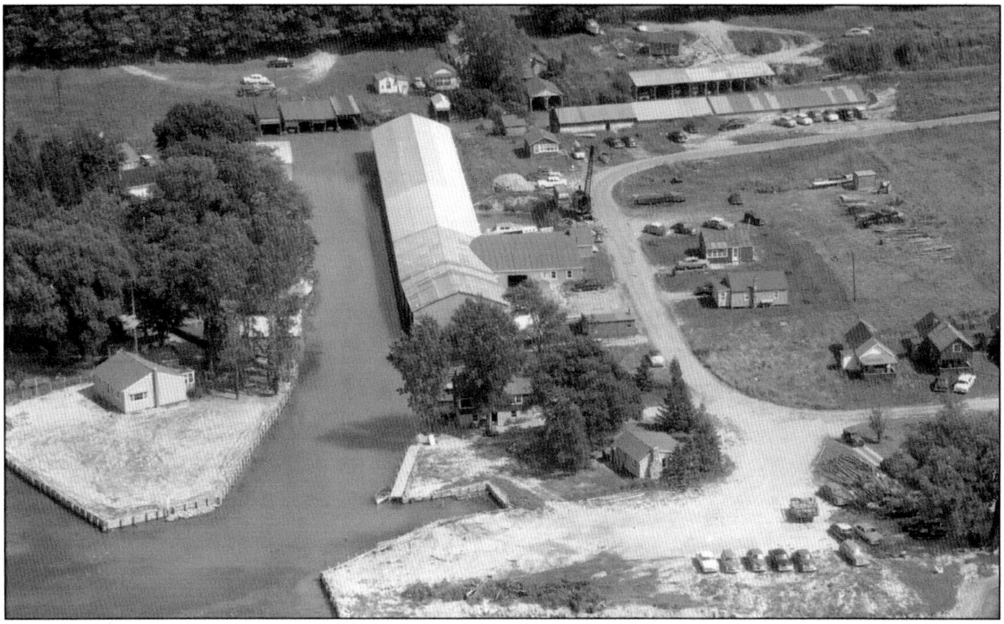

Reed Canal was dug into Graham's Creek for large boathouses, such as Cornell's boathouse and marina (center) and Harbor Marina (top right). The canal fill dirt was used to create more land in the bottom right of the photograph, where the Henderson Harbor Yacht Club would be located after it was established in 1948. (Church.)

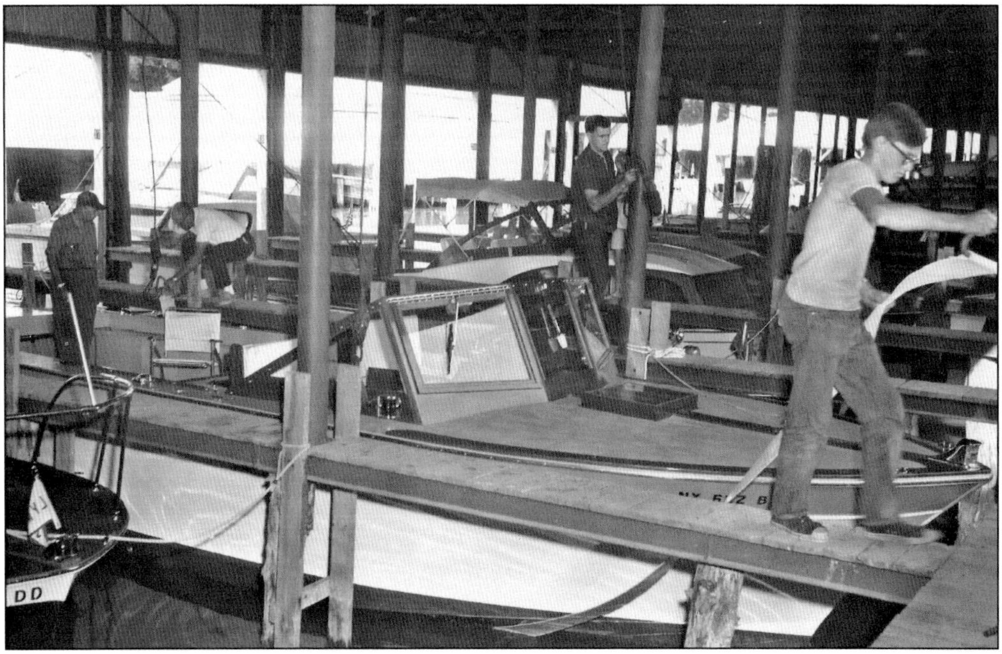

Preparing John Dunk's fishing boat *Boom Boom* inside Cornell's Marina in 1966, Gary and David Cornell joined their father, Clarence, in the family's marina business, which began as Phelps and Cornell at the end of World War II. The Cornell brothers have worked together at their full-service marina for more than 35 years. The *Boom Boom* was a 28-foot wooden boat custom built at Cornell's Marina and spent more than 40 years fishing from Henderson Harbor.

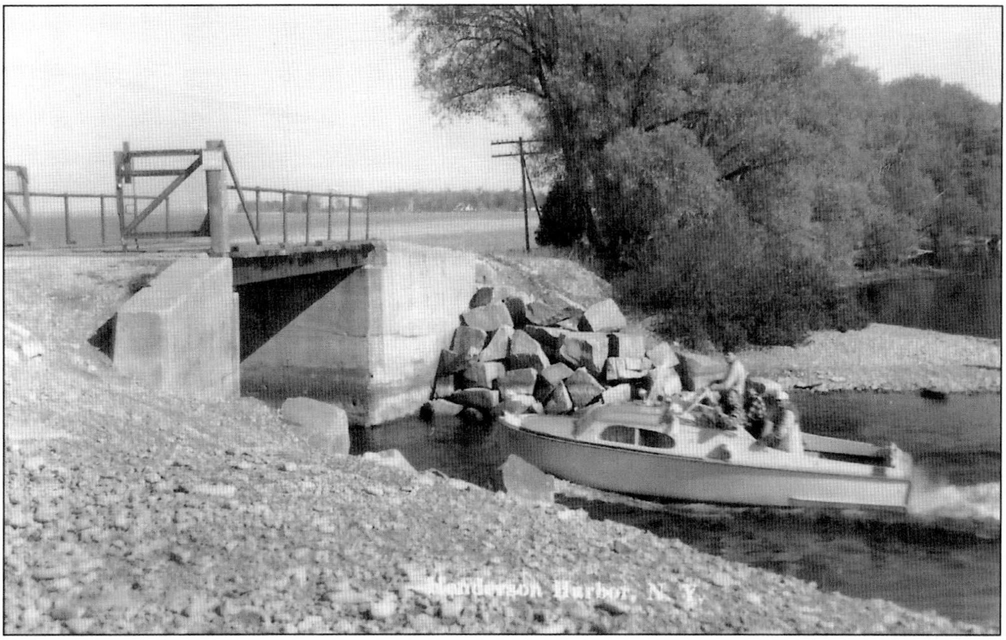

Upon leaving the marinas, it was a two-and-a-half-mile cruise across Henderson Harbor to Snowshoe Bay and the cut. This scene of a cruiser navigating the narrow channel through the cut is probably from the early 1960s. Prior to construction of the cut in 1927, fishermen hauled their double-ended rowing skiffs by hand over the gravel bar to get to the lake (left).

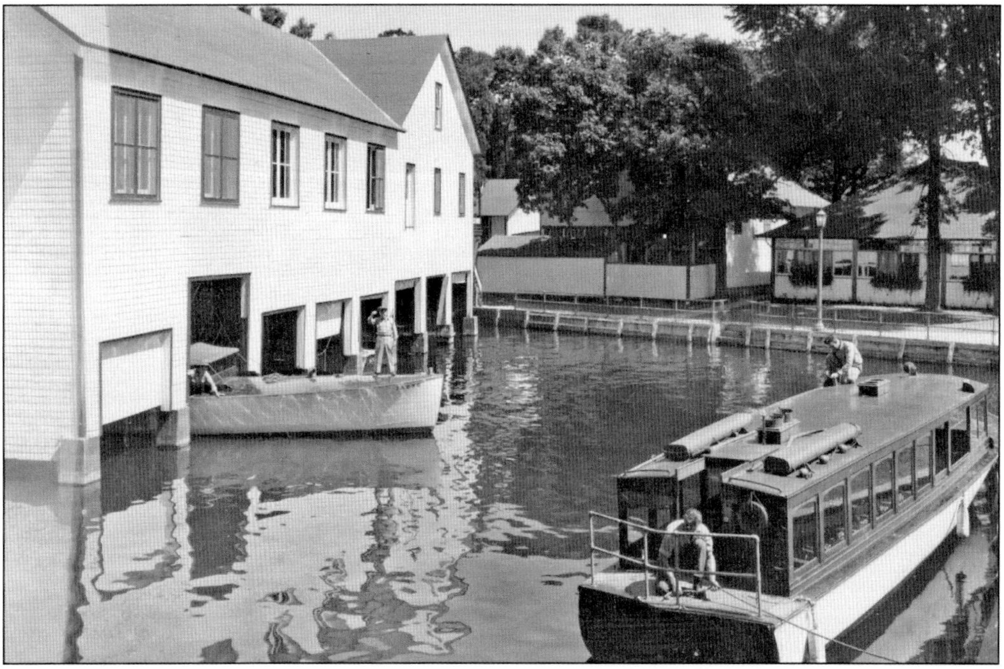

The boathouse at Association Island included eight slips and a large meeting room/dance hall on the second floor. Built over the large lagoon prior to 1920, the boathouse was often the center of activities on the island and the location for many dances, with partygoers arriving by boat every half hour from Henderson Harbor. (GE.)

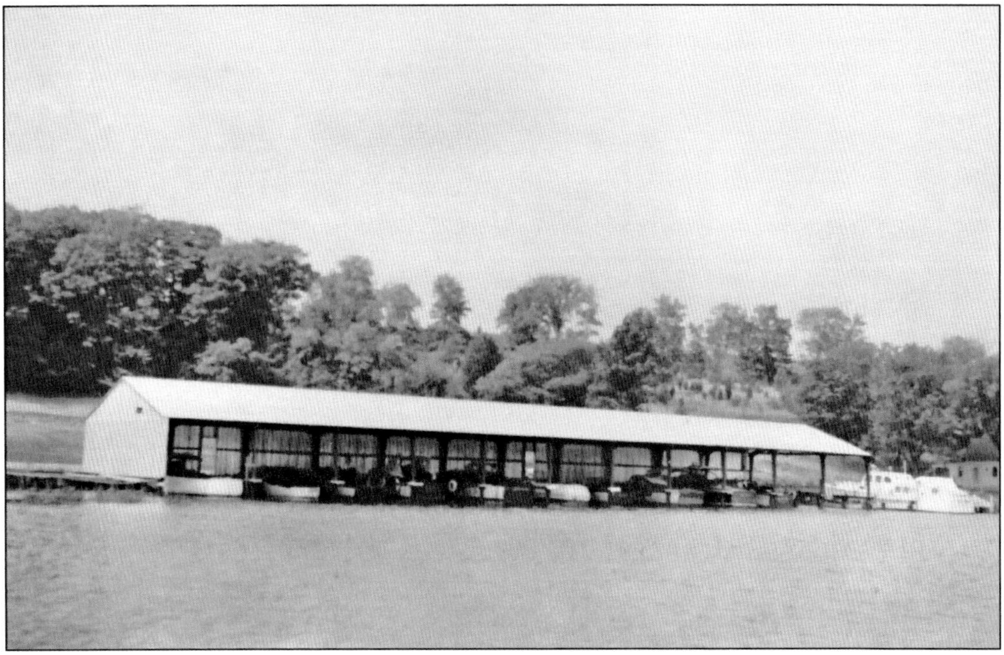

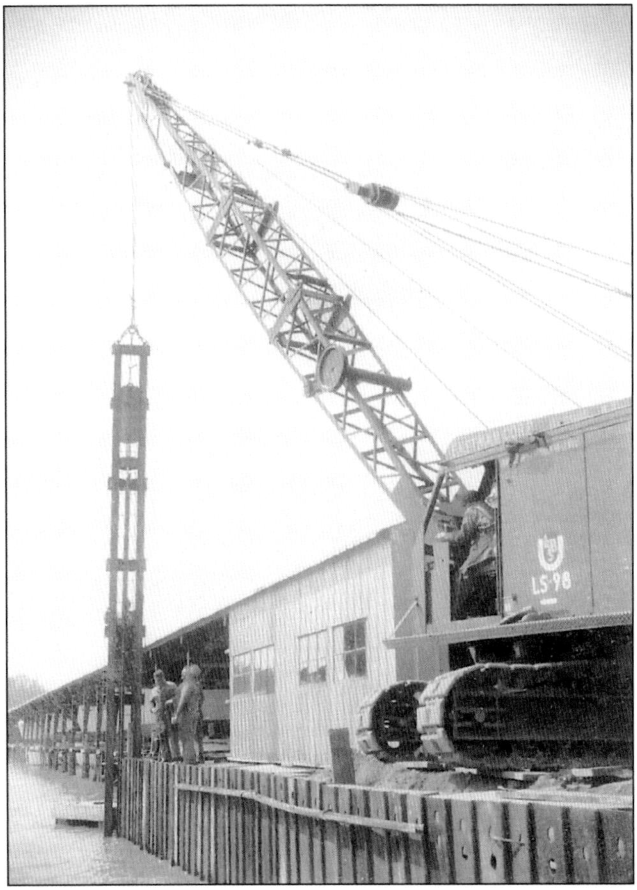

At the far southern end of Henderson Harbor, brothers Paul and Carl Eastman of Ellisburg built Eastman Marina. The largest marina in Henderson Harbor began with a 12-slip boathouse designed for cabin cruisers. The two slips at the far right would later become the marina bait shop, office, and store. Paul Eastman died in 1966, and Eastman Marina, owned by Eastman Corporation, was managed for many years by Glenn Dobbin. (Fran and Alma Eastman.)

Eastman Corporation of Ellisburg had all the necessary heavy equipment to construct Eastman Marina. Driving piles with Eastman's large Link-Belt crane in front of what later became the marina store and gas dock is equipment operator Wallace "Buster" Bettinger of Ellisburg. (Fran and Alma Eastman.)

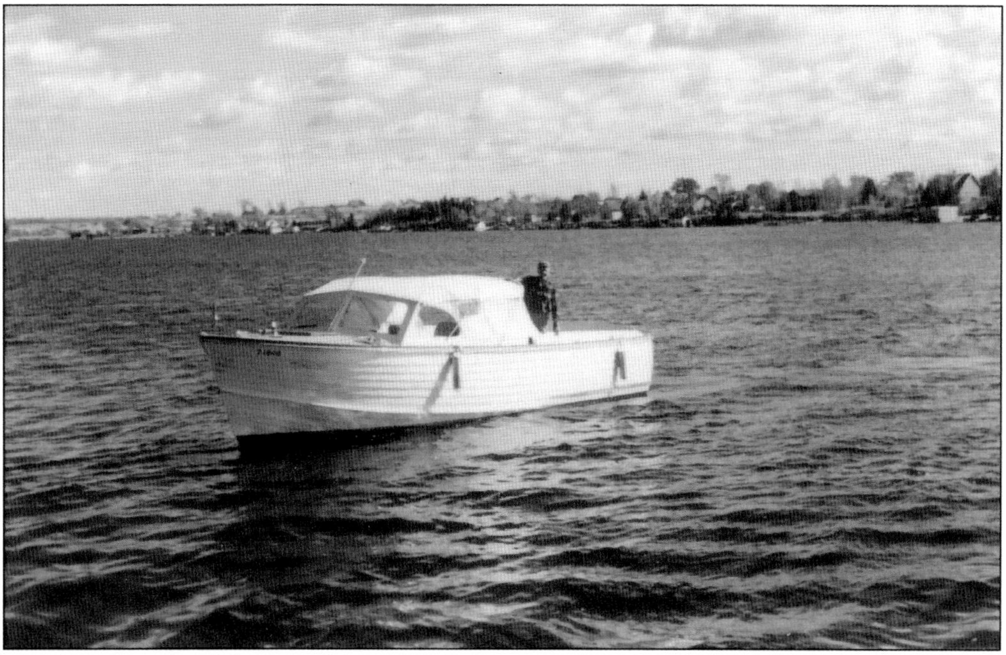

Henderson Harbor fishing guides, such as Fremont S. "Freem" Powers, offered their services on some of the best equipped boats on the lake. Powers owned the former Tyler's Inn property in the 1970s and guided for Erwin Dickey and Robert Marzolf. This is Powers in his 1950s Chris Craft, *Lucky I II.* (Susan Powers Washburn.)

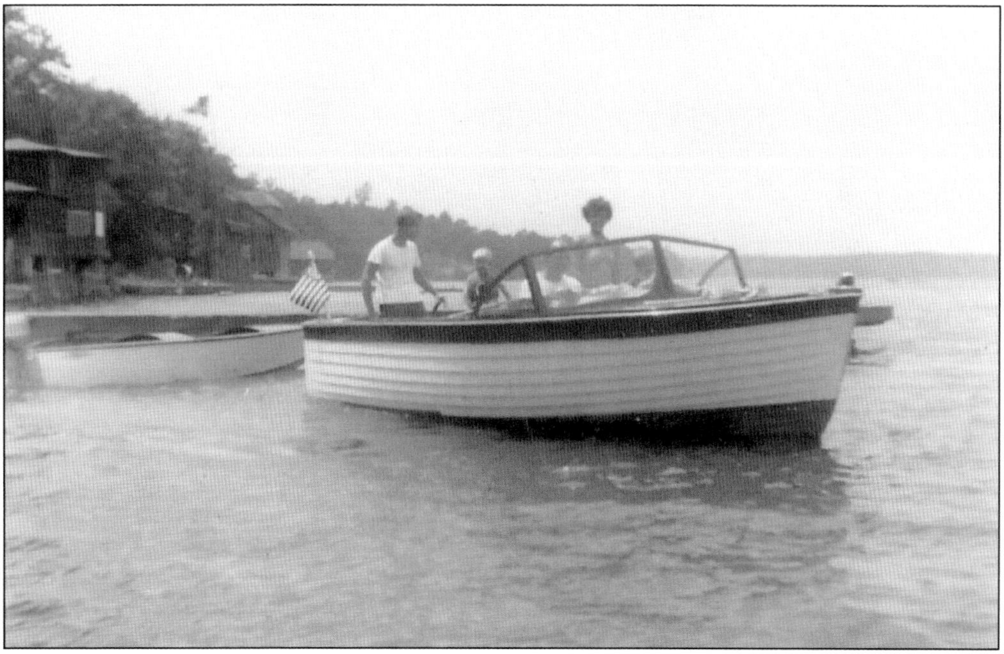

Lyman boats found a home early in Henderson Harbor. The Lyman Boat Company of Sandusky, Ohio, built its lapstrake wooden boats with large bows for the rough waters of Lake Erie. This 1948 Lyman owned by James and Mary Parke Manning of Henderson Harbor is an example of the early Lymans used for fishing and cruising on Lake Ontario. (Mary Parke Manning.)

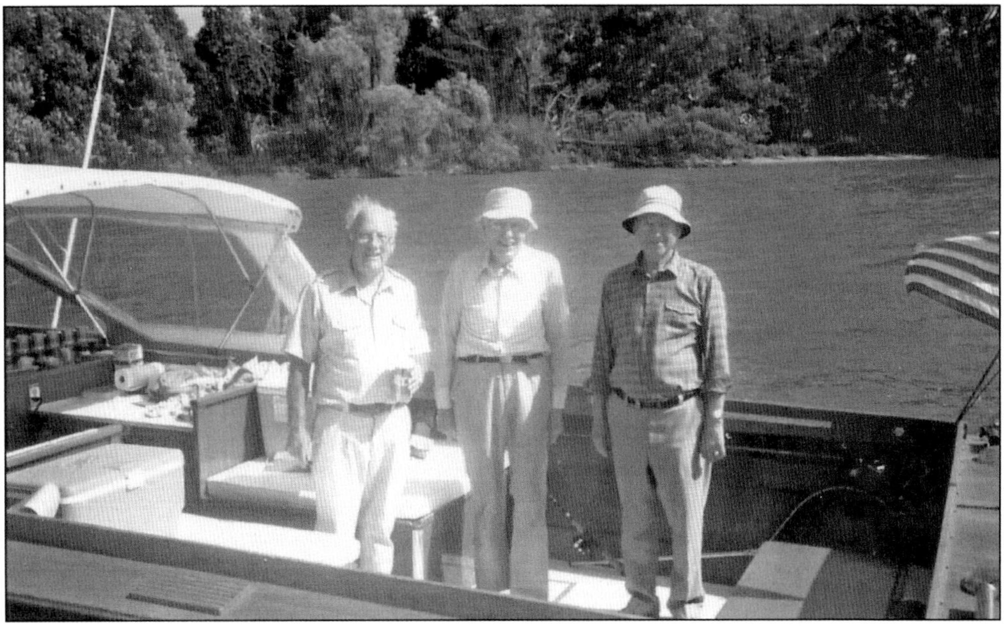

This 1971 Lyman Sportsman is tied to the PK Clubhouse dock at North Pond on Galloo Island around 1973. Larry Smith, Watertown truck company owner and Henderson Harbor summer resident (left), owned the PK Clubhouse for many years beginning in 1966. With Smith in his 30-foot Lyman, *Smith's Bonanza*, are Harold Evans (center) and Paul Severance. (Greg Smith, GallooIsland.net.)

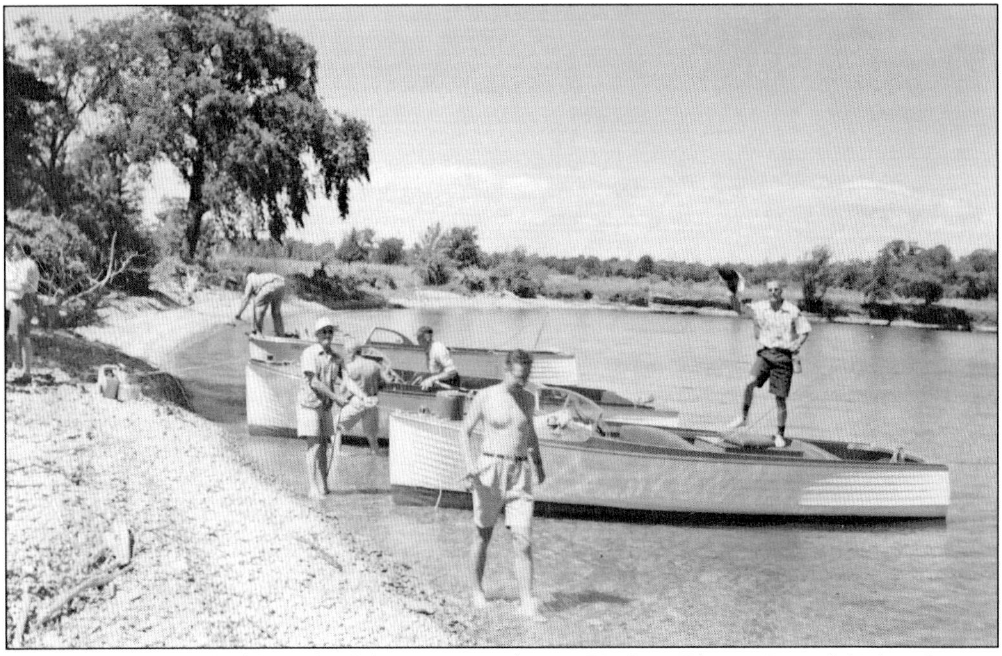

A Lyman was an ideal boat for fishing in Henderson Harbor. These 18- and 21-foot Lyman Islanders could handle the choppy waters of the lake and could easily be pushed onto the stony beach of Calf Island for a shore dinner. There are still many original Lymans in Henderson Harbor. (John D. Marsellus.)

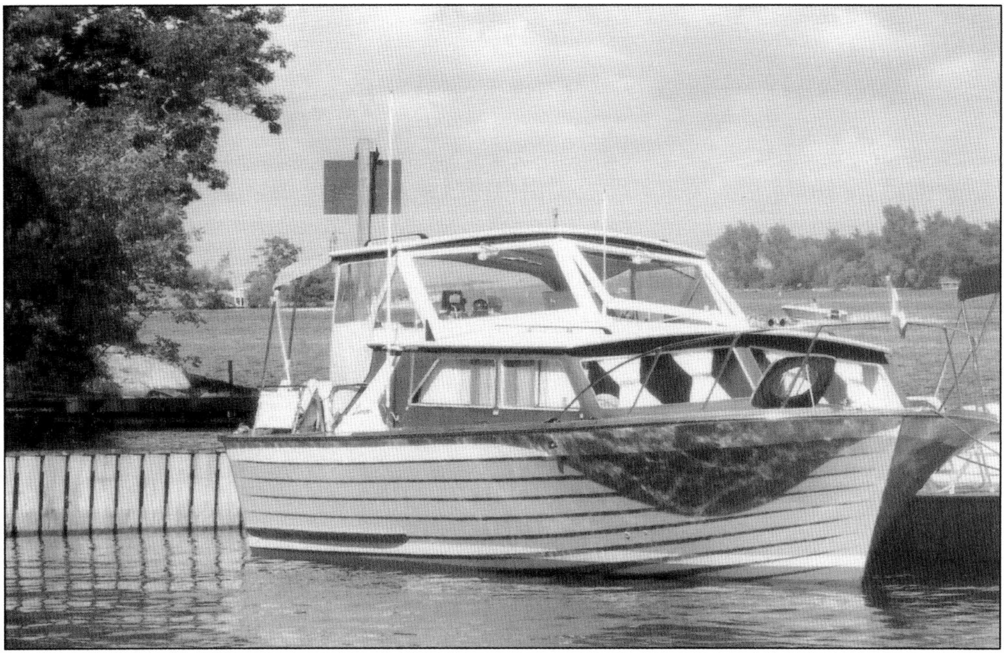

The 1967 Lyman express cruiser *Freebird* is moored at a dock on Mary's Island in the St. Lawrence River. *Freebird* is one of the largest Lyman boats in Henderson Harbor and often cruises throughout Lake Ontario, the Thousand Islands, and Canada. (Brian and Mary Bettinger.)

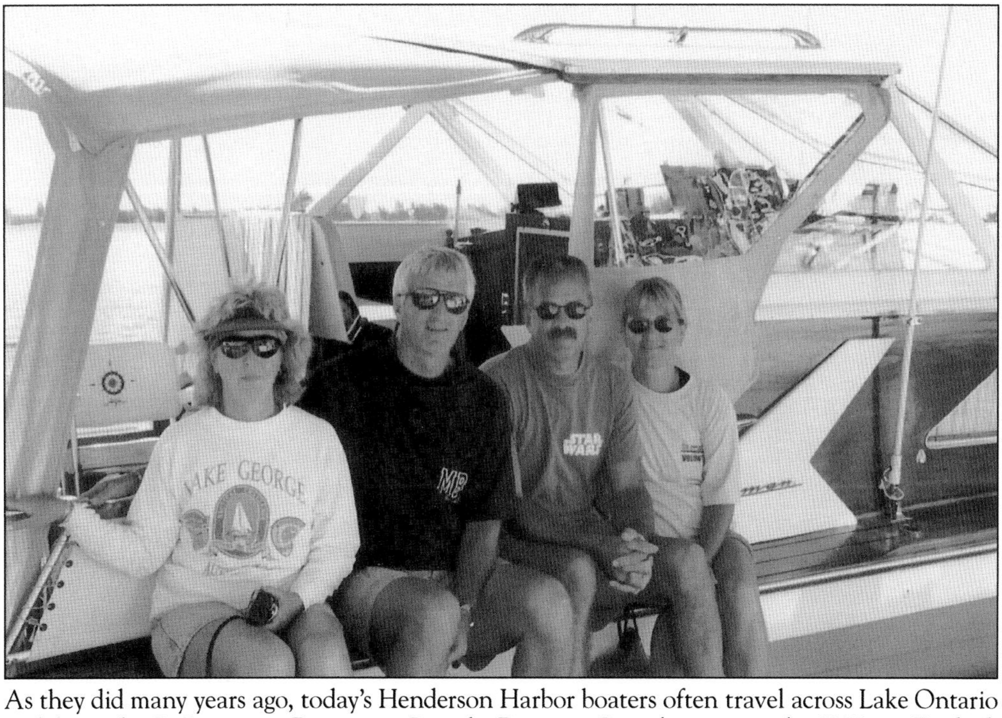

As they did many years ago, today's Henderson Harbor boaters often travel across Lake Ontario and down the St. Lawrence River into Canada. During a Canadian trip in the 1990s on *Freebird*, a 1967 Lyman Express Cruiser from Henderson Harbor, are, from left to right, Jeanne and Dan Lake and Brian and Mary Bettinger, the boat's owners. (Brian and Mary Bettinger.)